KESWICK
Ex-Taylor
HOWTOWN
PATTERDALE
GRASMERE
AMBLESIDE
CONISTON
WINDERMERE
BOWNESS
NEWBY
KINGS
MEABURN
Ex-Lyvenet
APPLEBY
SHAP
CROSBY
RAVENSWORTH
BROUGH
ORTON
KIRKBY
STEPHEN
NEWBIGGIN
TEBAY
SELSIDE
KENDAL
SEDBERGH

CW01667948

RIBBLE

Volume Two

An anthology

© T. B. Maund and A. A. Townsin April 1994.

ISBN 1 898432 08 2

All rights reserved. Except for normal review purposes no part of this book may be reproduced or utilised in any form or by any means, electrical or mechanical, including photocopying, recording or by an information storage and retrieval system, without the prior written consent of Venture Publications Ltd, PO Box 17, Glossop, Derbyshire, SK13 9FA.

Front Cover Illustration

A Plaxton Interurban-bodied Dennis Javelin prepares to pull into Manchester's Chorlton Street coach station on the 29th March 1994, three days after this new service was introduced in response to Charterplan's X43 service also operating from Manchester to Clitheroe. The branding of the vehicles for the MANCUNIAN Network 2000 Service is a clear pointer to Ribble's future in Greater Manchester.

Typeset and produced electronically for the Publishers by
Mopok Graphics, 128, Pikes Lane, Glossop, Derbyshire
Printed and bound in Great Britain

The British Bus Heritage

RIBBLE

Volume Two

An anthology

by

T. B. MAUND, FCIT

and

ALAN TOWNSIN

with additional material by

David Meredith

and

Duncan Roberts

Venture *publications*

INTRODUCTION

The enthusiastic reception given to Volume One by readers throughout the world has been accompanied by several valuable offers of new material for which the authors and publisher are very grateful. Thanks are also due to those who have taken the trouble to write to us. A table of Addenda is included but the authors must point out that there simply is insufficient space to include all the meticulous detail available. The wide-ranging nature of the material and also the availability of certain of the company's minute books have added to the dilemma as to what should be included and what should be left out.

Promises were made of additional treatment of the fleet and the depots and these have been included. However, the publisher has now been offered a comprehensive history of Ribble's principal subsidiary, W.C. Standerwick Ltd. and it was felt that it would do much greater justice to the subject if this were to be published as a separate work so the promised coverage of the Standerwick fleet has been omitted from the current volume. It is anticipated that the Standerwick history will be published later this year.

The authors then had to decide what else should be selected from the mass of available material. Regional albums had been considered at one time but there were many practical difficulties. The company's history was so complex in some areas that it would be impossible to deal with it adequately in a work of this kind. It was decided, therefore, to draw on David Grisenthwaite's meticulous research of the northern area of the company as much less has been published on Ribble's Cumbrian operations. Furthermore, although this part of the book is much abridged from the original, it was felt possible to give a reasonably coherent account of the growth of the Ribble network in the north and the politics and personalities involved.

Lists of operators acquired by the company have been published before but they contain several errors and it has not previously been possible to show how much was paid for them. So this was felt to be essential to a detailed history of this fascinating company.

Lastly two separate sections have been devoted to the working of the company's Traffic department and what went on at Britain's second busiest coach station – Blackpool Coliseum – in its most hectic days. Both of these include personal experiences of one of the authors.

T.B. MAUND
A.A. TOWNSIN

April 1994

This scene dating from 1959 shows 1507, one of the first batch of Leyland Titan PD3/4 models with Burlingham full-fronted bodywork dating from 1957, passing one of the former 'White Lady' PD1/3 double-deck coaches, repainted and demoted to bus work but still retaining full destination display, albeit not in use, on the bridge over the River Lune in Lancaster.

CONTENTS

RIBBLE today . . .

Ribble in 1994 is part of a very go-ahead and aggressive organisation, itself only in existence since 1980. Its vehicles have been operating Local Bus Services – the name given by the Transport Act 1985 to what were previously known as Stage Carriage Services – in Manchester. Since deregulation, Ribble's former Local express services, known by the Company as Limited Stop and identified by X prefixes, continued to operate from Chorlton Street coach station as other services continued to exist harmoniously with those of most other local operators.

After Ian Chapman's privatised Ribble passed to Stagecoach in 1989 Drawlane and Stagecoach 'exchanged interests' to rationalise their activities in Greater Manchester. This resulted in each operator enjoying a defined territory without local competition from the other. A period of relative calm came to parts of Manchester though meantime Ribble (Stagecoach) busied themselves elsewhere in Barrow, Preston – both the municipal company and Mercer's of Longridge being involved, and finally Lancaster as described in the text.

In 1993 the Secretary of State for Transport directed Greater Manchester PTA to divide its bus operating company into two parts in preparation for Privatisation. This Direction was in response to the PTA's protracted reluctance to sell the company – its was the last to do so. Strangely the Monopolies and Mergers Commission had permitted Stagecoach to bid for the southern company and British Bus for the northern but not the reverse. This arose from Territorial Overlap affecting perceived competition. When the two sections of Greater Manchester Buses were offered to Open Market Sale Stagecoach failed to secure Preferred Bidder Status.

The Hazel Grove, Stockport, terminus in February 1994 as the bus war between Stagecoach and GM Buses South gets under way leaving a line of GM double-deckers waiting in the winter sunshine as the Volvos hurry by.

– with Javelins at the sharp end

Consequently Stagecoach resolved to carve a section of territory by commercial means – the first visible result being the 192 Manchester to Hazel Grove route where a fleet of new vehicles based at Bredbury began to operate in 'fierce' competition with GM Buses South, running more modern vehicles, at more frequent intervals and at cheaper fares.

Eventually GM Buses South responded, after some three months, by introducing a competitive service over an established Ribble route through the Ribble valley. The immediate response of Stagecoach was to increase frequency, deploy effective marketing techniques and move some virtually new Javelin coaches into the fray. The Stagecoach Inspector at Chorlton Street, a veteran of earlier campaigns including the 192 service, provided a visible and clearly a vital part of the strategy.

The photographs reproduced on these two pages clearly show the competitive edge of the Stagecoach operation. Opposite, one of Ribble's new vehicles leaves the GM double-deckers quietly waiting in the Hazel Grove lay-by for any remaining passengers prepared to pay the higher fare to Stockport or Manchester, whilst, below, a newly-lettered Javelin, branded Mancunian to distinguish it from the existing service, lettered Ribble Valley Mancunian, passes a ten year old Plaxton Paramount carrying improvised boards in the windscreen to show its destination, on the competing X43. What relevance mention of Tours and Holidays on the side panels of Charterplan's Tiger may have is open to question, but there can be no question as to the relevance of Network 2000 on the Stagecoach vehicles and the significance of the brand name Mancunian.

Javelin passes Tiger during the latter's meal break. The Stagecoach Inspector admitted contemplating getting another packet of cigarettes to encourage the Charterplan driver to extend his lunch break !

FRONTISPIECE

This early post-war scene of one of the big staff outings requiring the provision of large numbers of coaches shows how Ribble managed to maintain good standards of appearance, even on such occasions when finding enough vehicles might be expected to bring out vehicles of standards below those chosen for scheduled services. The leading vehicle, with sticker indicating it was No. 16 in the convoy, was one of the oldest coaches still in service, RN 7587 being one of the first three of the batch of Leyland Tiger TS7 models with English Electric bodywork dating from March 1935, with fleet number 1421 applied to the cab front in the style adopted in 1946 – some of the paintwork appears to have gone a little dull but the brightwork is polished. Behind it is 1507 (RN 7757), another TS7 with generally similar body but built by Duple and dating from March 1936 – this vehicle is not quite so pristine, and, perhaps significantly, this was one of the vehicles that was to be rebodied in 1950, again by Duple but to post-war style and 8ft wide. Most if not all the other coaches visible are similar Tiger TS7 models of the 1935-37 period.

ACKNOWLEDGEMENTS

Authors and Publisher acknowledge assistance received from officials and Members of the Ribble Enthusiasts' Club and the Omnibus Society; Staff of the Lancashire County Record Office; M.J. Ashton, G. Bailey, A.E. Caine, D. Cowell, P. Deegan, W. Dodds, J. Dunabin, R. Greenwood, D.A. Grisenthwaite, R. Harvey, R. Hopkins, MBE, JP, J.B. Horne, W.R. Johnson, D. J. Meredith, C. Morris, D.F. Roberts, M.A. Shires, T.G. Turner, S. Watts, N. Witham.

Photographs have come from the Author's collections, and also from A.D. Broughall, A.B. Cross, R. Downham, R.N. Hannay, J.B. Horne, R. Hopkins, A.D. Maund, H. Melling, C. Morris, R. Marshall, H. Postlethwaite, J.A. Senior, the Senior Transport Archive, M.A. Shires, D. Waymann, R.L. Wilson, A.L. Witham.

Colour material has been supplied by J. Aldridge, G. Lumb, Photobus (from P. Eckersley, D.K. Kerrison, R. Marshall, G. Morant, A. Richardson), H. Piltz, J.A. Senior.

If anyone has been inadvertently omitted from these acknowledgements Authors and Publisher proffer their apologies.

THE CONQUEST OF THE NORTH

For many years, David Grisenthwaite has made a detailed study of bus services in Cumbria and this chapter is based on his researches. See the end papers for maps which illustrate some of the events described.

By their acquisition on 1st December 1927 of Lancashire and Westmorland Motor Services Ltd., over which they already exercised some management control, Ribble moved north into a very sparsely-populated part of Britain. In Cumberland and Westmorland, now combined as Cumbria, the average population density was below 64

Very different from industrial Lancashire was the northern part of Ribble's territory, often picturesque but much more sparsely populated. Express services to Carlisle and beyond were established in 1929, before the Ribble local service network was established in the Penrith and Carlisle areas. Here 877, one of the 120 Leyland Royal Tiger coaches with Leyland-built bodywork dating from 1951 climbs Shap Fell on the A6 road, heading for Carlisle on the X21 from Liverpool. This was quite a tough climb in those days before the M6 was built, the road rising to 1,300ft and reducing even one of these quite lively vehicles to second gear over the steepest stretch. Note the sliding roof, arranged to give two openings.

This view of three vehicles of the Lake District Road Traffic Co. Ltd. at Ambleside, probably dating from about 1905, is taken from almost the same vantage point as the view of Ambleside bus station about half a century later on page 50 of Volume 1 – the company's office behind the Clarkson steam bus in the centre of the picture was to be incorporated in the latter premises.
The two open charabancs have now been identified as Thornycroft petrol-engined models. The first entries of vehicles supplied to Lake District Road Traffic in a list of early Thornycroft chassis numbers copied from official records (apart from 349, which was a 4-ton steam wagon with tipping body dated September 1904) were 459-461 which were 24hp type 40 sold as chassis in January, April and May 1905 respectively, so these seem likely candidates for two of them – the vehicle on the right is EC 109, also shown on page 9 of Volume 1 (its registration going to another Thornycroft circa 1912). Note that this has a three rows of seats, while the other, also with EC registration but with number not visible, has four in a longer body. Likely candidates for the others of this batch are EC 115 and 116, known to have been Thornycrofts of LDT.
Two further 24hp type 40 chassis, 568 and 569, were supplied in April 1906, and it seems quite probable that these had the much neater later type of radiator with brass surround shown in that other view, one of which was EC 223, and hence EC 224 was probably the other.

per square mile, less than a sixth than that of Lancashire's; Westmorland's largest town, Kendal, had a population of only 14,000. Because of natural barriers, railway penetration was only peripheral as a consequence of which some of the earliest bus services in the land were to be found in the region.

The mail service between Penrith and the settlements along the northern shore of Lake Ullswater is said to have had an 8-seat Sterling car as early as 1899 though horses were mainly used for a few years longer. A mail contract between Windermere station and Grasmere figured in the activities of the Lake District Road Traffic Co. Ltd., formed by Bruce Rigg in January 1904. This became a Thornycroft stronghold, services being kept going through the 1914-18 War with gas bags. Further south, Fahy's service, with origins in 1906, though working mainly in the Lancaster and Morecambe area, was an early operator of Lake District tours by road.

This view of a Clarkson bus registered EC 131 may well show the same vehicle as seen in the top view. The print is marked British Railways and hence made after 1948, inscribed with a pencilled reference to Wolverton and negative date as 1904, so may have come via LMS sources. The reason for this is not known though there was a faint later railway connection, as a bus service operated by the Furness Railway between Ambleside and Newby Bridge in the winters of 1920/1 and 1921/2 was replaced thereafter by a Lake District Road Traffic service. The display of the maker's name on the Clarkson, and other clues, suggest that it may have been a delivery or demonstration journey – note the padlocked wooden box and can, probably of oil, secured on the roof. The vee-fronted body was characteristic of this early small Clarkson model.

Another view of one of the early Lake District Road Traffic Thornycrofts. This is a Thornycroft photograph, and may indicate that one of the three early chassis of that make was fitted with the closed body seen here or that alternative bodies were fitted in accordance with the season – such transfers were common at the time – note the route board for Windermere, Ambleside, Rydal and Grasmere.

Meageen Enterprise

In the coastal region, the Whitehaven Motor Service Co. Ltd. was formed by the Meageen family on 8th August 1912, its name being changed to Cumberland Motor Services Ltd. in June 1921 when the British Automobile Traction Co. Ltd. acquired 9,000 of the 18,000 shares, the money being used to finance a programme of expansion. The deal was done by W.S. Wreathall, who had served with BAT since the earliest days of bus services. He also sat on the Ribble board and was to play an important part in subsequent developments. Henry Meageen, the chairman of Cumberland Motor Services (CMS), held Wreathall in great esteem, mainly because he agreed to local control. CMS tended to model itself on Ribble but never with the same panache and son, Tom, who was managing director, often went his own way; he did not have the confidence of his father which limited CMS expansion, particularly in the direction of Carlisle.

In July 1925, Henry Meageen formed Westmorland Motor Services Ltd. by acquiring Rutter's Kendal Bus Services and Feirn (Anbleside) Ltd., a company formed in 1920, engaged mainly in touring. The Lake District Road Traffic Co. was immediately taken over and the company became public within a month. The company's main line, the Lancaster-Kendal-Keswick service, started on 15th July 1925, using 5 AEC Reliances based at Kendal (2), Ambleside (1) and Keswick (1). It was profitable even in winter despite competition from the Kendal Motor Bus Co. Ltd. between Kendal and Grasmere. The latter company had been started by B. Bracken and some ex-service colleagues in 1921 with a Ford T to carry workmen between Endmoor and Burneside and Bowston Paper Mills.

In February 1926, the name was changed to Lancashire and Westmorland Motor Services, businesses in Lancaster and Morecambe being purchased. F.C. Fahy, the owner of one of them, became managing director. Six months later, 8,556 £1 shares were bought by Ribble on the basis of £100 for 116 shares; 1,000 of them were registered in the name of H.E. Hickmott as nominee. A pooling arrangement was drawn up for services over common ground; this was extended to embrace services to Preston and Blackpool in due course, though at first L&W could not get licences in Blackpool. Ribble became more and more involved in the company's affairs, producing, for example, their timetables and it was a short step to complete absorption, a policy decision by BAT, which seems to have been unexpected as only a few months earlier, the extension of the pooling arrangement for five years had been discussed and charges for terminal facilities at Garstang and Preston were agreed at £200 per year. The purchase price was fixed by BAT at £75,000.

The operational problems in this sparsely-populated region were quite different and new techniques to solve them had to be learnt. Initially, this was not too difficult due to the traffic potential of the Lake District. Even in winter there were four through trips to Keswick, where

This Thornycroft of the early 'twenties is thought to have been in the fleet of Fahy's Ltd., though no vehicle with an appropriate registration number survived through take-over by Lancashire & Westmorland Motor Services into Ribble ownership in December 1927.

The Kendal Motor Bus Co. was a substantial competitor until its take-over in April 1930. The vehicle seen here, No. 29, seems as if it may have just been delivered unregistered on trade plates, judging by the lack of registration number and the expressions of the onlookers. It became EC 8331 and was one of a pair of Thornycroft UB models with Northern Counties bodywork dating from 1928. It became Ribble C921 and survived in the fleet until 1934.

one bus was out-stationed, with an hourly Kendal-Bowness service and an adequate though irregular Windermere-Grasmere service. Local services from Ambleside penetrated to Coniston and up Langdale.

For the 1928 season, partly to combat the competition from Kendal Motor Bus Co. (known locally as the K company because of the sign carried on the front of each bus) and partly to stimulate new traffic, an ambitious programme of through running from Lancaster was initiated. There was a half-hourly service from Lancaster to Windermere with hourly extensions to Bowness and Keswick; separate services from Windermere brought the frequency up to 15-minutes between Bowness and Grasmere and half-hourly Windermere-Keswick. Only in the summers of 1949-50, when buses ran every 20-minutes, was this level of service exceeded.

This was excessive but from it stemmed the regular pattern of services which still continue hourly from Lancaster to Keswick (halved in winter), augmented between Windermere and Grasmere.

Ribble and the K company competed on the most populous roads from the town with Ribble inheriting the successful Castle Grove-Romney Road and Highfield-Rinkfield town services started by Rutter who became the company's local superintendent, a position he held for over 25 years. The K company enjoyed a monopoly on the service to Burneside and Bowston but on the Endmoor road, Ribble ran both a local service and some Lancaster trips which were diverted from the main road. The Ribble offensive was relentness. From March 1928, a regular service to Grange-over-Sands and Cark competed directly with a 'K' service which had run since 1924 and the Endmoor route was extended hourly to Kirkby Lonsdale with six trips running beyond, two each to Skipton, Colne and Burnley. This replaced the diversion of Lancaster trips and was very much at the expense of the Kendal company which had enjoyed a monopoly on the route since 1922. With the later involvement with County Motors (see Vol. 1), through running across Ingleton was discontinued, the services to the east being linked to Lancaster instead.

At the end of the 1928 season, Ribble adopted a policy on some routes in the Kendal area of issuing return fares at single fares plus 1d, guaranteeing these fares until 22nd March 1929 and, in February 1929, announced a whole range of cheap return fares from Kendal, Kirkby Lonsdale falling from 1/11d to 1/4d and Ambleside from 2/3d to 1/11d. An office was opened in Windermere railway station (rent £1 per year) and in the Rothay Hotel, Grasmere. Plans were made for a garage extension at Ambleside costing over £5,000. The buildings were to be built in local stone to blend in with the surroundings and were completed during 1931-32, replacing the old Lake District Road Traffic Company's Wansfell Tower premises.

Ribble encirclement of the Kendal company was advanced further in May 1929 with the start of a new route between Kendal and Sedbergh over Roan Edge. This linked at Sedbergh with an extension to Dent of the service from Kirkby Lonsdale which Ribble took over from its subsidiary, County Motors (Lancaster) Ltd. The timetable was so devised that it was possible to travel between Kendal and Kirkby Lonsdale by this scenic route through the Lune valley. Further west, a new route in direct competition with the K company's seasonal Grange-Newby Bridge-Bowness service was commenced.

In August, the Kendal company raised additional capital up to £11,675 of the £15,000 authorised, in order to buy new buses. In October, they refused Ribble's offer of £26,000. Negotiations continued and in February 1930, Major Hickmott told the directors that management was disorganised and divided. An offer of £20,000 was made verbally and eventually the K company was bought for £21,000 plus a further £2,000 after twelve months if no competitor was licensed to ply for hire in Kendal. This was settled in October 1931 for £1,725. Ribble took over on 11th April 1930, thus avoiding another season of warfare.

As well as the lucrative Burneside route, Ribble gained services to the Lyth Valley and by the 'back road' to Bowness plus market runs to Grayrigg (ex Winders) and Kentmere and henceforth enjoyed a virtual monopoly in Kendal with the exception of one competitor, Fawcett's Dallam company of Milnthorpe, founded in March 1924.

A remarkably busy scene at Newby Bridge in the late 'fifties, with five Ribble buses visible at this rural junction near the southern end of Lake Windermere and no other vehicle in sight; it is suspected that there may have been some holding back of one or two of them to suit the Leyland Journal photographer. Royal Tiger bus 332 is bound for Ambleside on the 517, with Olympic 252 on the left running on the same route in the opposite direction, towards Barrow. A former 'White Lady' PD1/3, 1213, demoted to bus work, is seen arriving from Ulverston, together with two other Olympics, one bound for Grange and the other only just visible, disappearing round the corner towards Lakeside. This area had been the scene of some of the competition with the 'K' buses.

They plied from Arnside to both Lancaster and Kendal, being particularly energetic in their competition over the road between Kendal and Milnthorpe. Ribble retaliated with a service from Lancaster to Arnside via Milnthorpe which survived until withdrawn at the beginning of the 1939-45 war, never to be reinstated. The Dallam company was finally taken over by Ribble in December 1950.

The Penrith Services

Further north, a network of services of quite a different character had developed. Penrith, with a population of 8,350, was the gateway to Ullswater, and two hoteliers, George Armstrong of the George and Tom Siddle of the Crown had, ever since the late 19th century, provided horse-drawn coach services for their guests and others, to and from the lake. In 1920, they formed Armstrong and Siddle Motor and Transport Co. Ltd. with a nominal capital of £15,000 of which £4,200 was eventually issued. The business was initially very profitable and, by capitalisation, this was doubled to £8,400 in 1923. Both goods and passengers were conveyed between Penrith, Patterdale and Pooley Bridge, Thornycroft, Guy and Renault vehicles figuring in their early passenger fleet. They had contracts with the LNW (later LMS) railway and the Ullswater Steam Navigation Co. and considerable excursion traffic was developed. Joint rail, bus and boat tickets in many combinations were issued for a traffic which was bewilderingly variable and unpredictable.

In 1924, Armstrong and Siddle widened their activities in response to the market services being developed by carriers from the surrounding villages. A thrice-daily service between Penrith and Appleby was soon augmented and a route to Shap Granite Works was started in July 1925. In the following year the direct Appleby route was extended to Kirkby Stephen and a new Penrith-Appleby service commenced linking up the fellside villages, including Ousby and Milburn. For a time this route diverted via Melmerby, a successful but circuitous 26-mile trip compared with the 13.3 mile direct route. In September 1926, Sowerby's carrier service to Kirkoswald and Melmerby was acquired and converted into a regular bus service, followed by the Lyvenet Motor Service to Crosby Ravensworth which had been running for less than a year.

All this activity gave A&S a network of daily services centred on Penrith so that traffic originated in both directions instead of inward only. Nine buses were needed with a tenth in summer for the summer service across the Kirkstone Pass between Patterdale and Windermere which originated in 1925. Considerable duplication was needed

Kendal had been an important centre for Ribble's development as it expanded northwards. By no means large, it was becoming very congested by the through traffic on the main A6 road by the late 'fifties, especially in the summer. Here 953, one of the 1954 batch of Leyland Tiger Cub coaches with Burlingham Seagull bodywork, *en route* from Carlisle and Penrith to Liverpool on the X21 passes 1343, one of the final batch of Leyland-bodied Titan PD2/3 lowbridge buses of 1950 with platform doors, coming in from Lancaster on service 70. The Titan bears an advertisement for Ribble holiday tours 'from 7 guineas' (£7.35).

The Penrith-Patterdale service, with superb views of Lake Ullswater, was the only profitable route from the Armstrong & Siddle network when it was taken over by Ribble in 1929. Ten years later, Ribble was using Leyland Cheetah saloons of the batches with sliding roofs on the service and thereby helping to provide one of the most pleasant bus rides in the country. One of the initial 1936 batch with Eastern Counties bodywork is seen with most seats filled at Pooley Bridge, crossing the river Eamont as it flows into the lake, Patterdale being at the other end, amid the mountains in the distance. The comfortable Cheetah buses, with their smooth-running petrol engines, ran all the Penrith area routes until the early post-war period.

in summer. In 1927 a Penrith town service, to and from the Golf Club, and a Shap-Kirkby Stephen route via Orton, Tebay and the upper Lune Valley were started.

A&S had competition on the Patterdale service from George Taylor (Motors) Ltd. whose claim to be the pioneer they did not accept. The company had been formed on 10th December 1913 to continue an existing service by Taylor and had the Royal Mail contract until December 1926 when it was gained by A&S. His advertising became even more emotive and colourful and he started competitive services to Shap and Appleby.

In 1925, Tom Siddle wanted to retire and an approach was made to Cumberland Motor Services. In March 1926, after an investigation, they declined because of the appalling state of the mixed 14-vehicle fleet. In June 1927, Cumberland reopened negotiations, almost certainly at the behest of BAT, and eventually a deal was struck with takeover fixed for 31st March 1928. The asking price had been £14,000 but it changed hands at £9,077 including the business of George Taylor. The assets comprised 16 buses, six charabancs, a taxi, a lorry, the depot in Brunswick Road and an office in Middlegate. On the night of 19th March, the depot was destroyed by fire with three charabancs and five buses. A new completion date was fixed for 30th April and six second-hand Daimlers were transferred from the Cumberland fleet. A new company, Armstrong and Siddle Motor Services Ltd. was formed with a capital of £25,000 of which £15,700 was issued; £15,000 was held by Tilling and BAT and its nominees and £700 by Cumberland. This company started trading on 18th May 1928 by which time Bernard Mandale's Greystoke service had been acquired with one 26-seat Albion.

The timetable was rationalised in August when a new route to Melmerby via Winskill replaced the diversion on the Appleby service. In October, Henry Meageen bought Dr de Mello's business, operated by Moore and Baty, between Carlisle and Penrith which was then transferred to A&S. It was then logical for the BAT's Caledonian Omnibus Co. operations south of Carlisle to Cotehill to go to the English company and this happened in January 1929 when the route was diverted to Wetheral. The transaction took place on 18th December 1928, Caledonian receiving £425. In November 1931, Ribble discontinued the route to Wetheral on payment to them by United of £215; by this time Ribble had acquired Wright's (see Vol.1).

Territorially, the A&S operation was large with 258 route miles and a depot in Penrith (now rebuilt) and out-stations at the County Garage, Carlisle (2 buses), Sayers' Yard, Appleby (3 buses), Kirkby Stephen (1), Orton (later moved to Shap (1) and Patterdale (6). Only the Ullswater route was profitable but, even so, it was decided to continue A&S as a separate entity; however, control was transferred from Cumberland to Ribble from 1st April 1929.

Meanwhile, in September 1928, Cumberland had started, independently, a Keswick-Penrith service which necessitated a bus being out-stationed in the A&S garage.

From 14th June 1929, Ribble became a joint operator. This was initially the only Ribble service into Penrith but was of great importance as a feeder to and from the new Glasgow express service, providing a connection with the northern part of the Lake District. Ribble soon obtained the A&S licences from Penrith UDC but did not take over operations in their own name until September. The A&S acquisition yielded 28 vehicles of 10 different makes.

The A&S network was retained intact but only the Penrith-Carlisle service kept its regular headway, journeys on other services being tailored to meet a combination of local needs and economic bus scheduling. This was essential as the profitability of the A&S routes was abysmally low. A notable development was the extension of the Penrith-Shap service to Kendal; this ran throughout the year until 1932 after which the Lancashire-Scottish services provided the winter service on the Shap-Kendal section. The Saturday Kendal-Grayrigg route was extended through to Appleby in 1933 and a Sedbergh-Kirkby Stephen link established on three days a week in 1935. In the same year, two new Carlisle-Penrith services were started, replacing various village services and giving, in a highly economic fashion, vastly improved facilities to the inhabitants. Some of the pre-war workings were extremely complex. Thus in the summer of 1939, 17 buses were required to work the scheduled services from Penrith of which seven were allocated to the Carlisle-Kendal route. The Ullswater service required four buses, Keswick one and Southwaite-Carlisle one. The others were based at the various out-stations. Other local improvements were introduced and this network remained intact until the drastic cuts of 1971 with the essential framework surviving until 1984.

The purchase of Armstrong and Siddle for purely commercial reasons made no sense; in 1926, the business had made a profit of £299-14-4d (£299.71) in a full year's trading and the nature of its territory was such that little improvement seemed likely in the short term. The transfer of A&S to Ribble was, therefore, welcomed by Meageen. But this was part of a wider strategy by the BAT. Wreathall saw Carlisle as the jewel in the northern crown and Meageen, for the flimsiest of family and personal reasons, had failed to develop the opportunities which it presented despite the fact that Cumberland was the first of the Tilling or BAT companies to reach the Border City with a route from Maryport on 30th May 1921. Ribble also kept a wary eye on the ambitions of United Automobile Services Ltd. of Darlington, still staunchly independent until its purchase by the Tilling-BAT group in 1929.

The loss of, first, Lancashire & Westmorland and now Armstrong and Siddle was the price the Meageens had to pay for the retention of local control of Cumberland.

Lowther Street bus station in Carlisle, dating from 1935, had altered only slightly in this view of about 1949. Cumberland Motor Services occupied the premises just visible on the left, the style of which matched those used by Ribble on the right. At that date, Cumberland buses still entered in the foreground and loaded for Whitehaven or Skelton on the left. Ribble buses working out-of-town routes entered in the opposite direction from Lonsdale Street, just out of sight in the right background, to load as shown – the city services did not use the station. Out of sight, but just round the corner in Lonsdale Street, Caledonian had its small bus station. It later passed to Western SMT. Tiger TS8 2157, typical of Carlisle's single-deck allocation and bound for Hesket Newmarket on the 619, has just been moved up alongside the similar bus working as far as Bridge End, and passengers walk across to board it. Three Cumberland buses – a Leyland-bodied PD2, a Bedford OWB and a Brush-bodied utility double-decker – are parked outside the small garage that was that company's only operating base in the city. In the background, one of Ribble's then recently-rebodied Tiger coaches is parked between express service duties.

Wreathall and the BAT board were determined to minimise the effects of this local control by hemming the Cumberland company in. Nevertheless Meageen became a very rich man and it has been said that he had made a bargain with Wreathall that, at the appropriate time, Cumberland Motor Services would pass to Ribble. It is, indeed, strange that, effectively, the reverse has now happened.

Trams in Carlisle

Carlisle (population in 1931 – 57,000) was an isolated city seven miles south of the Scottish border with an extensive rural hinterland. A 3ft 6in gauge tramway system of 7.25 miles on six short routes radiating from the city centre and opened on 30th June 1900, had been refurbished in 1912 after purchase by Balfour Beatty. The new company, Carlisle and District Transport Co. Ltd., gained control of Richard Percival's bus services to Brampton, Longtown and Annan on 29th July 1924 but the only city service was to Blackwell.

Extensive housing development during the 1920s resulted in large suburbs growing beyond the tram termini and new bus services were started, the first being Bert Evered's route to St. Ann's Hill Garden City on 20th February 1922. By 1925, 32 operators were serving the city; some amalgamated to form Carlisle and District Motor Services Ltd., incorporated on 3rd September 1926 but, by 1920 there were 74 buses belonging to 47 operators plying for hire in the city. Traffic conditions became chaotic and the Corporation who, as mentioned in Volume 1, had ambitions to become a bus operator, called in the services of a consultant, A.R. Fearnley, general manager of Sheffield Corporation Tramways. He recommended a co-ordinated system under unified control.

By 1930 three other big companies besides Ribble and Cumberland had reached Carlisle. Caledonian, a BAT company, had started a service from Lockerbie in 1927 and their subsequent acquisition of T. Wood's Cumwhinton service and its transfer to A&S has already been mentioned. Scottish Motor Traction Co. Ltd. had come in from Edinburgh from 13th April 1929. In January 1930, United took over Robert Emmerson Ltd's Newcastle-Carlisle service, started on 24th October 1927.

The Carlisle Joint Transaction

Ribble was already present on the Carlisle city services by virtue of the purchase of Adair's service to Raffles from 17th December 1929 following the revocation of his licence by the Watch Committee. On 19th March 1930, the Tilling and BAT operators set up the 'Carlisle Joint Transaction' under the chairmanship of Leo Myers (the Ribble chairman) and Horace Bottomley of Ribble (and a former trainee with United) was appointed to conduct the negotiations on behalf of all the companies so that a unified operation could be established and the tramways and the independent operators could be purchased. Myers and Hickmott met Sir Joseph Nall of Balfour Beatty the same month and good progress was made towards the takeover of the tramway.

By the end of 1930, Carlisle Corporation intended to support the exclusive operation of the city services by Ribble; in addition to the Raffles route, there were to be four cross city routes and other changes. The local operators, led by Carlisle and District Motor Services, objected and submitted counter-proposals. This led the Corporation to revive the idea of municipal operation and, although it lacked the necessary Parliamentary powers, it prepared a scheme for a network of routes which extended beyond the boundary into the surrounding countryside. The rival proposals were then submitted to the Traffic Commissioners under the new Road Traffic Act, 1930 and, at a five-day hearing on 23-27th June 1931, the Corporation's plans were rejected. Fresh proposals prepared by the Joint Transaction were approved by the city council and accepted by the Commissioners. The tramway system and most of the local operators were purchased by Ribble on behalf of the Joint Transaction but the territorial boundaries were revised so that United had the city service to Botcherby.

Ribble operated most of the existing services under short period licences from 1st September and introduced their replacing services on 1st November 1931. Further modifications were made on 22nd November, following the closure of the tramway system the previous evening. There were eight services identified by the letters A to H. Three radiated from the Town Hall and the others ran across town. The network was revised and developed as various housing estates expanded and new service numbers with C prefixes were introduced in the spring of 1935 as part of Ribble's system-wide renumbering scheme.

During the war, highbridge utility Guy buses were used on the city services and this set the scene for the general use of this body layout after the war. Rebodied TD4s, new PD2s, PD3s and then latterly full-height ECW-bodied Atlanteans and VRTs ensured that the city services had a high standard of vehicle. Restrictions were imposed by the low bridge at Denton and plans to lower the road, made in 1939 (to the cost of which Ribble had agreed to contribute), were postponed by the war until 1954, after which much duplication was saved. Many extensions took place in the post-war period so as to serve new housing estates but, even when the services were completely revised on 8th June 1968 and given new service numbers in the 6xx series, some of the original routes remained. Not until the transfer of United's local operations by National Bus Company on 5th January 1969 did Ribble buses reach Botcherby; from 29th November 1969 that suburb became full integrated into the pattern of city services.

For over fifty years the Carlisle city services were to be the Ribble profit centre which helped to sustain the rural network of services throughout Cumbria. Stagecoach were to transform the area yet again when they took the Ribble business into their control but nonetheless W. S. Wreathall's vision back in 1928 was fully vindicated.

A DAY AT THE COLISEUM

This scene at the Coliseum coach station, Blackpool, dates from June 1954 but the operators represented and most of the vehicle types were still to be found in the slightly later period described in the text. Only a minority of the vehicles visible were from Ribble's fleet, as was apt to be so at some times of the day – a 'White Lady' PD1, and a PD2 with Leyland bus body are the only double-deckers and there is a Royal Tiger bus almost opposite them in the line on the left.
For the rest, there is a very strong Yorkshire presence, largely of buses rather than coaches, which may reflect one of the wakes weeks when whole towns took their holidays. Yorkshire Traction was always strongly represented and there are three of its red and cream Royal Tigers with Federation-type bodies, one nearest the camera, another in the centre foreground, and on the right of the vehicles in echelon at the loading platform – there are also some older Tiger PS1 buses from the same fleet. The two Daimler CVD6 coaches with Plaxton bodies in the foreground, with a Burlingham Seagull coach behind them, were from W. Pyne & Sons of Harrogate, having worked on the J16 service from that town. There are also two Bristol L-types with ECW bodies from West Yorkshire's fleet.
The two light-coloured buses were Tiger PS1 models in the cream and blue livery of County Motors of Lepton near Huddersfield, part-owned by Yorkshire Traction, to whom they would be on hire. The Leyland-MCW Olympic at the platform on the right, very like Ribble's examples, was a Yorkshire Woollen District vehicle – that concern, based in Dewsbury, used a maroon livery at that date.

This account is based on a typical day at Blackpool Coliseum coach station, the busiest in the provinces, on an August Saturday about 1960.

For the District Traffic Superintendent (DTS), planning for the day had begun almost two weeks earlier when he had submitted to Head Office a voluminous form known as X3/3D (no one seems to know why it was called that!). It consisted of a statement of resources and duplication requirements for this Saturday. The resources were depicted in the form of a straight line graph indicating the availability of uncommitted vehicles. The estimated needs were calculated by the records of what happened in previous years, the calendar of holiday dates for various towns and, in conjunction with Head Office, advance bookings on services with pre-booking facilities. But the Ribble dogma of catering as far as possible for unbooked passengers presents many problems which have to be solved by the man on the spot. Every depot submits an X3/3D and a special section at Head Office allocates the resources to the needs and returns a copy to each depot. Frequently, some of the requirements still have a blank square against them.

The X60 service connecting Manchester and Blackpool was immensely important and needed careful attention to make sure the huge numbers of passengers that could build up were carried efficiently and with minimum delay. Here 1248, one of the second batch of 'White Lady' double-deckers, with East Lancs body on Leyland PD2 chassis, heads for Manchester from Blackpool. In the accompanying account, this Blackpool-based vehicle was being used on the Keswick service, for which double-deck capacity was also useful. The lorries in the background, with an ERF leading, belonged to British Road Services.

On the Friday evening, the DTS has had a meeting with the Senior Inspector and other inspectors who will be on duty on the Saturday morning. Staffing and tactics have been discussed including what are seen as weaknesses and the best way of dealing with the problems which may develop. It is agreed that the Senior Inspector will come to work in civilian clothes so that he can move about quickly, avoiding the endless enquiries from passengers. Even the gas meter men give the station a wide berth in summer as anyone in uniform is a target for enquiries! The meeting is attended by the inspector who looks after 'the Coast', the section of route between Blackpool and Preston via Lytham St. Annes. There are 11 stops on this section and it is essential that sufficient accommodation be left. The policy is 'if we're going to be mucked up, let it be in one place where we can see it, not at half a dozen places round the coast'. There are also coach-air passengers from the Isle of Man and Jersey to be picked up at Blackpool airport where a senior conductor will be on duty to look after things and advise the Coliseum staff of any late running planes. The regular Yorkshire Traction inspector also joins in. He comes every Saturday in the high season, sometimes just for the day on the J7 but today he has come on Friday's J12 so that he can help with the morning departures. He is well known to the Ribble staff who welcome his assistance.

The supervisory system at the Coliseum is complex as it is not a Ribble station, being owned by Blackpool Omnibus Stations Ltd. in which Ribble holds 50% of the shares and the rest by the principal users. BOS has its own manager, enquiry office staff, one inspector and several general workers who man the left-luggage room, change the indicator boards on the platforms and sweep up. It might be said that BOS are responsible for space and Ribble for movement. BOS staff decide which platforms will be used and also supervise, where necessary, the loading of services in which Ribble has no interest. These include the Lancashire United 'dailies' to small towns all over South Lancashire and the various North Western and Crosville services to Cheshire and North Wales.

The First Two Hours

To the relief of all concerned, Saturday dawns cloudy and fine. Wet days make everyone miserable and slow up the job; sweltering heat is almost as bad, sapping the energy of the control staff and seemingly making the concrete harder than usual. It's 8.15am and the passengers are starting to gather. The 8.15am X60 for Manchester – never a busy trip – is reversing from the stand. The back of the station is already full of local excursion operators' coaches hired for the day and an inspector is instructing the drivers. Six move over to the Coach Park where passengers for the 9.30am to Glasgow are already assembling. A group of Blackpool depot conductors, with overnight bags, are waiting to be allocated hired coaches for Scotland on the basis of three vehicles each. The cumbersome ticket system whereby every return ticket has to be exchanged makes this arrangement essential even though they will all return empty on the following day. They usually arrange to check one on the stand, travel with another and arrange to meet the third somewhere on the road.

Another three coaches are now on the Newcastle stand on platform 9. Northern General has sent a regulator to assist the loading – a senior conductor from Worswick Street who knows the job backwards and can handle the drivers well. Separate queues are organised for Consett, Stanley and Sunderland, nominally on feeder services from Durham, but through coaches will be run. This service loads also at Talbot Road bus station and the inspector there has already asked for assistance. The service coach is a Blackpool depot Tiger Cub which will go there and back in the day. On other days of the week, the service leaves an hour later, spending the night at South Shields. A second driver will take the coach to Lancaster, returning as passenger, in order to comply with the drivers' hours regulations.

The 8.40am J1 to Leeds, which starts from Talbot Road, is arriving headed by a lowbridge PD1A double-deck (2493) loaded for Burnley. A coach is rostered for this trip plus the 2.45pm Bradford duplicate but it was used for a Scottish duplicate on Friday. The rule on peak summer Saturdays is that coaches are only used for duties which must be coaches. The DTS has arranged with Scout to do a Salwick works trip and otherwise rearranged the bus duties to release the double-decker in the morning; the afternoon part will be covered by a Skipton depot coach whose crew will take back a Blackpool coach coming down from Newcastle. The 8.30am Leeds service coach is, surprisingly, a Seagull coach of S. & J. Wood, driven by a retired Ribble driver who worked the route regularly; it is allowed to go through almost empty to clear passengers round the coast.

The tempo is now increasing. The 9.10am Barnsley and Wakefield services are being loaded by the Yorkshire Traction inspector. The Barnsley service coach is a Blackpool-based Yorkshire Traction coach manned by a driver and conductor who have worked together since the war ended and dislike each other intensely! The Wakefield leg is normally served by a feeder from Halifax but Hebble have sent an AEC Regal service bus through. Inevitably four seats are lost to luggage which is loaded through the rear emergency door. Two Jackson's Holiday Tours and a Marshall's coach act as duplicates. The X9 Oldham service queue is divided into two – one for Oldham and the other for points up to Manchester via Bury which are catered for by a rostered Blackpool double-deck PD2 (1351) which will return as a duplicate on X60. The service coach is a Yelloway Burlingham Seagull bodied AEC Reliance. The two vehicles clear comfortably.

Other coaches have arrived for Glasgow duplication – Braithwaites of Sedbergh, Bibby's of Ingleton and Titterington's. Coaches from the north are hired when local sources are exhausted. They will only be used one way so the cost is the same. The service coach, a black and white Guy LUF of Western SMT, is kept out of sight for the time being as some seats must be left for traffic boarding *en route*. It looks as if the 30 duplicates provided for Glasgow will not be enough. Filling odd seats is always a problem and, with this level of traffic one unfilled seat on each vehicle adds up to another coach. The inspector has dealt with it before and strides to the back of the queue, consulting a clipboard as he goes. 'What's your name, madam?' he asks a new arrival. 'Mrs Macdonald', she says. 'Come along, we've been waiting for you; your seats are on that coach at the front. Hurry up and you'll be in Glasgow for dinner time!' The couple fall for it and two of the odd seats are filled. 'They do have their dinner at seven o'clock in Glasgow, don't they?', he says in an aside to a colleague. The DTS has no doubt that some of the queuing passengers should travel tomorrow but they cannot stay in their boarding-houses and have to be moved somehow. Fortunately he has taken a chance and hired two additional coaches from Jackson's that Head Office knows nothing about and these are directed to the Coach Park to clear the queue.

The X60 queue has now been divided into three including one for Nottingham and another for Great Yarmouth. There are sufficient bookings to justify a through coach for the latter and North Western have sent a Leyland-bodied Royal Tiger. This is an unlicensed but legal service formed by linking together three routes – Blackpool-Manchester, Manchester-Nottingham and Nottingham-Great Yarmouth – with a separate ticket for each section. The Nottingham coach is a Ribble Manchester depot Royal Tiger with a Blackpool crew who will bring back a North Western vehicle from Manchester.

Platforms 1 and 2 are now busy and the Middlesbrough passengers are loaded on the rear of the station. This is a one coach affair with bookings strictly controlled by United even though it is worked by Ribble Blackpool depot. The driver will take the Royal Tiger coach to Hawes, bringing back the 9.30am from Middlesbrough manned by a Blackpool driver out-stationed there for the summer. Traffic congestion at Lancaster and Kendal is starting to affect this service and delays are passed on to the southbound vehicle. Next year the drivers will work through to avoid annoyance to passengers held up at Hawes waiting for the driver from Blackpool.

The queue for the 10.0am to Liverpool is taking up a lot of room as there are separate queues for Liverpool, Cheltenham, Bristol and, this week, Llandudno. It is a particularly heavy week for West of England traffic and Bootle depot have sent four Royal Tiger coaches which will run through to Cheltenham. Two Blackpool depot PD2 duplicates for Liverpool are scheduled for 9.30am to spread the load and get substantial numbers of people out of the way. They are sure to be loaded both ways as Liverpool is one of the few places from which day traffic comes on Saturdays. Two more will be needed before 10.0am but have been laid on from Fleetwood depot. The

Yorkshire Traction's presence was always strong. Here that company's 803, a 1949 Leyland Tiger PS1 with Brush body to the BET Federation design, standard in the fleet, is seen on arrival at Blackpool. In the background is 854 from the same company, a Dennis Lancet III with similar body, already parked up against the wall of the adjoining Blackpool Corporation bus and tram depot. A problem with the use of such vehicles on express services was the lack of space for any luggage that would not fit on the internal overhead racks, forcing the sacrifice of the rear row of seats to its carriage, as mentioned in connection with a Hebble AEC Regal in the text above.

Such was the pressure on the X60 that double-deckers were hired in from any possible source reasonably placed in relation to the route. Here the Stalybridge, Hyde, Mossley and Dukinfield Joint Transport Board, inevitably known by its initials SHMD, has sent its No. 4, a Daimler COG6 with Northern Counties body dating from 1939, at some date during the 'fifties. By then, this was quite an old a vehicle for such duty, though this type, which had the Gardner 6LW engine giving lively performance, was actually quite 'civilised' and quiet-running, with comfortable seats and moquette-lined interior panels. Some Lancashire United Leyland Tigers, also of pre-war date, are parked alongside.

service coach will run through to Bristol, the Blackpool crew working the X71 service from Liverpool Pier Head with a Liverpool vehicle which will make tomorrow's Bristol coach. From Preston, the Llandudno coach, a Blackpool Tiger Cub, will duplicate the X35 service from Colne but this is a tricky operation as the 10.0am Liverpool queue is sure to hold passengers who have booked to North Wales on the Crosville service from Liverpool and they must not be loaded on the X35. The through coach does not run every week – just when the bookings make it worthwhile – but the driver has been specially selected as he has done it before and can be relied upon to sort out the passengers round the coast.

On platform 2, Edinburgh passengers are being loaded, mainly into hired coaches of Blackpool operators. The demand is not as heavy as for Glasgow so passengers for the Lake District booked on both the Glasgow (9.30) or Edinburgh (9.50) times are queued alongside. Blackpool depot's solitary PD3 (1711) is loading for Keswick and a White Lady (1248) is being kept out of sight at the back to follow on. The Lakes traffic is always an unknown quantity and double-deckers are used as far as possible. The Edinburgh service is an AEC Reliance coach of Scottish Omnibuses manned by an Edinburgh crew based in Blackpool for the season. They are given half a load and sent out to clear passengers at Poulton-le-Fylde, Gt. Eccleston and Garstang. They will drive north until they meet the southbound coach on the road, usually somewhere between Keswick and Bothel, change over and return to Blackpool.

There is a brief panic when it is thought there is a serious overload for Edinburgh but at least 30 passengers in the queue are for Wigan and St. Helens, a service scheduled at 2.00pm. The problem of passengers arriving hours early is a serious one at the Coliseum. They have to be out of their accommodation and have nowhere to leave their luggage so turn up and stand. The station luggage room has been full since Friday evening. The Wigan people will be moved long before 2.0pm but at present they have a low priority.

It is now 10.0am and everything has been cleared on time. This is regarded as the first stage of the day's proceedings and a good omen. 'We shift 5,000 people before breakfast', say the inspectors and it's true if you don't have your breakfast until after 10.0am!

The inspector who has supervised the Scottish loadings now has to telephone details of every vehicle through to a control office at Morecambe who collate reports on all the Scottish services from Liverpool, Manchester, Bolton and Preston. Morecambe will see few of them but records of what are going north are essential for dealing with southbound traffic next day. The fax is 25 years in the future so the phone call is a lengthy one. Eventually Morecambe will have to telephone a consolidated report to Carlisle which is the main control point.

Congestion Problems

The X60 queue is now lengthening and BOS staff alter the linking chains to provide two more barriers. There is a 15-minute service so it will take care of itself with a standman/conductor filling up the odd seats from further back in the queue and recording departures on this and other services. The queue for the 10.55am to Leeds is also getting longer and, as this is on the station exit road with no barriers, it soon straggles and gets in the way. Fortunately a Boddy's (of Bridlington) coach, on hire to West Yorkshire, arrives bringing with it the West Yorkshire conductress who will spend the day at Blackpool handling the tickets on all the hired vehicles. Her day started at her Ilkley home at 5.0am and she has already checked at least 12 coaches on the 6.30am departure from Leeds which runs regularly on summer Saturdays though it is not in the timetable. Ribble inspectors can more or less forget about the Leeds queue as she is as good as two inspectors and will shout if in trouble. Boddy's coach goes straight on to the stand immediately and will depart when full. Two more coaches arrive, an OB of Eddie Brown of Helperby and another of Wray's. The latter is sent through to Talbot Road to duplicate the 10.45am to Leeds. Many of these hired vehicles will do two Leeds or Bradford-Blackpool return trips in the day.

Space problems are now mounting. A driver has parked a Leigh Corporation double-decker in the space needed to unload the Lancashire United 'dailies' and disappeared. Loudspeaker appeals are ignored. It is on hire to North Western and the inspector wants to load it for Manchester but it appears to have some kind of automatic transmission and he cannot move it. In fact it is an AEC Regent III with preselective gearbox, but he's never come across one before. Difficulties of this kind are common. Drivers want tea breaks and the station cannot spare the space to park their vehicles. Eventually he reappears and truculently puts the bus on the stand. He has no conductor so it is loaded 'Manchester first stop' and a Ribble stand conductor deals with the tickets. There are through vehicles to Derby at 10.0am and 12.00noon which do not attract much traffic, probably because Trent often allocate uncomfortable Leyland-bodied Royal Tiger buses to them. The 10.0am, manned by a North Western crew, has left on time but the 12.00 will almost certainly be late because of the traffic congestion in Preston.

There are so many people queueing, mostly with suitcases, that it is almost impossible to move about. The DTS, summoned to the telephone, finds it easier to walk right round the outside and enter by the main entrance in Tyldesley Road. There is a commotion outside the ladies' toilet where the turnstile won't work. The coin-box is full so the manager takes a large toffee tin and the problem is solved as a cascade of pennies is released.

Traffic congestion at Preston and elsewhere is now seriously affecting arrivals. A North Western duplicate on X60 is used to cover the 12.00 Derby on time and when the Trent vehicle arrives almost an hour late, the crew is sent back passenger to Manchester and the vehicle is kept to cover the 1.30pm Nottingham which has a Blackpool crew. Duplicates are starting to arrive from Liverpool. One, a Bootle depot PD3 arrives already showing 'X183 St. Helens' on the destination indicator. The crew, both old servants, work this 'special' every Saturday and have been sent back via St. Helens so many times that they have come to expect it! Their 72-seat bus clears much of the 2.0pm queue and Wigan depot duplicates accompanying the X193 service from Widnes should take care of the rest. The crews of two other Bootle depot duplicates are told to report back at 6.0pm, as their buses are used to fill in late-running X60 departures with Blackpool crews between 1.0pm and 2.0pm. If these do not leave on time, the whole evening service will be disrupted as many duties do two Manchester trips with a meal break in between. Other Liverpool area duplicates will accompany the 2.15, 3.15 and 5.15pm departures.

Heavy Arrivals

This is the busiest time for arrivals and the control staff have their work cut out to prevent the traffic on Lytham Road, including the frequent trams, from being held up by buses which cannot get into the station. The problem is not made any easier by the activities of boys with barrows, offering their services to carry luggage, and taxi drivers parking at crazy angles. Many vehicles required for later departures are sent to the overflow parking ground at Bloomfield Road from which their departure will be strictly controlled, instructions being sent by field telephone.

The senior inspector confers by telephone with the North Western inspector at Manchester, explaining what he has done on X60. One late-running North Western crew will not be back to work their next trip – the 2.37pm Manchester-Liverpool – so our man suggests he uses the 2.45pm Manchester-Blackpool crew to cover this as the bus which should work it is being held at Blackpool to cover the next Derby or Nottingham trip which is seriously late. This knowledge of other companies' workings is a unique attribute of the Blackpool Ribble inspectors and a valuable aid to solving problems on these busy days.

The BOS manager has arranged with Blackpool

The Coliseum premises are seen here in the form in which they were taken over after the purchase of the business of Wright Bros (Burnley) in January 1934. That concern had leased them, but Ribble was then able to buy the property. Blackpool Omnibus Stations Ltd was formed, with Ribble as 50% owner and the remainder shared by associated major operators of services to Blackpool, on 14th May 1934. Until demolition began in late 1935 the huge 'Collosseum' building, latterly used as a skating rink and visible in the background, remained and only a booking facility for coach travel could be provided on the site. The entrance in the centre, with the new company's name in much smaller lettering than 'Coliseum Garage', was surrounded by an alphabetical list of 60 places to which bookings could be made.

Royal Tiger coach 804 arrives at the Coliseum on the J1 from Leeds, its passengers mostly having left their seats to get out, though a lady in the front has yet to move. Behind, the driver of a West Yorkshire SGL-class Bristol LL5G bus, one of those with 8ft ECW body on a 7ft 6in chassis, doubtless duplicating on the same service, has parked by the platform. He is already jumping out, perhaps glad to do so, having had to work quite hard on the hilly route via Bradford, Keighley and Burnley over the Pennines, making frequent gear changes to make up for his vehicle's limited power from its Gardner 5LW engine. The Ribble driver would have had a much easier trip with the Royal Tiger's O.600, though he would have needed to take care in the descents, where that model's brakes were apt to be a little marginal in relation to the greater power.

Corporation Transport for the hire of the old Blundell Street tram shed and this week the 1.55pm Yorkshire Woollen District service to Dewsbury and Ossett is being loaded there. This relieves pressure on the main station and is a blessing in wet weather. In Walter Luff's time as Corporation manager, the Transport Department was hostile to Ribble but Joe Franklin is much more friendly and doubtless glad of the extra revenue. On exceptionally busy days, the Corporation bus garage and yard which adjoin the Coliseum have also been used.

Skipton depot crews arriving on the X16 from Skipton and the X7 from Southport are warned that their coaches will be used by Blackpool crews, one for the 2.40pm Huddersfield duplicate (which returns as service at 7.5pm) and the other for the 2.45pm Bradford duplicate.

Afternoon Departures

The 2.0pm X9 for Oldham departs on time, worked by three North Westerns: two Bristol L duplicates and a Weymann-bodied Leyland Royal Tiger. Several duplicates on the 2.40pm Yorkshire Traction Doncaster service have already left well ahead of time. Coaches of Leon of Finningley, Rossie Motors and Ward Bros (Lepton) are loading together with Yorkshire Traction service buses running through to Ryhill and High Green. A queue barrier is marked up for the 4.15pm Newcastle to prevent early arrivals getting in the South Yorkshire queues. Some Northern General duplicates have already arrived but have been sent to the parking ground as there is no room for them at present. Loading for Leeds and Bradford is continuous with a pair of West Yorkshire Bristol L service buses on the stand, an SG and a longer SGL. The West Yorkshire conductress has already detailed a Bristol LS coach to accompany the J1 service vehicle, which has started at Fleetwood and has little accommodation for passengers round the coast and at Preston. The J6/9 service via Skipton, which runs at 2.45pm on Saturdays instead of 7.0pm on other days has plenty of accommodation.

The Coach Park is now busy with North Western services to Stockport, Macclesfield, Northwich and adjoining towns and Crosvilles for Wrexham and Newcastle-under-Lyme. An elderly lady's demand to know where 'Binns's bus' starts from causes some head-scratching until it is realised that she wants Durham District Services, every bus of this United Automobile Services subsidiary carrying a 'Shop at Binns' advertisement.

The 3.0pm J16 to Harrogate is a Pyne's Daimler and clears comfortably. Next to it on platform 1, the 3.10pm to Middlesbrough via Skipton is loaded by its own conductors. Ribble calls this service X6 but to United it is 200. No one sets foot on board unless prebooked and the United conductors are entitled to a seat even if it means leaving a passenger behind. The Northern General regulator sorts out his passengers as he has blue Sunderland District duplicates which might as well be loaded for the town of that name. Traffic is relatively thin and some buses are sent direct to Lancaster to load the traffic from Morecambe.

Passengers are now thinning out. On the back of the station are Blackpool depot double-deckers which have arrived late from Manchester and will be put back as the Bootle depot buses return. The late turn inspector juggles them to ensure that the 'last Manchester', due back in Blackpool at 1.11am, does not run out of fuel, consumption being increased by idling in congested traffic. The scheduled bus leaves the garage at 4.55am, working first an express to Preston via Lytham St.Annes which gives connections for the 7.30am West of England departures from Liverpool, returning to Blackpool empty. It then works the 6.45am, 11.30, 4.0 and 8.30pm trips to Manchester, a colossal mileage of 428 for a double-deck bus in one day. By substituting another bus for the 4.0pm trip, there will be no danger of a fuel problem later on.

Sweeping-up Time

An air of relative calm now descends on the station and the BOS workers have brought out their long brushes and are sweeping up the day's debris. The ladies' toilet turnstile cash-box is emptied again!

There is a sigh of relief as the first of three Blackpool depot Royal Tiger coaches arrives early from Newcastle.

A scene from the early days of the Coliseum as the staff outing of Littlewood's arrives. Some 5,500 passengers were carried in 180 coaches on 23rd and 24th August 1939, just over a week before the outbreak of war. The series of parallel barriers were designed to be able to cope with large outgoing crowds by chaining off so that queues could be doubled back, but the arrangement was unpopular in bad weather and the roof was extended in 1950. The vehicles visible are mainly 1936-7 Tiger and Cheetah coaches and one or two Cheetah buses, all in spotless condition and mostly with sliding roof open, bearing identification numbers on stickers in the bulkhead window. Also among the parked vehicles are a couple of Yorkshire Traction Tiger buses on the right, and some Crosville Tiger coaches can be seen in front of the taller building in the background.

This will be given to the Skipton crew working the 4.40pm X7 to Southport and if it is late, the changeover is tight as it needs to be cleaned and fuelled.

Before going off duty, the senior inspector calls for the arrival records and estimates what duplication will be needed for evening departures. He consults with the DTS about the arrangements for Sunday as the weather forecast is favourable.

The Evening Traffic

The first duplicates from Scotland are arriving – two red and cream Western SMT coaches from Inchinnon depot and, surprisingly, a Ribble Royal Tiger coach from Ulverston depot. The conductor explains that they should have been loaded to Manchester but, as frequently happens, the inspector at Glasgow seemed to have no knowledge of Lancashire geography. This time there is a complication, as the coach is scheduled to duplicate the night service from Manchester to Glasgow with another crew. The men are given an hour's break, then take a through load to Manchester on X60.

A Blackpool depot Tiger Cub arrives from Edinburgh. This, with two others, has worked hard for over 24 hours, duplicating the 5.15pm from Blackpool to Liverpool on Friday with Cheltenham traffic, then the Liverpool-Edinburgh night service, turning round immediately on to the Edinburgh-Blackpool service – a total of about 470 miles. Three crews were sent up to Edinburgh as passengers on Friday morning and three others relieved the original men at Preston on the way north. This highly efficient arrangement works every weekend in the summer.

The arrival platform is now getting busy again with arrivals from Yorkshire, Scotland and various Lancashire towns. The Bootle PD2s, back from Manchester are handed back to their crews to duplicate the 7.5pm X71 and 8.0pm X61 to Liverpool. There are also Standerwick Royal Tiger and PS1 coaches from London, Coventry and Birmingham, setting down passengers and then continuing to their terminus at Chapel Street.

From 7.0pm a mixture of White Ladies and red double-deck buses arrives from Great Harwood, Darwen and Blackburn on services X8/18. These bring in evening excursionists and are still known as the KCRs from the name of the company taken over in 1934. Some of the buses return at 8.0pm, those not needed being held over to the 11.30pm departure. The inspector arranges with his Blackburn colleague for some of the 8.0pm buses to be returned for the 11.30pm traffic but Blackburn depot is chronically short of staff and this is not always possible. It is not unknown for a Blackpool depot bus to be sent to Blackburn on the 11.30pm X8.

The X60s are now running to time but there are some strange buses, the product of make-do-and-mend at the Manchester end during the day. An open-platform Lancashire United Guy Arab makes the 8.45pm X70 to Manchester via Westhoughton and Swinton. The last Liverpool at 9.5 just clears. With one or two duplicates, the quarter-hourly service clears the Manchester queue easily and the inspector makes sure that the last bus at 10.0pm leaves dead on time. There should now be a lull until the 11.30pm KCRs but the inspector has a problem as a flight has been diverted from Leeds/Bradford airport to Blackpool and the airline want to hire a coach to take the passengers on to Yorkshire. His colleague at Talbot Road eventually finds a driver who is willing to go. He is a relatively new man, not used to going to Yorkshire, but the inspector crosses his fingers, makes out a work ticket and sends him on his way.

The KCRs often attract a rowdy element but a friendly policeman, the son of an ex-Metropolitan officer who now works at Ribble Head Office, strolls round whenever he is on late duty. He is a man of enormous physique and his mere presence seems to have a calming effect. At 11.29pm engines are revved up, a few drunks are bundled aboard and the last buses of the day leave dead on half-past. The platform lights are switched off and another hectic summer Saturday at the Coliseum has come to an end. In a few weeks time, when the Illuminations are switched on, the days will be even longer.

It was certainly the case that by 1963 people had given up taking their Lions to the Coliseum. Leopards however were coming into their own. Two interesting vehicles which would certainly have appeared at the Coliseum in the 'sixties would have been Nos. 1060/1 (821/2 YEH). New in 1963 to the Michelin Tyre Company, these vehicles were originally used to show the merits of 'X' radial tyres, then a new product for PSVs. Here they can be seen in their original colours whilst the lower view shows the Distance Measuring Equipment with which they were equipped, during a road side tyre change.

Facing page:

Seen in Liverpool is Leyland Titan TD5 2057 (RN8622) built in 1939 and originally fitted with a Burlingham 53-seat lowbridge body. The vehicle was rebodied by Walter Alexander of Falkirk in 1949. The close similarity to the Leyland product of the period is noteworthy. The original appearance can be seen on page 88 (upper).

A Red . . .
. . . and pleasant land

The final traditional single-deckers were 20 Tiger PS2/5 buses delivered in 1950. These were the equivalent of the double-deck PD2s which had entered the fleet in some force. Although originally numbered 2780, CRN 980 had been re-numbered to 230 under the 1950 scheme.

Ribble's operating territory showed as rich a variation as any in the land. From the lakeland splendours of the north through the variously genteel or slightly brash Fylde down to the industrial grime of Lancashire and Merseyside.

What's more the buses were painted Red ! Cherry Red to be strictly accurate with some cream relief varying down the decades. Coaches and latterly dual-purpose vehicles too, showed a similar bent, although, usually, in a reversed style with cream predominating. However applied, vehicles clearly belonged to Ribble or one of its Associates. Wherever these were viewed – on a humble works duplicate, the extensive network of Express Services or indeed prestigious Holiday Tours, a Ribble group vehicle needed little introduction. The company's reputation was sealed.

The fleetname lettering too, was reassuringly familiar and even the lesser known subsidiaries such as Auty's Tours of Bury reflected the style, as is shown in the photograph of Leyland Tiger Cub 979 on page 70 of Volume 1. The minor changes of appearance over the years passed almost unnoticed and it was not until the late 'sixties that the lower case fleetname in a modern typeface took over.

The apparent vehicular tranquillity belied the fact that the company was in fact in the vanguard of technical development. The Leyland plant in Lancashire was ideally placed for this collaboration and the practice of the company becoming a test bed for Leyland developments continued up to May 1986 when a Leyland Lynx 901 (C544 RAO) was received on behalf of the National Bus Company. The fleet list over the years reads like a litany of Leyland models – few being missed. However, Ribble always remained loyal to its suppliers, at least whilst it was responsible for its own fleet. The 'sameness' which becomes apparent in the 'fifties reflects this aspect. Clearly the suppliers for their part took the company's requirements seriously – Burlingham supplied various coaches to the Seagull pattern through the 'fifties in versions to suit differing uses and after a brief flirtation with Duple (Midland) and Harrington, Plaxton assumed the mantle. This pattern continued throughout the first three generations of the 'Panorama' era until the National Bus Company gradually assumed the control over ordering.

Titan 1405 (HRN 45) is an air braked PD2/13 of 1955 carrying Metro-Cammell highbridge bodywork equipped with platform doors.

Typifying both Leyland's double-deck production and Ribble's image of the day is Titan PD2/3 2756 (CRN 849) apparently on a private working. In the bright sunlight the Ribble livery and fleetname convey the 'feel' of the fleet.

Whilst BMMO (Midland Red), under Donald Sinclair's charismatic leadership, produced the first viable underfloor engine design (the S6) Ribble quickly sought to catch up. The company's engineers worked closely with the Sentinel company in what some would have described as a brave or even fool-hardy endeavour. However, the resultant STC4 and STC6 buses proved to be fairly successful and certainly led full lives in the Carlisle area. STC6 number 285 of the second batch is seemingly engaged upon a Private Hire working in its adoptive city.

Leyland Motors was stung into action by the simple expedient of running the Sentinels past the Works Gate. The reaction was certainly quite impressive with no fewer than three alternatives for the discerning operator. Ribble took batches of each option, the first in a very long line of Leyland underfloor engined single-deckers. The left lower view shows integral Olympic HR44 264, (DRN 128) in the Pennine town of Settle, bound for Sedbergh, whilst on the right is Saro bodied Tiger Cub 411 (FCK 843).

The third member of the Leyland trio of underfloor-engined models designed was the Royal Tiger PSU1. Number 224 (ECK 586) is a typical Leyland-bodied vehicle. It is seen heading for the picturesque village of Cartmel, in Lancashire, as the area was then called. Cartmel is also the home of an elusive racecourse which once enjoyed a degree of infamy. This contrasts with the internationally known course at the other end of the company's territory – Aintree.

Ribble took many coaches based on early mid-engined chassis. Royal Tiger No. 127 actually formed part of the associated Standerwick fleet but was identical to 'Ribble' badged examples in this pioneering class. Even at this time Ribble group vehicles were fitted with full bus-type destination equipment above the windscreen. In the 1960s this was to become commonplace – with the clearly inaccurate description 'Bristol Dome' given – because of the space problem caused by a front mounted radiator.

Later deliveries were based on the lower powered but lightweight Tiger Cub. Late model Burlingham Seagull coachwork was fitted to 1013 (LCK 727) seen on service X21. This was the last batch of single-deck vehicles built by Burlingham to be bought new by the company.

As the evolution took place rear platforms gained doors. As the PD2 gave way to the PD3 in 1957, entrances moved to the front with sliding doors, full front, enclosed radiators and an open bulkhead behind the driver. In some designs this would have led to complaints about intrusive noise levels but the smooth running Leyland O.600 was not a significant problem in this area. The early PDR1 Atlantean broke the mould, though Metro-Cammell maintained their premier position as body builder. Quite apart from the coach variants the Atlantean appeared to have captured the hearts and minds of Ribble management, but the PD3 and even the dubious Albion Lowlander profited from the early unreliability of PDR1 series Atlanteans. Strangely the unreliability of new designs in service was to be a normal feature of operators' lives in the very near future. Even greater change was afoot, for by 1966, Bristol Commercial Vehicles had gained orders from the company for its highly acclaimed RE single-deck bus - though the coach version was not as well received, possibly because of an element of NBC policy creeping in. The solitary Leyland Panther of 1964 remained just that. The initial order for the Bristol VRT is, however, more enigmatic. Ribble had some choice in the matter, a low-height Atlantean with conventional upper deck was available, but elected to take Gardner-engined Bristols. The model received an obviously unfriendly welcome, but nonetheless, central policy took over and the model established its hegemony.

To many, Ribble Motor Services will always evoke memories of successive generations of double-deck coaches of varying degrees of sophistication. The PD2 variant is represented by now preserved White Lady 1247 (DCK 218) seen here on the Stray at Harrogate after a Trans-Pennine run.

Burlingham bodied the first batch of PD1 based 'White Ladies' and remained a key supplier of double-deck bodies in the 'fifties – indeed until it withdrew from the market. Titan PD2/13 1462 (JCK 536) is seen in Ormskirk, an important agricultural centre in west Lancashire. Yet another of the contrasts to be found in the traditional territory of the company.

Burlingham remained a supplier of the new style double-deck bodywork to Ribble and 1958-built PD3/4 1600 (LCK 763) is seen *en route* to a fitting place on service H4. Although *avant garde* in some ways, the fitting of a synchromesh gearbox maintained a link with the past. By now the original gold fleetname transfers had given place to cheaper ones in a yellowish colour. Full lining out had long since disappeared.

A later PD3 is 1765 of the penultimate batch in 1962. By now Burlingham bodies had given place to Metro-Cammell and the Pneumo-cyclic gearbox was fitted.

Scout management had pursued an engineering policy close to that of Ribble, but with a touch of individuality. Eventually the vehicles came into the main fleet but their BMMO/Leyland enclosed radiators and half cabs made them immediately distinctive, despite the Burlingham body. Number 1978 (MCK 371) is bound for Burnley on service 152.

The front engine double-deck era came to a close with what was one of the least happy designs of all time. The Albion Lowlander was an amalgam of PD3 front-end structure and a low-height rear axle section. Alexander hardly excelled itself in this design of body to complete the ensemble. Nonetheless, a full life-span was enjoyed by the type. Number 1852 (UCK 852) is seen.

Ribble territory expanded and contracted as demonstrated throughout these two Volumes. The times up to NBC formation were those of expansion and up to 1977 continued thus. Then came the setting up of the National Travel companies to operate, successfully, Holiday Tours and Express Services. Financially this policy failed through the inevitable conflict between the marketing companies and the service providers over the split of the revenue – particularly where loss-making services were involved. As a result of this express territory came back in the early 'eighties as indeed did a locally-managed Holiday Programme run in conjunction with the highly successful 'National Holidays' business. This spawned the re-emergence of the Kingfisher and Sandpiper titles. The NBC Group was perhaps at the zenith of its corporate strength when came the transfers demanded by Nicholas Ridley chronicled elsewhere. After Privatisation, the new management owners both expanded and contracted the areas of influence. The recently recovered express work was sold, with the better coaches, to Amberline of Liverpool who were later taken over by Crosville Wales. On the other hand, by acquiring BET's new minibus business in Preston and Manchester, Ribble grew in vehicle numbers. Stagecoach had different views with further transfers between Ribble and northern compatriot Cumberland Motor Services and exchanges with British Bus around Greater Manchester. As this volume goes to press Ribble is spearheading the Stagecoach Group response to its not having secured the purchase of GM Buses South in the belated Privatisation of the last PTC to survive.

As with many fleets the Atlantean arrived in 1959 – – and is still there today. An early 'Box Look' Metro-Cammell highbridge 1614 (NCK 355) displays the modern image fleetname introduced in the late '60s.

Ribble had always had a problem with low bridges and the unhappy PDR1/1 with sunken upper deck gangway was acquired to meet the need. The second vehicle of the type to enter the fleet was 1657 (NRN 557) in Bolton. Notice the traditional Ribble plaque fleetname in place on the dash panel.

After a period of consistency, Ribble turned back to Alexander for a small batch of traditional low-height double-deckers. This batch of steel-framed H-type bodies was to be the only work placed with Alexanders apart from the M-type Leopard until the Stagecoach era. Number 1875 (CRN 875D) is seen in its original Ribble company livery *en route* for Blackburn.

The first Atlantean era was brought to an end with the delivery of this batch of Northern Counties-bodied PDR1/3 variants. This bodybuilder had never really enjoyed any success at Ribble and this batch did not herald any change in that respect. Number 1959 (ECK 959E) is seen on home territory near Preston. The BET pattern windscreens are still fitted to new Volvo double-deckers entering the Company's fleet in 1994.

The rear-engined double-deck bus finally returned to favour to facilitate one-man-operation. Four of the original 'Box Look' Atlanteans were converted to this pattern and enjoyed long lives as a result. A few even had their destination gear rebuilt so that the driver could change displays from the cab. This modification made the vehicle look even worse, especially when adverts designed to go either side of the traditional displays were plastered on. Number 1647 (NCK 636) is seen at Blackpool.

NBC was criticised for deleting the white reliefs on single-deck buses. Memories are short, for in the 'sixties BET encouraged subsidiaries to do the same. This Leopard PSU3 looks dire in overall Cherry Red in 1966.

The beginning of what was ultimately to be the end of the Leyland association came when the company itself ordered ten Bristol REs. The ECW bodies were to that company's standard outline although they had Ribble destination gear, not a Tilling or BET design which came later. The bodies were noteworthy in having Deans centre doors of a continental design. When opening, these moved outwards away from the body and around the door pillars to leave the full width of the aperture clear. This is 225 (FRN 225F) at Fleetwood.

HOW THE TRAFFIC DEPARTMENT WORKED

In the early days when the company was relatively small and geographically compact, the organisation was rudimentary, the Managing Director, (Major Hickmott), the Engineer, (Capt. Betteridge) and the Secretary, (at first Harry Cumming then R.T. Ebrey), controlling the day-to-day affairs of the company with the help of foremen, inspectors and clerks.

When, from 1927, the company started to break out of its Lancashire heartland, delegation of various functions became essential. Communications both by road and telephone were much more basic in those days and many of the problems which arose in the course of bus operation needed immediate decisions.

When existing businesses were purchased, clauses were often built into the contract guaranteeing employment for named individuals and jobs of similar status had to be found for them. Many of the people who joined Ribble in this way were able and dedicated employees. They sometimes continued in their old jobs but ran Ribble buses instead of their own as in the case of Mr J.E. Coward, Secretary of the Furness Omnibus Co. Ltd., who conscientiously controlled Ribble's affairs in the Furness area for 25 years. Others were moved away to look after depots elsewhere or to Head Office. Many of these people became valued long-serving members of the staff.

However, there were people who could not, or would not, fit into the rather bureaucratic organisation which grew within Ribble. These were often men with scant respect for the finer points of bus licensing who had been accustomed to taking short cuts and maximising profits, sometimes at the expense of their passengers. Trips would be missed on competitive services if a lucrative private hire offered or there was a special event which promised richer pickings. These practices were completely contrary to Ribble's policy of meticulous regularity and reliability.

Others were guaranteed a job for a limited period and this did not necessarily reflect on the person's ability. In this category was Thomas Robinson who became Traffic Manager when Kenyons, Coleman and Robinson's stage services were acquired in December 1926. He had a five-year contract and as KCR was still in business as a coach operator, there was a potential conflict of interests.

These circumstances led to Ribble having to adapt their organisational structure to the people available so that some areas were managed differently from others. On the traffic side, there gradually emerged a system of district (later called area) superintendents, responsible for a group of depots each controlled by a resident inspector or traffic supervisor (later called district traffic superintendents). The abilities of these officials varied greatly. The case of one area superintendent, who was rumoured to have served in the armed forces with Major Hickmott in World War I, encapsulates the company's policy towards its old servants. In the company's early years he had worked tirelessly as a cleaner, conductor, and inspector and it was men like him who were responsible for welding together the many acquired operators into a corporate whole and exploiting the new opportunities which emerged. In 1928 his salary was £275 per annum. He probably worked 70-80 hours a week and quite literally never took a day off except a short annual holiday, right up to the end of his working life. However, he can only be described as totally incompetent in later life. He was short-sighted and deaf but spurned both spectacles and a hearing-aid. He lived in complete fear of 'Them' (the senior management) and refused to delegate, constantly frustrating his district superintendents by interfering in their work and not keeping them informed of what he was doing. He was such a hopeless driver that only cars which had been discarded by others were allocated to him! Somehow, he survived in his job until two years after retirement age because the company's record system was not geared to ensuring that people retired on reaching 65. His problem was just that he could not cope with the rapid changes of the post war years. Senior management was aware that he was not quite up to the job but he had become so much of an institution that, despite his inadequacies, the company nursed him along as a reward for years of loyalty.

The degree of authority delegated to an area or district superintendent in one place might be quite different from that applying elsewhere, being based on the abilities of the individuals concerned. The purists would, no doubt, condemn this lack of standard procedures but it was an eminently practical solution to the problem of absorbing disparate individuals, many of whom had local connections and abilities of enormous value to the company. During the 1939-45 war, some depots were given virtual independence from their areas, for the very practical reason that there was insufficient petrol available for the area superintendent to visit them in his car.

In the early days, the company insisted that all correspondence should be handled at Head Office so, if a member of the public wrote a letter of enquiry or complaint to, say, Blackburn or Lancaster depots, he received his reply from Head Office. This probably originated as empire building on the part of John Swarbrick, chief traffic clerk, whose conscientious approach to his job demanded the highest standard being applied to every letter. Eventually, as the company expanded, the sheer weight of correspondence demanded a different approach and certain depots were classed as 'correspondence depots'. The criteria were not the size or importance of the depot but the perceived ability of the incumbent to write an acceptable letter and, perhaps, the availability of a typewriter.

The engineering department, after functioning with one or more mobile assistant engineers, eventually adopted the same regional approach with area engineers controlling depot foremen most of whom were eventually redesignated depot engineers. The traffic and engineering areas did not coincide for many years as it was argued that the needs of the two departments were different. Area superintendents numbered between three and seven at different times but, eventually in the 1960s, there were four areas for both purposes.

The Secretary's department's had no representative at area level, dealing direct with senior cash clerks (later senior depot clerks) who were responsible for the cash, tickets, lost property and mileage recording. Once more, the purist would be offended by the flexible nature of the depot organisation for the senior depot clerk, (responsible to the Secretary through the head of Ticket Audit), was the recognised deputy of the district traffic superintendent, (responsible through the area superintendent to the Traffic Manager), and both had to deal with the depot engineer whose responsibility was to the Chief Engineer, through the area engineer. Yet this unorthodox arrangement worked admirably until comparatively modern times when a greater need for cost control led to the district superintendents being upgraded to Depot Managers with responsibility for all the depot's functions.

In the formative years, the company chairman was involved much more with changes in the management of the BAT subsidiaries. Leo Myers who was chairman until 1930 personally conducted negotiations with various bodies sometimes with unfortunate long-term results for the company. When he resigned on 1st May 1930, W.S. Wreathall became chairman and Ashton Davies of the LMS, vice-chairman. Wreathall personally appointed F.A. Dickinson as Traffic Manager in 1931 without consulting Major Hickmott, who was on holiday at the time. Dickinson had been with the Llandudno Blue company which was swallowed up by Crosville (of which Wreathall was also chairman) and a job had to be found for him.

Head Office Organisation

Of all the large regional bus companies, Ribble was probably the most centralised, a policy which afflicted it with a vast bureaucracy. In retrospect, it is wonderful that the company achieved such eminence despite the vast burden of paper generated from Frenchwood Avenue! One negative result was the creation of too many able specialists, people with an expert knowledge of only one or two small facets of the company's operations. Many of these people would have functioned much more efficiently if their experience had been widened.

The move into the new office block at Frenchwood on 6th September 1937 triggered an enormous increase in the numbers employed, a classic example of staff expanding to fill the space available! At Frenchwood, there were four main departments which had varying degrees of impact on day-to-day operations. The Traffic department was the most monolithic of all with sections, each controlled by a senior clerk, dealing with particular functions. One dealt with extended tours, excursions and private hire. While depots could issue quotations at rates recommended by Head Office, all acceptances had to be forwarded to Head Office who, in due course, issued the Work Ticket and sent it to the depot. Only jobs booked late were exempt from this rule and all used Work Tickets were forwarded for a check against payment and for filing. Needless to say, there were literally mountains of these. The weakness was that the competition in different areas varied so much that standard rates did not make sense. This was particularly true of the seaside towns where, in winter, there were too many coaches chasing too few jobs. It was too easy for a district superintendent who wanted a quiet life to ignore

Carlisle became a major operational centre for Ribble from 1931, with a series of local services (which for many years had C-prefix route numbers), yet the scheduling was carried out 88 miles away by headquarters staff in Preston, who may never have visited the city. The Titan TD4 in this unusually quiet scene in the city centre, perhaps on a Sunday morning, is bound for Blackwell on the C15 – the photograph dates from soon after the vehicle was rebodied by Burlingham in 1947, when such buses were sent to work the bulk of the Carlisle routes, remaining there until new PD2 models began to replace them in 1955. The car parked by the railway station approach in the foreground, possibly in use as a taxi, is an Armstrong-Siddeley.

THE RIBBLE RUNNING SHEET

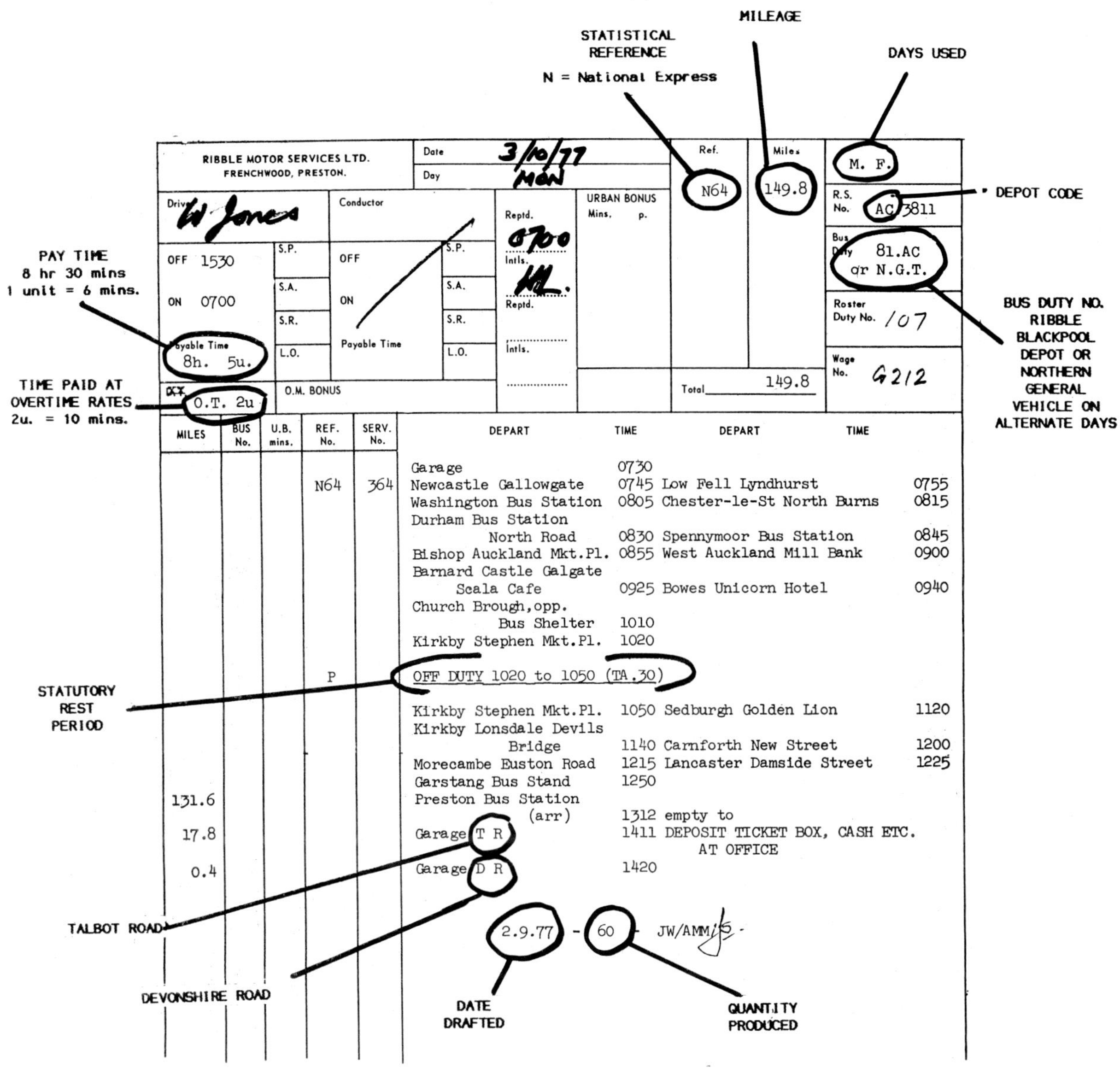

Ribble used a unique document known as a Running Sheet which combined the functions of running board, time sheet and mileage record. In the days of crew operation, both driver and conductor would be issued with a copy of the same document though the signing on and off times would be slightly different.

The general arrangement of a Running Sheet is shown in the accompanying illustration. They were prepared by Head Office Schedules department and held in racks at the depots, marked with the sheet numbers and days used so that a day's set could be drawn quickly.

Many running sheets had spaces for the insertion of extra trips which had to be initialled by an inspector. Special duties were written out by hand. Some depots kept special sheets in skeleton form on which departure times could be inserted to save time in the office.

After use, the depot clerks would sort the sheets and use them to record payable time for drivers and conductors and mileage run. The latter had to be recorded against both routes and vehicles. In both cases only variations from the standard schedules were recorded. Thus additions were made for extra trips and deductions for trips missed for any cause.

As far as is known, the system was unique to Ribble and Pennine (which was run like a Ribble depot). Scout went on to the system when acquired in 1961.

the private hire market on the grounds that the standard rates were not competitive. On the other side of the coin, the expertise of the tours specialists produced extended tours programmes of the highest quality.

Centralised Rostering

The largest section was Schedules & Rosters with over 30 staff at one time. It dealt with drivers' and conductors' rosters for the whole company with sub-sections of roster clerks corresponding with each of the traffic areas and producing all the rosters for the depots except holiday week variations which were done locally. Nowadays, the concept of day-to-day operations in Carlisle being worked out by clerks in Preston who may never have visited the border city, seems like lunacy and there is no doubt that much was lost because the people doing the job usually had no local knowledge whatsoever. The job consisted of planning the duties (with due regard to statutory limitations on drivers' hours), assembling them into bus duties which were drawn on a straight line graph, writing up the Running Sheets (see illustration) and then building them into duties. When a new roster was complete, the depot roster representatives, one driver and one conductor drawn from the local trade union hierarchy, would be sent to Frenchwood to agree to it. Their reactions varied in direct relationship to the militancy of the local union membership. All the Running Sheets then had to be typed on stencils, checked, run off and distributed to the depots. An enormous quantity of paper was used in this exercise.

A periodic exercise was the updating of the Service Schedules, enormous working timetables written in pencil for ease of alteration, which nevertheless were usually out of date. All minor alterations between roster changes required by depots had to be submitted to Head Office for processing.

After each major roster change, a statistical base was calculated for each depot, the key elements of which were miles per actual hour and miles per payable hour. In the first instance, this gave some check on the efficiency of the clerk compiling the roster but the main purpose was to check on the efficiency of the depot's use of manpower. Serious variations from the base had to be explained away by local superintendents.

Another job for Schedules & Rosters was keeping check on the miles run by each partner in the many joint service pools. Mileage details were supplied monthly by Ticket Audit, and balances kept. When serious deficits or over-runs were noted, some initiative was taken to rectify the imbalance. The Vehicle Allocation function was originally included but it was separated when its role became increasingly more complex. It decided what vehicles each depot should have and, in summer, allocated the company's resources at summer weekends by the procedure mentioned elsewhere. This involved constant liaison with the many joint operators and its head, Norman Miller ('Mr Miller Traffic' as distinct from 'Mr Miller Secretary') became a well-known telephone voice throughout the land. Movements of vehicles between depots were also organised by this section.

Fares and Contracts

All fare tables were compiled by the Fares Section, a relatively small one whose duties increased enormously after 1951 when fares increases became frequent. Ammunition had to be prepared to present to the Traffic Commissioners, involving the calculation of rates per mile and average fares for given distances. With so many joint operations, Ribble was inevitably affected by increases introduced by its partners. A tedious job was checking to ensure that no anomalies were introduced because the fares had been changed only on one section of a long route. Anomalies could consist of an ability to perform a journey more cheaply by re-booking at an intermediate point or the emergence of different fares for journeys between the same points by different routes. When increases became very frequent, fare books were replaced by separate sheets. Someone devised a plastic holder for them, designed to fit on the conductor's cuff. Needless to say, these soon broke on impact with seat-backs and handrails and were little used.

Ribble issued season tickets (usually called contracts in the north) on a vast scale. These were ordered and paid

Ribble operated numerous routes jointly with other operators. In the area around Leyland, J. Fishwick & Sons, based in that town, shared the working of many routes with Ribble, including seven running into Preston, as well as works services. Many of the vehicle types operated were similar, but the lowbridge version of the MCW Orion body, as seen here on a Fishwick PD2 at the firm's garage, was not found in Ribble's fleet. Relationships with old-established independents were often friendly, but an eye had to be kept on the mileages run to ensure that they were in accordance with the agreements in force.

Works services formed an important part of Ribble's activities, especially in the days when hardly any factory workers had their own form of transport, save possibly a bicycle. Wet weather produced long queues, as here at Leyland just after the 1939-45 war; pre-war Titans load under the eye of an inspector and a Tiger coach awaits its turn, with blinds set for the W12 to Preston. In 1952, works services listed as running to Leyland – either for Leyland Motors or serving other companies in the town comprised four from Wigan, twelve from Preston or other nearby places, four from Chorley and two from Blackburn.

for at enquiry offices but every one was prepared at Head Office. When the County Councils introduced a policy of paying for school contracts, the same procedure was adopted and an enormous volume of work was created just before each school year began.

Perhaps the least popular section with area and depot management was General which dealt with staff matters and complaints from the public. Its senior clerk also acted as the personal clerk to the Assistant Traffic Manager who usually dealt with the trade unions, the appointment or regrading of inspectors and disciplinary appeals which could not be settled at area level. To many at the depots, the General section was the ultimate of Ivory Towers, with little or no appreciation of the problems encountered in the real world in which the buses actually ran. The principles current in 1939 were often applied to conditions in the 1950s when staff was short and men no longer jumped through hoops when commanded.

W.J. (Joe) Hart, when Assistant Traffic Manager, was famous for delivering long, boring homilies preceded by 'I remember the time...' and occasionally related to his experiences with Parsons Motors of Chorley where he had originated in 1925. But he dealt very shrewdly with some situations. There was a particularly troublesome depot union chairman, an articulate man who had joined as a conductor and later trained as a driver. Joe had his own little group of mobile inspectors who reported only to him and carried Senior Inspector rank. He instructed the depot to send this union chairman to his office at 9.30 one morning. When the man returned to his depot at 4.30pm, he was dressed in full Senior Inspector's uniform, having been recruited into this select body. The ATM had realised that here was a man who had to have power and was not particular how he got it. He certainly got his own back for all the trouble that the man had caused in the past and if there was a job to be done on Shap at midnight on a frosty winter's night, there was no doubt who would be detailed for it! Eventually the man resigned, left the area and was soon active in the union elsewhere.

Licensing and Publicity

Another important section was Licensing which expanded greatly after the Road Traffic Act 1930; it had its own suite of offices on the first floor presided over by Ted Holding with Geoff Dawes doing the routine appearances in the Traffic Courts. Specialist lawyers were employed on the trickier cases and F. Lustgarten, Bill Blackhurst and Douglas Walker became well-known names in this field. Ribble guarded what it saw as its interests relentlessly and opposition to another operator's application sometimes landed the company with an expensive, loss-making service. One wonders how many lost causes would have been pursued if these adventures had been properly costed in the modern sense.

Publicity was also a complex undertaking producing not only the familiar timetable booklets and hundreds of throw-away leaflets but much of the paraphernalia which adorned the public enquiry offices, a staff artist being employed for many years. In earlier times, route number cards and other destination equipment was designed and manufactured in quantity. In the 1950s and 1960s, under George Bell, a lifelong employee whose father had been an inspector at Lancaster, the Publicity department produced its own travel films which were shown at free public and private shows throughout its operating area.

DEPOTS AND BUS STATIONS

Ribble was a substantial property owner, the directors' policy being to own rather than to lease wherever possible. As the company grew, especially during the late 1920s and early 1930s, there was a constant shortage of garage accommodation and as soon as one problem was solved, another arose elsewhere. As early as 1928, the capital expenditure on property was £44,000, a not inconsiderable sum in its day. Later, much larger sums were involved on single properties. In the early years of the 1939-45 war Ribble, like many companies who experienced an increase in revenue and enforced reduction in expenditure on wages and maintenance, was awash with money. Much was invested in residential property, some for occupation by key staff members but the majority as a safe haven for money. Late in 1942, 63 houses in Maghull, near Liverpool, were bought at auction for £26,775. They were gradually sold off after the war for almost four times their original cost.

The company appointed its first qualified architect, Cecil Quinn, in June 1927 at a salary of £7 per week and during his long service with Ribble, he placed his individual style on many elegant buildings. His small department became responsible for a planned programme of maintenance work.

AINTREE (AY)

Because both Liverpool and Bootle depots were full to capacity in 1945, it was decided to build a completely new depot and a site in Ormskirk Road, Aintree was obtained in 1946. Post-war bureaucracy caused endless delays and it was not until 6th July 1951 that the garage was formally opened. The brick building had a capacity of 90 vehicles of which 52 were originally transferred from Liverpool and Bootle. Modern maintenance facilities including Ribble's home-made version of the Essex bus washer were amongst the equipment installed. A large parking area was useful for accommodating the large number of additional coaches used in summer and for race day parking. Both depot and area offices were accommodated in an administrative block to the south of the garage.

North Western took over in September 1986 but closed it in February 1989 when the allocation was moved to the former Crosville depot at Love Lane. However, within two years, the Merseyside Development Corporation wanted Love Lane for redevelopment and Aintree was reoccupied, becoming the company's third head office in five years.

AMBLESIDE (BJ)

When Lancashire and Westmorland Motor Services were acquired on 1st December 1927, Ribble inherited a wooden building known as Wansfell Tower garage. A new depot, attractively built of local stone, upon which the company was congratulated, was erected in Compston Road in 1931-32. Also acquired was the office at the Market Cross which had been the former registered office of the Lake District Road Traffic Co. Ltd. since 1904. This remained as offices after the adjacent bus station was built, using local stone, in 1952 on land purchased in 1930. The office was unusual in that it doubled as a railway booking office. The bus station was also built to blend with the local architecture. In April 1981, Ambleside became a sub-depot of Kendal but was closed in May 1989, before the takeover by Cumberland Motor Services. An office in the Rothay Hotel, Grasmere was also inherited in 1927. It was rented at 11/- (55p) per week and closed at the end of the 1948 season.

BARROW

The Furness company's office in Ramsden Square was taken over in 1930 and remained open until damaged in an air raid in 1941. A new office in Schneider Square was opened in June 1953. It later moved to Church Street but went back to Furness House, Schneider Square in 1966 jointly with Barrow Corporation. Emlyn Street garage was opened on 26th October 1986 to accommodate the fleet of minibuses operated in opposition to Barrow Corporation. The premises were too small and a rented yard in Ironworks Road was also used for a few months in 1988-89. With the acquisition of the Barrow municipal undertaking from 26th May 1989, operations were transferred to their Hindpool Road depot. On 18th June 1989, the company's Cumbrian operations were transferred to Cumberland Motor Services.

BLACKBURN (AG, AH)

The original garage at Foundry Hill came with the purchase of Pendle Motor Services in 1926 but it soon became inadequate and Dock Street warehouse was rented from the Leeds and Liverpool Canal Co. Additional premises were acquired in 1928 at George Street East. It was decided to develop the site partially to accommodate 50 buses at a cost of £12,000 and the new garage was opened in 1930.

In 1936 an extension to George Street was put in hand and it was decided, also, to rebuild Foundry Hill with new offices and a staff club and this was completed by 1938 when an office in Darwen Street was closed. Part of the roof of George Street garage was raised in 1960 and it was extensively rebuilt during 1985. In the course of its various extensions, the garage was extended to include the street which ceased to exist! Foundry Hill was closed for redevelopment of the area. In modern times, Blackburn became a minibus depot but is also one of the company's three main maintenance centres.

BLACKPOOL (Devonshire Road) (AC)

Numerous small garages, acquired with other businesses, were occupied in Blackpool and in 1935 plans were drawn up for a new garage to be built on land owned by Standerwick's in Devonshire Road, at a cost of £24,344 including equipment. It was opened in 1937 and accommodated both Ribble and Standerwick coaches. The latter had been housed at King Edward Garage, Chapel Street, Kent Road and various small garages in the town and all these were retained for the time being. Land on the north side, purchased in 1954, was used for storing delicensed vehicles and extra parking was available on the forecourt.

The garage was requisitioned by the Air Ministry from 7th October 1939 to 24th September 1945 and the Dickson Road and Kent Road garages followed in October and November 1940, putting the company in some difficulty.

In the 1950s the summer allocation was about 30 Ribble and 70 Standerwick coaches with Yorkshire Traction, Scottish Omnibuses and Western SMT coaches in every night. This made it rather full but, when Scout was taken over in December 1961, somehow or other, room was found for about 25 Scout vehicles! When use of the Gay Hostess double-deck coaches was at its height, the staff achieved amazingly quick turn-rounds, cleaning and servicing several vehicles and toilets and restocking the larder, in the space of less than an hour. During the winter, in addition to normal maintenance work, painting and refurbishment work was undertaken, using, to some extent, Standerwick coach drivers.

The depot's foundations were unstable and, with the decline of services, it was closed and demolished in 1987, the residual coaches being accommodated at the Coliseum bus station where basic servicing equipment was installed.

BLACKPOOL (Talbot Road) (AC)

This depot was offered to the company in a near-complete state in 1932, having been built for some other purpose. It cost about £7,000 and about £2,000 was spent to complete it and provide pits, etc. Being only 600 yd from Talbot Mews it was very conveniently situated. It came into use in 1933. After Devonshire Road was completed it operated only service buses and, for many years, only double-deck buses were housed there.

Talbot Road garage, Blackpool, is seen here in September 1993, in use by J. Abbott & Sons Ltd., coach operators, after Ribble had closed it in 1988. In earlier times some of its buses had clocked up nearly 6,000 miles per month on the X60 service to Manchester, calling for high standards of maintenance.

It supplied buses for the X60 Manchester-Blackpool service and, in the 1950s, achieved the highest mileages on the system for this type of vehicle – approaching 6,000 miles per month. If a particular bus was lagging behind the average mileage for its type and age, it would be sent to Blackpool to catch up, much to the chagrin of the Depot Engineer, who was often faced with the task of bringing a bus up to the standard whereby it could reliably do such mileages. It was a small shed with an allocation of about 30 vehicles and ran into trouble when 36ft long saloons replaced some of the double-deckers and, at the same time, work was transferred from Preston depot. Some land adjoining the garage was purchased in 1965 to relieve the congestion.

The depot offices, opened in 1928 in Cookson Street, alongside Talbot Road Bus Station, were moved to the first floor of the garage in 1952. The enquiry office moved to Travel Corner at the corner of Talbot Road and Abingdon Street, which was under Standerwick management. The depot was closed on 13th August 1988, following the loss of BNFL Salwick contracts and other work, the residual operations being transferred to Fleetwood, Preston and Lancaster. Talbot Road garage was later occupied by J. Abbott and Sons Ltd., an old-established coach operator.

BOLTON (AS)

A small depot was established at Bolton in the mid-twenties, a garage in Charles Street being rented at £7 per week. By 1928, several buses were being kept in other garages in the town and premises were bought in Goodwin Street for £4,500. The building was completely reconstructed at a cost of £8,250 and occupied late in 1929.

The original offices in Albany Chambers were transferred to Victoria Square. After the acquisition of Christy's and Snaylam's businesses in 1938, their separate offices on Moor Lane bus station were extended to form one block and the Victoria Square premises were remodelled as an enquiry office.

The depot was closed as an economy measure in April 1981, its fleet being shared between Blackburn, Burnley and Chorley, but was reopened on 26th October 1986 when deregulation enabled new services to be started in and around Manchester. In September 1990, the allocation had reached 90 vehicles and by 1992 it was the company's largest depot.

BOOTLE (CL)

The original Bootle depot at 507 Hawthorne Road was owned by Garlick, Burrell and Edwards, and was acquired with the Merseyside Touring Co.Ltd. in February 1930. In January 1933, it was decided to cover over most of the open space and erect a new building capable of holding 75 vehicles at a cost of £11,000. The new depot built on the site bore a family resemblance to several other Ribble depots of the period, reflecting the influence of the company's Architect, C.D. Quinn. Its roof was supported on steel trusses with a wide span and largely uninterrupted floor area. Maintenance facilities for the whole Merseyside fleet were provided. The building was further extended in 1935 and 1937.

The garage entrance was opposite Staley Street and the yard adjoined the Leeds and Liverpool Canal. It was Ribble's largest depot, with space for 107 vehicles, some of which were parked outside, radiator heating equipment being provided in 1947. In the summer, the additional coaches brought the depot fleet up to 130 and an overflow parking ground was found on a former football field nearby.

In the post-war period, some congestion was relieved by acquiring additional offices in a building opposite the garage and, in 1948, a body shop was opened at Fazakerley in a former barrage balloon hanger, 80 ft. in height. A false canvas ceiling was fitted to cut down heat loss. The shop could handle all body work for the Merseyside depots and Wigan.

In October 1979, the original depot was closed and operations were moved to new premises costing £750,000 at 499 Hawthorne Road, about 300yd further south. The two-acre site was almost 50% larger, consisting mainly of open-air parking with covered maintenance facilities occupying about one third of the site. It was of the 'swimming bath' type with 10 pits equipped with compressed air, low voltage power points, exhaust extractors and waste oil disposal equipment. The drive-through fuelling and cleaning bay was in a separate building with 25,000 gallon fuel tanks above ground, shielded by a wall embellished with the NBC logo. The workshop was designed to service the Liverpool and Southport depot fleets of almost 50 vehicles in addition to its own.

It was taken over by North Western in September 1986 and for a time was the registered office of that company. The original premises remained unused until 26th September 1992 when they were occupied as a bus garage by Liver Line Travel Services Ltd. When this company came under the control of North Western in July 1993, the depot had gone full circle.

BURNLEY (AK, CA)

When Burnley depot opened on 10th October 1923, the four Daimler buses were accommodated on a site close to the later Olympia Street garage, the offices, which were candlelit, being in Boot Street. New offices were rented in Grimshaw Street in 1925 and remained there until 1934 when the Parker Lane premises were taken over with the Wright Brothers business, together with a garage in Turf Street.

In 1926, century-old premises were obtained in Trafalgar Street. Originally occupied by textile machinery merchants, they had been partially burnt down about 1925 and were thoroughly renovated as a garage for 42 vehicles (code AK). Later it became necessary to find additional accommodation in Olympia Street which was used for coaches (code CA). The Turf Street garage of Wright Brothers was adapted as a repair and maintenance depot, undertaking major docking and accident repairs. The Springfield Mill site was bought in October 1939 but the war prevented anything being done. In 1951 it was exchanged for the old Gas Works site and in 1958, new premises in Centenary Way, built and equipped at a cost of £125,000, replaced all three of the old buildings. A joint Ribble-Standerwick travel office was opened at 25 Albert Road, Colne on 31st March 1954. The Cattle Market served as the bus station in Burnley for many years but, as part of the town centre redevelopment scheme, a new bus station adjacent to Centenary Way was brought into use on 29th June 1964.

In 1989, following the rundown of both local and express services in the area, Burnley depot was closed, space for the remaining vehicles being rented in the Burnley and Pendle Transport depot at Queensgate, between Burnley and Nelson.

BURY (BY)

The Millett Street garage, with accommodation for 20 vehicles, was acquired with Auty's Tours in 1956 and continued to operate mainly as an excursion, tours and private hire depot under the Auty's name. Coaches were occasionally supplied for express service duplication and, if a conductor was required, it was supplied by another depot. The office was raised to the status of a Ribble booking and enquiry office. Bury depot was disposed of in 1975 when the Bury excursion business was sold off to Yelloway Motor Services.

CARLISLE (BR)

Until the autumn of 1931, Ribble kept their three Carlisle-based buses at the County garage. Their first office was the former Armstrong & Siddle premises in Cecil Street but they soon moved to 48 Warwick Road and then to Percivals' old office at 5-7 Lowther Street. The company's original Carlisle depot in Corporation Road belonged to Carlisle and District Motor Services, one of the businesses acquired in 1931. Access was difficult but it was enlarged and improved to a capacity of 58 vehicles in 1952. When the fleet outstripped this number, some buses were parked overnight on Lowther Street bus station which was opened on 7th June 1935. The northern side was leased to Cumberland Motor Services who opened an office and built a small depot for six vehicles; this was demolished about 1968. The Ribble office, built on the south side near their departure platform, was enlarged in 1939 but, when Western SMT started using the station in 1968, following closure of their Lonsdale Street depot, the office was leased to them and Ribble and Cumberland ran a joint office in the former Cumberland office. Earlier Ribble wanted to build a central bus station to be used by all operators but United and Caledonian would not agree.The Bowness-on-Solway outstation, accommodating two buses, came with the business of White Star Motors. A new garage was opened at Willowholme on 5th November 1968 and is still in use by Cumberland.

When Ribble took over the United operations in January 1969, they acquired Scotch Street bus station (built 1938) and the ex-United routes were run from there until they removed to the Ribble station on 6th March 1971. The United depot at Peter Street was never used by

Ribble. After the closure of Western SMT's Carlisle depot in 1981, Ribble provided accommodation and maintenance for 15 out-stationed vehicles.

Chorley garage in the early 'fifties, with a rebodied Tiger TS8 coach and a PD2 posed for the photograph. Within (below), a row of Cheetah and TS8 buses are washed by hand. Note that some are in the old livery and some in the new, with only the waistband as relief to the crimson.

CHORLEY (AR)

The depot in Eaves Lane had been the base of Parsons Motor Services which had been merged with the Chorley Auto Co. shortly before that business was acquired by Ribble in 1925. The Chorley company also had a garage in Windermere Road and an office at 4 West Street which was also ex-Parsons. There was originally accommodation for 10 buses. The roof of the Eaves Lane building partially fell in during 1929 and it was extended to hold a further 10 vehicles when the repairs were done. There was a further extension in 1937 to reach its maximum capacity of 50 vehicles. Additional premises in Brooke Street were used for minibuses from 1986 to 1989.

The bus station was built on the Cattle Market and opened on 21st May 1928, replacing a number of stands in West Street adjacent to the Town Hall. It comprised an island platform with offices etc. with unidirectional bus tracks on each side. A major improvement scheme was authorised in 1942, but abandoned due to war conditions. When 8ft-wide buses were introduced, the tracks proved to be too narrow and the station was closed for demolition on 21st September 1964. New offices were included and it reopened on the same site on 15th April 1965.

Chorley bus station as rebuilt in 1965, with a new Leopard/Plaxton coach visiting before the opening.

CHURCH (BW)

Rishton and Antley Motor Services originally owned this depot which was always called 'Church' but, in fact, was in the Antley district of Accrington, and it became a Ribble depot when the R&A subsidiary was wound up at the end of 1930, continuing in use until 1946. It had been intended to replace it with a new depot in Hyndburn Road, Accrington where Holme Mill was bought in November 1937. A £13,000 rebuilding scheme was approved and the fuel tanks had already been put in place in 1939 when further work was deferred upon the outbreak of war. After the war, the project was abandoned in favour of greater utilisation of Burnley, Clitheroe and Blackburn depots. An enquiry office was opened in railway property at 131a Blackburn Road, Accrington in 1950.

CLITHEROE (AL)

This scene inside Clitheroe garage on 5th July 1981 is fairly typical of the late NBC era. The vehicles seen were 1809, a lowbridge Atlantean dating from 1962; 321, a Marshall-bodied Bristol RESL of 1971, and 832, a National 2 of 1980.

The original garage in Pimlico Road, acquired from Pendle Motor Services in 1926, had a capacity of six vehicles. It was a wooden structure built on land leased from the Co-operative Wholesale Society and, when the lease expired at the end of 1929, the site was bought for £2,000. A new garage was then built to hold about 37 buses. This was more than the usual fleet allocation and up to 10 delicensed buses were often stored there. From 1943, leased premises at 14-18 Wellgate were used as depot offices; these were purchased in 1950. Clitheroe became an out-station of Blackburn from 26th October 1986 and is still in use.

DALTON-IN-FURNESS (DT)

The garage at the corner of Station Road and Beckside Road had housed the fleet of Furness Omnibus Co., acquired in 1930, but was too small and was replaced by new premises at Ulverston, opened in 1933. An office remained at Beckside until April 1944 and the garage was used as an out-station until 1968. The Furness company also had an out-station at Lindal and this was retained by Ribble for a time.

DARWEN

A depot in Gillibrand Street, Darwen served as a minibus out-station of Blackburn from 1986 to 13th August 1988.

FLEETWOOD (BC)

The garage and office in Birch Street, which were taken over with the business of Lawrence Motor Services Ltd. in 1931, were extended in 1932. More land was bought in 1938 and a further extension, including an office block costing £4,500, was added in 1939 to bring the accommodation up to 34 vehicles. The depot supplied buses for the Fleetwood and Thornton Cleveleys local services, the Fleetwood-Preston and Cleveleys-Preston local services, running through to Wigan for a time. There was no regular express operation. When Blackpool (Talbot Road) depot closed in 1988, various services from Blackpool were operated from Fleetwood. However it, too, closed on 27th April 1991, 12 minibuses being out-stationed at Fleetwood docks. It was brought into use again in December 1993.

GARSTANG (AF)

The small shed at Garstang was originally the property of J. Storey and Co. (Castle Motors) which was acquired by Pilot Motors in June 1926 and passed into the hands of Ribble four months later. It was a dilapidated building with accommodation for eight vehicles and, in 1929-30, it was rebuilt to hold 12. It doubled as a garage and bus station and, in post-war years, had an allocation of eight vehicles. In the mid-fifties, it became, in effect, a dormy shed, buses being changed over for fuelling, cleaning and maintenance by pre-arranged procedures at Blackpool, Preston and Morecambe. It closed as an operational depot in 1989 but remained in use as a store until 1993.

GRANGE-OVER-SANDS (BV)

When the stage carriage services of the Grange Motor and Cycle Co. Ltd. were taken over in July 1951, Ribble acquired the rather rudimentary Hampsfell Road garage. The demolition of the building and erection of a new structure was under consideration when the coaching side of the business came on the market in 1958 and the coach garage at Albert Road was then used for all operations.

KENDAL (BG)

A garage in Station Road was taken over with Lancashire and Westmorland Motor Services in 1927 and other premises, Longlands garage, Shap Road, came from the Kendal Motor Bus Co. in 1930. From 1947 to 1952 the latter was used as a bodyshop in an effort to make up arrears of body maintenance incurred during World War II and 243 vehicles were dealt with. A new garage was built on the Station Road site at a cost of £57,900 and opened in 1959, Shap Road then being closed.

An office in Highgate dated from the Lancashire & Westmorland takeover on 1st December 1927. Buses departed from various stands in Highgate, Stricklandgate and later Sandes Avenue where, during the 1960s, vending machines were installed to ease the problems of catering on the Scottish services, particularly at night. Some services had to lie over in South Road, three-quarters of a mile from the town hall and this became a terminus from as early as 1926. The Kendal one-way traffic scheme was put into effect in March 1968, stands being moved around until the opening of Blackhall Street bus station and office in 1972; this was rebuilt on a more modest scale in the 1980s. Kendal is now a major operational and maintenance centre for Stagecoach.

KESWICK (BH)

Keswick depot was the property of Cumberland Motor Services Ltd. It was opened in 1927 and the bus station was completed in 1933. After the Lancashire and Westmorland takeover in 1927, Ribble kept one bus in Tithebarn Street but used the Cumberland premises from 1928. Vehicles lay over in the depot from 1931.

The Cumberland depot was extended in 1952 and improved further in 1961 from which date the office became a joint Ribble-Cumberland affair, replacing separate ones. The original Ribble office had been at 37 Main Street. For several years Ribble stationed one or two buses for stage carriage operations and three for express duties. A Standerwick vehicle was also out-stationed there from 9th April 1952 until the London service was extended to Whitehaven.

LANCASTER (BA)

The garage built at Skerton, Lancaster, seen in September 1930, shortly after it came into use. The policeman appears to be signalling to a vehicle about to emerge into the busy road. In the other doorway a Lion PLSC is just visible.

There were originally two garages in Lancaster. Skerton garage was used by Lambsfield Motors who took their name from 'Lamb's Field' on which it was built. It was an unsightly temporary building and Lancaster Corporation pressed the company to rebuild it but this was resisted until the land could be purchased. It was bought for £2,000 in 1929 when it was decided to build a new garage for 48 vehicles at a cost of over £9,000; this came into use about May 1930. The County Motors depot in Dalton Square was used until 1934 and was eventually sold to Lancaster Corporation for £4,250 on 10th May 1939. Some services terminated at Dalton Square and others at a Corporation-owned bus station in Damside Street. The Corporation opened the new Damside Street bus station on 1st April 1939. The depot became a sub-depot of Morecambe.

LIVERPOOL (AW)

The company's original two Liverpool-based vehicles were accommodated in private yards, originally, it is believed, in Vauxhall Road and later, it is thought, in a yard in North Street behind 127 Dale Street which was acquired in 1927 with Collingwood Motors. Ribble made some alterations to these premises with a view to converting them to a coach station but the city council disapproved and eventually the plan was abandoned but it was not until 1957, when the city council complained about dilapidations that the premises were demolished, the site being sold to a brewery in 1960. There were also two separate garages in Collingwood Street, No. 4 Collingwood Street, capable of holding 15 27ft.-6in. vehicles and No. 38. In 1930, the latter was combined with No. 36 which had been acquired with the Merseyside Touring Co. and 36-38 together had a nominal capacity of 22. Number 36 was severely damaged in the May 1941 air raids and remained without a roof until 1957 when it was repaired with a view to its later sale, almost two-thirds of the cost being met by the War Damage Commission. Space problems had been alleviated by the purchase of a 625 sq.yd. site adjoining No. 36 in 1947. The cramped, old-fashioned buildings were operationally inconvenient and the coming of 30ft.-long vehicles aggravated matters further. All docking and repair work had been done at Bootle for many years.

In 1939, a 12,000 sq.yd site at the corner of Harlow Street and Grafton Street, Toxteth was purchased for £10,700 and plans were drawn up for a new garage estimated to cost £41,700 but the outbreak of war led to the scheme being shelved. The choice of site, at the south end of the city, far removed from any Ribble route was a strange one and it is not surprising that there was a change of heart after the war. The land was not sold until 1953 – for £200 less than originally paid.

The allocation of 35 buses and coaches was transferred from Collingwood Street to the new Skelhorne Street bus station in mid-1960 and, towards the end of that year, Collingwood Street was finally vacated when the docking facility at Hilbre Street was brought into use. On 18th January 1961 the premises were auctioned and the whole area was later cleared to make way for the Wallasey Tunnel approach roads.

The depot offices were moved to the Merseyside Touring Company's premises at the corner of Islington and Fraser Street and remained there until 1960 when the two-level Skelhorne Street bus station was opened on a sloping site. The purchase of the site from the LMS railway for £30,000 had been agreed in 1941 after years of discussion but was abandoned because of wartime uncertainties. The site was eventually acquired for £38,000 in 1955, delay being occasioned by uncertainty about Liverpool Corporation's planning intentions and outrageous development costs.

Skelhorne Street coach station, (the upper level with access from Hilbre Street), was opened in April 1960 for express services and tours. The lower level, a typical Ribble nose-on bus station in Bolton Street, was opened in three stages in June. The total cost was about £190,000. The Hilbre Street docking facility was handed over to National Travel (North West) on 23rd March 1980, the remaining 12 stage-carriage buses being transferred to Bootle. In September 1986 the whole complex was transferred to North Western who closed it down on 11th September 1989. It stood empty for over two years before being partly demolished for redevelopment as a night club and ultimately, it is said, as a hotel.

MANCHESTER (AV)

A small garage was situated in Trumpet Street, adjacent to Lower Mosley Street bus station; as vehicles became longer and wider, entering and leaving was difficult as Trumpet Street was very narrow. Several vehicles were parked on the bus station parking ground in Great Bridgewater Street. The date when the garage first came into use is unrecorded but it was well before the outbreak of war in 1939 and possibly ten years or so earlier. The original allocation was just two coaches, one for Glasgow and one for Keswick in summer and Kendal in winter. In the heady late 'fifties, as many as 24 vehicles were based in Manchester one summer.

The site of Lower Mosley Street bus station was purchased jointly by Ribble and North Western for £24,000 and a new private company, Omnibus Stations Ltd. was formed with a capital of 35,000 £1 shares of which Ribble held 12,500, North Western 12,500 and other operators the other 10,000. The depot offices were located on the first floor of the bus station, the booking office being manned by Omnibus Stations staff. An additional city centre booking office was opened at 5 Albert Square in 1957.

When the original North Western Road Car Co. was broken up in 1972, Ribble took over certain express service operations and the Hulme Hall Road garage. When National Express was formed, these vehicles, many of which were initially owned by Ribble, operated from this base. The pure Ribble presence was eventually reduced to six Leopard coaches which were dispersed to other depots after operation on 7th November 1980.

MORECAMBE (AZ)

The depot, in South Avenue, was quite new when acquired with Lancashire and Westmorland Motor Services in 1927. An adjoining open yard was frequently used for storage. The depot was closed after 22nd August 1993 when the allocation was moved to the former Lancaster City Transport depot at Heysham Road.

The company used the municipally-owned Poulton Hall coach park as a terminus for many years. In 1930, a scheme to use the Midland station forecourt on a £10 p.a. lease fell through but an alternative scheme was put forward for a bus station at Euston Road railway station. This was opposed by Morecambe Corporation who probably did not want to lose Ribble's custom but an appeal against a planning decision was successful. The station came into use in the summer of 1936. The site was improved by the addition of platforms and shelters in the post-war period; additional land for parking was acquired and the freehold was bought from the railways for £9,800 in 1953.

ORMSKIRK (AX)

A new garage, bus station and offices were built at the corner of Moor Street and Knowsley Road, Ormskirk and opened in 1937. The garage had a nominal capacity of 12 buses and 13 were based there from the day it opened. It closed in October 1974 when Skelmersdale depot opened. A 1978 proposal to demolish two houses to give better access to the bus station was opposed by local residents and, eventually, a new bus station lower down Moor Street was opened by Mr Kenneth Clarke, then Under-Secretary for Transport, on 4th December 1981. It was built on the site of a municipal car park and there was provision for car parking within the horse-shoe shaped bus track. The station was intended to be phase 1 of a road-rail interchange but, so far, funds have not been found to move the railway station.

PENRITH (BK)

The garage in Brunswick Road was acquired with Armstrong and Siddle's business in April 1929, having been rebuilt following a fire the previous year. That company also owned a filling station, acquired from George Taylor, in Middlegate, on the A6 road in the town centre and this was demolished and offices were built on the site. These replaced the original A&S office across the road at No. 13. The Penrith terminus had been in Middlegate until June 1928 when the Penrith council insisted that it be moved to Sandgate because of congestion. Stands were marked out and Ribble took 14 at a cost of 1/6d (7½p) per week each. In later years there was mounting pressure to extend car parking in Sandgate, at the expense of the buses, and after the death of the well-known Penrith independent operator, Ernest Harkness in February 1971, his premises at Sandgate Hall were compulsorily purchased. His small bus station was then enlarged and a new bus station opened in 1972.

The town offices were moved to a hut at Brunswick Road depot in the 1980s and Penrith was reduced to the status of an outstation of Carlisle on 18th May 1985. The depot is being offered for sale by Stagecoach, the buses being parked at Gilwilly at the time of writing.

PRESTON (Park Road) (AA)

This was the company's original Preston depot, built on land known as Lang's Yard, purchased in 1919 and opened in 1921. Its site has long disappeared under new roads but it was conveniently situated to the town centre. Its capacity was about 30 buses and, as services were expanded, it soon became too small, additional workshops being rented in Crown Street pending completion of the new Central Workshops at Frenchwood in 1927. Adjoining these was a new depot in Selborne Street and both depots continued in use. Park Road was closed as an economy measure early in the war but reopened in 1942 to deal with the producer-gas fleet. It was closed in 1952, the site being required for new roads.

PRESTON (Selborne Street) (AB)

This depot was contiguous with the Central Workshops in Frenchwood Avenue but administered separately. The building contract for £11,933 was let in May 1927. It was difficult to operate as, for many years, all but the east end was suitable only for single-deck buses and there were inevitably some accidents and near misses. Extensions were made in 1929 when the Central Workshops bodyshop was also built. The depot was a long, narrow building with the entrance at the east (Manchester Road) end and the exit at the west end. Extra parking was available along the wall outside. In 1938, plans were drawn up to convert the central works body-shop into a double-deck garage, the new bodyshop being built at a higher level with access from Frenchwood Avenue. More accommodation was provided for double-deck vehicles after the war when the roof was raised bodily on jacks after a scheme for a new garage on an adjacent site had been rejected, and the old bodyshop was incorporated in the garage in 1962. It continues in use.

Tithebarn Street Bus Station

When The Pilot Motors was taken over on 1st October 1926, Ribble acquired property in Tithebarn Street, Preston. The company was under pressure from the police due to buses being parked in the street overnight because of lack of garage accommodation but it was decided to convert the site into a bus station. Some adjoining premises were bought and demolished and the company reached an agreement with Preston Corporation whereby the stands in Town Hall Square and Jackson Street would be vacated on the understanding that they would not be allocated to any other operators. The station which, initially, was very much smaller than its later form, came into use in October 1927. Breakell's warehouse was acquired on 1st November 1928 and demolished to make room for an extension which included accommodation on the first floor which it was first intended to let out as a cafe. However it was found more convenient to move the depot offices from 4 Lancaster Road and this was done in April 1930.

At first there was a separate exit on to Lord Street as a building on the corner of that street was not acquired for demolition until 1934. The 55 Division Club building was eventually acquired in 1937, enabling covered queue barriers to be installed at the Lord Street end. The express services were originally concentrated on one platform alongside the old Empire theatre and in post-war years the position became intolerable, drivers of coaches finding it physically impossible to reach the platform. Lord's Walk coach station, approached from North Road, was opened on 2nd April 1955, accommodating express services and local buses working the Longridge Road and ex-Viking routes.

The depot and public enquiry offices were originally at 4 Birley Street in the town centre but were transferred to 4 Lancaster Road in 1921. The booking office was moved to new premises at 30 Lancaster Road, bought at the end of 1928 for £3,750. Both stations were closed on 22nd October 1969 when the new municipal bus station was brought into use.

Many photographs of scenes at Tithebarne Street bus station, Preston, were taken over the years. That reproduced above gives an impression of the extent of the site, and the pressure on loading space. It dates from 1936-37, one of the English Electric-bodied Lion LT7 buses of 1936 being seen towards the far end of the line. The other vehicles include three Lion PLSC and various Lion or Tiger models of the 1929-31 period, with a 1931 LT2, C1146, and 1926 Lion C167 nearest the camera, the latter withdrawn in 1937. The three Titan double-deckers are thought to be two TD1 and a TD2, the latter in the middle and just identifiable by the opening emergency window at the rear of the upper deck.

The lower view, from a higher vantage point at the opposite end dates from 1956 – on the right, the covered queue barriers at the Lord Street end are visible. Nearest the camera, 1358, one of the 1952 batch of Titan PD2/12 buses with Leyland bodywork of 1952, reverses off the stand bound for Burnley on the 150 service. Behind it, a similar bus is on the same route but going in the opposite direction, to Morecambe. Most of the other double-deckers are PD2 models of various types, but at this end of the stand, 1909, a 1938 TD5 with 1947 Burlingham highbridge body can be seen alongside a 1956 PD2 also by Burlingham. The coaches are a Burlingham Seagull and one of the Leyland-bodied Royal Tigers. Note the Lion Ales Blackburn-registered Albion lorry in the right foreground, and that the street is still cobbled, as was often the case in Lancashire towns at that date.

SEAFORTH SANDS (AY)

Seaforth Sands depot was acquired with Waterloo and Crosby Motor Services in 1928. It had originated as the Liverpool Overhead Railway's tram depot in a building which housed the railway's carriage shed on the upper level. Ribble reduced the W&C fleet and based some of its own buses there, the Liverpool-Crosby-Southport services being partly run from Seaforth Sands and partly from Liverpool (Collingwood Street). But as the traffic grew, the depot became increasingly congested. However, it was not possible to close it down until Bootle depot had been rebuilt in 1934.

SKELMERSDALE (AX)

As the New Town of Skelmersdale developed, several local services were needed. Ormskirk depot, which had been overfull from the day it opened, was unable to cope and operation from Wigan involved wasteful dead mileage. It was decided to close Ormskirk depot and replace it with a new depot in Neverstitch Road, Skelmersdale, with accommodation for 50 vehicles. This was a modern structure with servicing facilities under cover and a large parking area. It came into use on 20th October 1974 and is still used by North Western.

SKIPTON (AP)

A garage in Broughton Road, about two miles from the town centre had belonged to Old Bill Motor Services, acquired in 1928. In 1931 there was a scheme to reconstruct it at a cost of £5,250 but this shelved in favour of a plan for a joint garage with the West Yorkshire Road Car Co. Ltd. which fell through. In 1933, a temporary building for five buses was erected next to the old premises which remained in use. Eventually the depot was rebuilt on the same site in 1938. Offices were originally situated in High Street. The street stands in Caroline Square were transferred to Waller Hill bus station when it was opened on 8th May 1950. The exact date of closure is in some doubt. The Skipton-Eastby/Bolton Abbey services were transferred to the West Yorkshire Road Car Co. on 23rd May 1976 and the depot was closed and sold to Pennine Motor Services. However, for a variety of reasons, they did not use it themselves but let the premises to a tenant.

SOUTHPORT (CS)

A municipal bus station at Coronation Walk was opened on 1st January 1933 and staffed by Ribble. Traffic into the resort was substantial but never reached the levels experienced at Blackpool or Morecambe. It is surprising, therefore, that Ribble was persuaded into such an expensive scheme as the purchase and adaptation of the ex-Cheshire Lines railway station in Lord Street. British Railways asked £80,000 for the property. Ribble thought £20,000 would be needed for alterations and offered £60,000. The price paid was £72,500, £8,000 being voted for alterations but this was self-delusion as the cost of filling in the ground between the platforms and providing road access could not be avoided and the final bill was £30,000. The

Southport had one of the most unlikely-looking bus stations that could be imagined, and even when the premises were built as a railway station for the Cheshire Lines Committee in 1884, the Victorian fondness for elaborate clock towers was given unusually free rein. A modest notice reading 'Ribble Bus Station' appeared over one of the entrance archways in this photograph taken just after the conversion for use by buses in 1954.

company drew rents from various shops and stalls though the need to provide an arrival platform altered the pedestrian flow and one tenant demanded the cancellation of his lease. The licensed refreshment room was run by the company, the Secretary's name, Harold Westall Miller, appearing over the door.

It opened as a bus station in the summer of 1954 and as a depot in September, relieving pressure on Ormskirk, Wigan and Bootle. But its spacious Victorian interior was never utilised to the full. It passed to North Western in September 1986 and was closed and sold for redevelopment as a shopping centre on 3rd October 1987, the facade being retained.

ULVERSTON (CD)

Following the take-over of Furness Omnibus Co. in 1930, the company found their Tarnside garage to be inadequate and purchased land at The Ellers on the site of an old sawmill for £6,500. About the same amount was spent on a new garage and offices which were opened in January 1933. Dalton depot was then reduced to the status of an out-station. Ulverston was taken over by Cumberland Motor Services in 1989 and closed on 6th February 1990.

WIGAN (AT)

When Ribble first started operations in Wigan in 1922, two buses were garaged with Northern Counties, the bodybuilders. In 1926 a portion of premises in Wallgate owned by Middleton and Wood was acquired and a new garage was completed in 1928 on this site. Adjoining land was purchased in 1940 for £8,000 but a full reconstruction had to wait until 1971. The depot and enquiry offices were in Hope Street, adjoining the Market Square bus station. The depot is still used by North Western.

Within, the railway origin of Southport bus station remained obvious. This scene dates from June 1954, just after it was reopened in its new form. Alongside a couple of Royal Tiger buses and a PD2 was one of St. Helens Corporation's AEC RT-type double-deckers, built to complete London Transport specification, and on the jointly operated 349 route to that town, one of many instances where municipal buses worked alongside those of Ribble. The St. Helens undertaking used the large indicator box intended for intermediate route details to show the service number, accounting for the very prominent but incorrectly set display visible.

WINDERMERE

An office in Windermere railway station yard was established in the early 1920s by the Lake District Road Traffic Co. and passed to Ribble with Lancashire & Westmorland Motor Services in December 1927. The rent was £1.00 per annum after Ribble became railway-associated and possibly before that. It was closed as a wartime economy measure in January 1943, reopening in summer only from 1949. A joint road-rail enquiry office was established in 1956; it finally closed about 1970.

BREDBURY, near Stockport Greater Manchester

Opened at a Volvo dealership at the end of 1993 to house the Stagecoach (Manchester) fleet.

OUT-STATIONS

Ribble had numerous out-stations to avoid unremunerative dead mileage. These included Alston (from 1969), Appleby, Bowness-on-Solway (see under Carlisle above), Carlisle (County Garage) until 1931, Cartmel (until Grange joint operation 1938), Chipping, Cumwhinton (ex-Wrights, for about 6 weeks), Grange-over-Sands (until 1938), Hawes (1932 only), Ingleton, Kirkby Lonsdale, Kirkby Stephen, Kirkoswald (from autumn 1932), Knott End-on-Sea, Millom (Cumberland depot), Patterdale (acquired with Armstrong & Siddle but may not have been used by Ribble),Sedbergh, Shap (Simpson's Garage),

NON-OPERATIONAL STORES

The former Eccleston Motor Co.'s premises at Eccleston, Cadman's garage at Orrell (sold 1946) and the Rishton & Antley premises at Rishton (sold 1966) were retained as stores for delicensed vehicles for many years. Later, storage space was rented in a hanger at the former Royal Naval Air Station at Inskip, near Preston.

DEPOT SYMBOLS

Before the 1939-45 war, each bus carried a coloured depot code on the offside rear of the lower deck. The system fell into disuse during the war and was not revived. The symbols were additional to the letter codes indicated in Volume 1. The latter were used on company running sheets and, in post-war years, were carried on small plates on new coaches starting with the Royal Tigers but not extended to other vehicles. At holiday weekends, they were displayed also on paper labels with the bus duty number, to assist traffic control staff.

Depot	Code	Depot	Code
AMBLESIDE	Green Diamond	KENDAL	Purple Circle
BLACKBURN, George Street	Yellow Square	LANCASTER, Dalton Square	Red Square
BLACKBURN, Foundry Hill	Yellow Triangle	LANCASTER, Skerton	Red Diamond
BLACKPOOL	Green Triangle	LIVERPOOL	White Diamond
BOLTON	Purple Square	MORECAMBE	White Square
BOOTLE	Red Triangle	ORMSKIRK	Blue Triangle
BURNLEY	Blue Circle	PENRITH	Pink Diamond
CARLISLE	Pink Circle	PRESTON, Park Road	White Circle
CHORLEY	Green Square	PRESTON, Selborne Street	Black Square
CHURCH	Yellow Diamond	SEAFORTH SANDS	Green Circle
CLITHEROE	Pink Square	SKIPTON	Blue Diamond
DALTON	Blue Square	ULVERSTON	Purple Diamond
FLEETWOOD	White Triangle	WIGAN	Red Circle
GARSTANG	Yellow Circle		

The early days of deregulation produced some peculiar vehicle uses. Leyland Atlantean AN68/ECW 1422 (RFR 422P) is seen here in privatisation livery bearing 'New Ribble' posters and the Kendal 'Info-line' phone numbers. Unfortunately it is actually operating deep into Greater Manchester Buses territory at Chorlton. Clearly a portent of what is still to come.

Alas . . .
Red no More!

Duple Midland bodied NRN 169 was new to Scout in 1960 but had transferred to Ribble as its 1072 in 1968. Ribble attention to detail had seen the fitting of the customary name plate to the dash panel.

This early Leopard with Harrington Cavalier 32-seat body was used for touring when new. With air suspension and Chapman reclining seats these were amongst the most comfortable vehicles of their day. Number 1040 (PCK 622) seen when new in 1961.

The first Plaxton Panorama bodies came in 1964, again on the now ubiquitous Leopard PSU3. This particular batch of vehicles had 49 seats and a two-speed axle for Express service. In all these views of coaches it is noteworthy that Ribble had adapted their livery to suit the line of each model whilst retaining the Ribble 'look'.

Ribble's coaching activities always appeared to be the jewel in the crown. Whilst the buses scurried about their mundane local tasks, successive generations of coaches proceeded about the Kingdom, in almost majestic fashion. True there were the seaside-bound coaches heading from industrial Lancashire to the Fylde, but many more exotic destinations (in their day) graced the fronts of sundry Tigers and others up to the day of the aristocrat of coaching, the 'All Leyland' Royal Tiger. So too, the bodies changed; Burlingham gained most from the forced closure of Leyland's bodying activity but appeared to throw all away, as the Seagull design waned, from its earlier refinement, by 1958. There were brief flirtations with Duple (Northern) and Harrington in succession, but it was Plaxton who stole the day. If the original Panorama produced for Sheffield United Tours was good, then the Elite was little short of unsurpassed, even to this day. The curved glasses of the Elite were mimicked but never excelled.

All Change!

Maybe the cry of the conductor at a terminal point in the days of crew operation, but in fact 1972 marked the end of Ribble's comfortable evolution. When F. A. S. (Freddie) Wood became chairman of NBC in 1972 he quickly signalled the corporate approach to vehicles and appearance. Quite simply 'Red' companies had the 'choice' of Poppy Red, and their 'Green' brethren, Leaf Green. Coaches too came in a unified form – white – with large (10in.) red and blue National fleetnames: at first the only acknowledgment of the owning company was a 1 in. grey fleetname over the front wheel arch with a house colour underline. A 3in. red block name was

Enter the Elite. Starring at the 1968 Earls Court Commercial Motor Show were two Ribble Group vehicles. The prototype Bristol VRL double-deck coach and the Plaxton Panorama Elite single-deck. This is 964 (HRN 964G) at Blackpool. The Ribble coach livery has again adapted to the new style with considerable success and the lower case fleetname has made its first appearance on a coach to enhance the elegant modernity.

The Elite's predecessors had been the Panorama 1 or 2. Number 791 (ARN 791C) is a Panorama 1. The livery sat less well on this 1965 version but this was remedied by 1966. This involved the front of the roof being painted Cherry Red. The lower case fleetname has been added.

All Change indeed! National White has arrived and this 1966 Leopard/ Panorama 1, 870 (ECK 870D), has not benefited. The styling for the livery was carried by consultants using an Elite vehicle. Overall white at least did not jar on that model's simple lines but on anything which had mouldings for reliefs, as here, the livery simply did not work.

quickly allowed to assuage the roar of disapproval from the companies. Buses too carried a standard style fleetname in 5in. block capitals. Somehow Ribble did manage to retain 3in. fleetnames on front and rear.....

Similarly freedom to specify vehicle design all but disappeared; influence alone survived. Vehicles henceforth were to be ordered merely by one of several available layouts and descriptions. Thus came Bristol VRTs, sundry Leopard coaches, a few Leyland Atlanteans to supplement VRT build at times of high demand for double-decks, and many Leyland National single-deckers. Subsequently, Leyland Olympians, Tigers and standard issue double-deck coaches became the order of the day. The NBC Group influence survived until the end of 1987 with deliveries of various minibuses – particularly the Mercedes Benz L608D vehicles. These came as part of a very successful NBC coup in securing the whole of this German manufacturer's 'run out' build at what can only be described as 'advantageous' prices. Group synergy did have benefits !

As the 'eighties had begun so National Bus had made a forceful response to the changes in licensing of bus services. To practical purposes, the Right Honourable Norman Fowler had heralded the new regime in 1980. Deregulation of Express Services promoted an unsuccessful challenge to National Express but, more importantly, it removed British Rail's ability to stifle competition by a statutory right to object to competing services. It was in the area of competition to BR's inner suburban services around the country that much growth ensued. NBC responded to growing disorder amongst its subsidiaries in promoting non-standard 'Marketing Liveries' for such enterprise, by introducing what became known as the 'Venetian Blind' Livery. In basic terms, National Express gained a new layout identifying itself quite specifically, and local subsidiaries generally, were to be permitted to adopt a specified layout **in their own choice of colour.** Perhaps surprisingly, Ribble management under Ian Chapman did not readopt traditional colours. Surprisingly, because by this time Ribble had become a leader in restoring/recreating vehicles of days gone by.

Albeit painted cream, the 1962 Atlantean coaches were nonetheless officially dubbed the 'White Lady' class. This livery did little to hide their membership of the 'Box Look' family, but they certainly demonstrated their fitness for medium distance Express service. Air suspension was fitted to the front axle. Number 1283 (RRN 432) is Manchester bound.

In 1972 the double-deck coach had no place in NBC minds of the day, for no equivalent of the 'local coach' livery was to be found in the original Corporate Identity Manual. Bus livery was therefore the order, although their prime use did not change. This unfortunate is 1267 (RRN 416) on service X23 – Manchester to Clitheroe.

The dual-purpose Leopards had originally enjoyed their own version of the Coach Livery as shown by 827 (CRN 827D). Whilst the body shell was uncompromisingly that of the standard BET product of the day, extra brightwork and cream window rubbers combined to give an almost majestic look. Certainly no passenger seeing one approach could consider that an adapted bus was to be his transport.

Another victim of the Local Coach/dual-purpose livery was Ribble's extensive class of dual-purpose Leopards bought during the 'sixties as the adoption of one-man operation gained pace. Marshall-bodied 1818 (CRN 818D) looks ill-at-ease in Poppy Red and white. The unfortunate custom of showing 'White Blank' as the destination has crept in.

A night scene at London's Victoria Coach Station, probably taken c1970. Two of Harry Tennant's coaches await departure for the north. A Gay Hostess Atlantean and the prototype Bristol VRL coach stand alongside a Plaxton Panorama-bodied Leopard. Very shortly afterwards, Ribble livery and the company itself were to take their leave of the Coach Station, albeit the latter only temporarily.

Although the application of NBC liveries to certain existing vehicles was always to look wrong, contemporary models when freshly painted at least looked the part. Amongst the first NBC Group orders were a batch of Park Royal-Roe/ Atlantean AN68s of which Ribble obtained a large share. This well-balanced design formed a class which was to serve Ribble into Deregulation, with the addition of numerous second-hand examples from Southdown and others. Number 1362 (GBV 140N) is seen in Lancaster.

The main livery schemes introduced by Ribble retained the white base, with Poppy Red primary relief, and grey providing the 'Venetian' stripe. It must be admitted that 'Timesaver' in particular became an effective trading style with some degree of subsidiary banding on individual services. For a period blue stripes in standard style were used.

As privatisation approached, companies were permitted to select their own liveries. Ribble took a version of the Poppy Red, white and grey, with yellow Fleetnames in NBC standard lettering to identify the Company. This image was to be the last before the successful Management Buyout 'A' Team sold its operating interests to the Stagecoach Group in April 1989. Thereafter Stagecoach stripes became the order with a fleetname 'Ribble Buses'. Various other marketing styles have since appeared with scant reference to Ribble.

The newly independent Ribble did not exist long enough to place any orders for new full size vehicles so it can only be a matter of conjecture what these might have comprised. Latterly the Stagecoach Group influence was even more dominant than that of NBC. The 'white and stripe' vehicles which have come to Ribble have certainly been of very high specification but apart from the 'Ribble Buses' name to be found on them, could equally have been at home from Peterhead to Brighton. Ribble's parent company, Stagecoach Holdings, has become a darling of the Stock Exchange since a successful floatation in 1993. However this is in no small measure due to the efforts of Ribble people, in adapting to yet another regime, since 1989.

After the sameness of the 'seventies, the 'eighties saw the Ribble coach fleet in a kaleidoscope of colour. The Leopard was at its zenith though Tigers were prowling.

Upper left: 1093 (YFR 493R) is seen on home territory in Preston in the NBC local coach livery of Poppy Red and white in April 1984.

Upper right: 1124 (WCK 124V) at Blackburn in September 1985 is in blue Timesaver colours in NBC style. This voluntary move from red took many by surprise but was short-lived.

Upper centre left: Seen at the Coliseum in March 1985 is an early Dominant-bodied Leopard 1062 (XTF 823L) in a peculiar version of Kingfisher colours. Applied in the style of the NBC Venetian Blind livery, it lacks the relief stripes.

Upper centre right: The sole Duple Dominant 4 bodied Tiger, 1150 (A150 LFR), itself a Leopard replacement, has worn many liveries. On this occasion in 1984 it is in overall white with red Ribble names over the rear wheel arch. Some variations on this livery had red and blue stripes.

Centre left: The red and grey Venetian Blind livery replaced many of the early variants – with a wide variety of fleetnames according to intended use. Here ex-National Travel (West) number 1253 (HNE 253V) approaches Preston whilst working a National Express duplicate.

Lower left: The top of the range livery was that of the five Sandpiper Plaxton Paramount 3500 Tigers of Southport garage. Number 1003 (BRN 3Y) is in Lancaster in 1987.

An attempt was made to revive Ribble extended tours in the 'eighties. Number 158 (B158 WRN), a member of a short-lived batch of Tigers with Duple Laser 2 bodywork, wears a livery based on the National Holidays livery of the day. This livery was not perpetuated either.

The coaching revival also brought a wealth of different vehicles – mostly on lease. Another short-lived batch was of Duple Caribbean high-floor Tiger coaches for National Express contracts. Number 145 (B145 ACK) is seen. Note also the unusual two-line destination display.

Double-deckers were not neglected in the revival of coaching. A 'Blue' Olympian 2156 (A156 OFR) works on the Lancashire Express service in 1985.

A tourist service, which continues under Cumberland auspices today, is the 'Lakeland Experience'. Started in 1983 using an MCW Metroliner whose use on express service had been refused by the trade unions, Olympian coaches subsequently took over together with some open-toppers at a later date. Number 2156 (A156 OFR) is seen again, this time at Kendal, newly repainted in summer 1988. It is to be hoped that the passengers are waiting for another service as the door of 2156 is firmly closed and the driver is absent while they stand on a chilly day.

Top: Typifying Lakeland Ribble country is this standard Leyland National Mark 1 in 1983. Notice the unapproved Ribble fleetname on the dash panel.

Upper centre: This Leyland National came into the Ribble fleet when the company finally took the the Barrow municipal business in 1989. Number 758 (NEO 831R) gained 'Chapman' fleetnames and is seen Preston-bound at Poulton-le-Fylde.

Below left and right: The minibus era is exemplified by Mercedes Benz L608D 544 (D544 RCK), part of the NBC mass purchase described in this book. Zippy number 6 (D416 FRV) is part of the fleet taken over from United Transport Buses in Preston.

Foot of page: Three Dennis Javelins came to Hampshire Bus as a Stagecoach Group experiment. After a while their 63-seat capacity Duple 300 Bus Bodies attracted them to Ribble services in the Fylde. This view was taken at Lancaster in September 1993. Stagecoach style fleet numbers have appeared – 3in. black numerals at each corner of the front and rear. Number 1135 (F135 SPX) is seen in Lancaster in September 1993.

Above: Ribble continued its experimental work for National Bus right to the end. The left view shows the first Olympian for NBC, 2100 (DBV 100W) at Cleveleys in 1984. NBC's only Lynx also joined the Ribble fleet. Later it was despatched to join Stagecoach Group's only Lynx, in the Cumberland fleet, seen appropriately in former Ribble territory at Windermere.

Above: The Management Buyout in 1988 raised hopes and great effort was put into promotion of this success. Number 1414 (RFR 414P) shows the 'Chapman' livery together with posters praising the participants in funding etc. The location is poignant – Lancaster in 1989. Three years later, in Stagecoach days, an acrimonious battle was fought over the municipal operation in the town. Stagecoach won.

Right: An evocative view immediately prior to privatisation. Number 1841 (TCK 841) the PD3 meticulously restored by Ribble Engineering is seen with red/grey/white Olympian 2176 (C176 ECK). No such sentiment extended into the Stagecoach era: 1841 was passed to Cumberland Motor Services as a driver trainer, shorn of its registration number (now AAO 771A) and latterly apparently fitted with an O.680 engine. The PD3 can also be seen on page 63.

RIBBLE ENGINEERING

Methods of looking after buses have changed greatly over the years, just as have the vehicles themselves. The good reputation Ribble built up in the early days had much to do with reliability and attention to the look of the fleet on the road, as well as the standard of comfort offered, and this philosophy was to remain characteristic of the company. Nowadays, large in-house engineering facilities are out of fashion, swept away under the combination of competitive and financial pressures that tend to prevail today. Modern vehicles generally do not need, nor do they lend themselves to, pulling apart on a regular basis in the way once not only normal but logical with older technology, even though they can still suffer their own types of fault, sometimes very expensive to rectify.

Yet it would be hard to deny that Ribble's central works and the methods used at the depots served the company well in the days when there were 1,000 buses or more to look after, spread over an area which stretched from Liverpool to Carlisle, and some of them garaged 80 miles from headquarters.

As explained in Volume 1, reliability of service had been a guiding principle from the beginning, and though it may have been no more than proximity that first influenced Ribble in the choice of maker for its buses in the manner then common even among members of the major combines, the relationship between Ribble and Leyland worked well from its beginning in 1923.

By the early 'thirties the fleet was largely composed of modern Leyland Lion, Tiger and Titan models of sound design, offering good comfort by contemporary standards. After 1931 only small numbers of coaches from acquired businesses were taken into stock and, by about 1935, very little of the variety of vehicles added to the fleet as other concerns were bought out in earlier years remained.

Clearly, this approach to the composition of the fleet gave a good basis for methods that ensured that it both behaved and looked well, but a methodical approach, with more than a touch of the military thinking quite common in bus companies with many of their management drawn from men who had been officers in the 1914-18 war, was also very evident.

The central repair works in the headquarters site at Frenchwood Avenue, Preston, was completed in 1926, although extended in later years, and thus the methods based on its availability were established just as the first big standardised fleet of Leyland Lion PLSC models was beginning to be built up. At first, the body shop was part of the adjoining but separate Selborne Street garage premises until a new body shop within the main works was built in 1938. It was standard practice from the beginning to remove bodywork from chassis at major overhaul, and this continued to be Ribble's preferred method right up to the era of such models as the Leyland Leopard, by which date it had become quite rare. It had applied to the succeeding generations of Leyland Titan from the TD1 to the PD3 but the Atlantean, with its closer structural relationship of chassis and body framing and general complexity of air and electrical systems made separation impractical. The true integral-construction vehicle such as the Leyland National simply continued this trend to its conclusion.

In the days of the Selborne Street body shop, once the bodies had been lifted the chassis were then driven into Frenchwood works for attention and, when their overhaul had been done, were tested in chassis form before going back for the overhauled body to be mounted. Even in later years the view was held that this method enabled the specialists in the fields of mechanical and body overhaul to do their respective jobs unhindered by the needs of people whose methods of working were necessarily different. Although this eventually came to be considered

It was standard practice until the 'sixties to lift bodies from chassis at major overhaul. Here the Leyland lowbridge body is being lifted from the chassis of 2580, a Titan PD2/3 model. The photograph, showing a scene at the subsidiary body shop at Fazakerley, near Bootle, appeared with an article on Ribble body overhaul practice in the January 1951 issue of 'Leyland Journal' – the vehicle had been new in September 1948, making removal in little over two years seem rather early by the standards of that period, unless there had been accident damage. At that stage, overhaul of post-war Leyland bodies had just begun, and it had been found that very little needed to be done, leading to a decision to widen overhaul intervals.

Acquired vehicles, 1925-31

Acquisitions made between 1925 and 1931 included, as far as can be ascertained, 590 vehicles, only a little short of the new vehicle intake over that period of 649. Many were sold off quite quickly and a few, finding their way into other fleets within Ribble's expanding area, were then acquired for a second time, making it difficult to balance the totals. The number of Leylands included was 238 (40%), reflecting the strong following for the make among operators in the north-west as well as Ribble's desire to add almost all to its fleet. As to the other 60%, in these days of standardisation it is hard to believe that the vehicles were made up of 30 different makes, as tabulated herewith.

1.	Tilling-Stevens	50
2.	Daimler	38
3.	AEC & ADC	36
4.	Albion	34
5.	Guy	34
6.	Maudslay	32
7.	Thornycroft	24
8.	Vulcan	20
9.	Bristol	9
10.	Karrier	9
11.	Minerva	9
12.	Dennis	7
13.	GMC	7
14.	Chevrolet	5
15.	Beardmore	4
16.	Pagefield	3
17.	Reo	3
18.	Bean	2
19.	Burford	2
20.	Crossley	2
21.	Dodge	2
22.	Gilford	2
23.	Halley	2
24.	Overland	2
25.	Fiat	1
26.	Laffly	1
27.	Morris	1
28.	Napier	1
29.	Republic	1
30.	Saurer	1
	Unknown	3

The variety reflects both the wide choice of makes on the British market at that period but also the different criteria of many independent operators, in some cases much influenced by first cost or quick delivery and rarely by factors such as the merits of standardisation. Even those attempting to choose on a long-term basis often found it difficult to assess which makes and models would prove reliable, except by trial and error. Even greater variety could be found among vehicles Ribble chose not to acquire.

Of the vehicles listed, only a few remained in the fleet for more than a year or two, notably most of the Tilling-Stevens Express B10A2 models and the Bristol B type coaches acquired from Merseyside Touring Co; the AEC Renown 411 and 413 from Pendle and Lancashire & Westmorland that went to, and briefly returned from, Merseyside Touring; some Thornycroft from Kendal Motor Bus; some of Rishton & Antley's Maudslay ML4B, and some of the Albion buses from Carlisle operators. Very few remained in service longer than four years and almost all had gone by about 1936, though six of the ex-Carlisle & District Albion PMA28 of 1931 remained in stock until sold early in 1940. By contrast, Leylands were mostly kept much as if bought new, though there were occasional exceptions, presumably where in poor condition on purchase.

Of the lesser-known acquired makes, GMC, Chevrolet, Reo, Dodge, Overland and Republic were of American origin, while Minerva, Fiat, Laffley and Saurer came from Belgium, Italy, France and Switzerland respectively. The numbers reflected the immense variety available to operators in the 'twenties, but there were specific influences, such as the preferences of some of the larger companies taken over and probably to some degree an element of local loyalty to such firms as Vulcan, made in Southport; Pagefield, of Wigan, and Crossley of Manchester. In Carlisle and Cumberland, the Scottish influence was appreciable, with Albion, made in Glasgow, and Beardmore of Paisley as instances.

no longer valid, it was an attitude shared with London Transport and a reflection of the blend of high standards and a radical approach with what could be a conservative view on some topics often found in such organisations.

A description of the methods used in 'The Commercial Motor' of 11 February 1938 reveals that at that time 'up to eight' buses were brought in for overhaul each week. The fleet had just reached the 1,000 mark, and such a throughput would thus allow overhauls with an average frequency of 2½ years, though the wording suggests that the full capacity was not used continuously and may have been subject to variation to some degree. In any case, in common with most operators, it was being found that such frequent overhaul was becoming unnecessary and intervals were widened in later years. In the period just before the 1939-45 war, Ribble was selling off vehicles of standard types after eight or nine years or so, and it seems probable that they would have been overhauled to Ribble's high standards twice in that time – it is hardly surprising that many were to have extended lives in other fleets, though this was also partly due to the effects of the war.

The method used in 1938 was for the chassis under overhaul to be stripped of its units which were then completely dismantled and reconditioned. In regard to engines, reboring or resleeving cylinders and regrinding crankshafts was carried out as found necessary, the unit exchange system not being used at that date. It is significant that Ribble was establishing its own modifications, an illustration being a simple baffle which was being fitted to reduce lubricating oil consumption on the many Leyland overhead-camshaft engines then in use – it deflected oil being splashed from the camshaft away from the valve stems.

In later years, overhaul methods were modified as vehicle design altered, and unit exchange was later adopted when it became the most economic system of dealing with items such as engines with a generally predictable long life. Even so, the complete vehicle normally continued to retain its identity, the body generally being refitted on its original chassis even though individual units were liable to be exchanged.

Over the years, fundamental changes in design had their effect on maintenance and operating methods. Analysing the situation in early 1938, the only oil-engined (diesel) buses then in the fleet were about 85 comparatively new Titans of types TD3, TD4 and TD5. Over 90 per cent of the fleet was still petrol-engined and maintenance methods biased accordingly, it being significant that the description of the Frenchwood Avenue premises refers to seeing the various tools and appliances 'with the exception of the oil-engine equipment, which is at Liverpool and other depots'.

Ribble was one of the last bastions of the full-sized petrol-engined single-deck bus, in the form of the Leyland Cheetah model of which it was by far the largest user. The intake of 121 examples with ECW bodywork in 1938 were the last that bodybuilder produced on new petrol-engined chassis – some of the English company fleets had been fairly late in accepting the diesel engine, not infrequently still specifying petrol units for coaches but Ribble's final 40 Cheetah buses of 1939 effectively rang the curtain down on the British company petrol single-deck bus, save

Emerging newly overhauled from the workshops at Frenchwood Avenue late in 1950 is 2344, a Titan TD7 that had entered service in May 1940. Harry Tennant, by then Chief Engineer, reported at the time that Leyland metal-framed bodywork of the type shown gave a cost saving at overhaul after ten years service of up to 40% in man-hours as compared to timber-framed bodies of similar age. As usual at that date, it had been fitted with the 'hexagonal' destination display and lost its upper-deck cream waistband. This vehicle remained in Ribble's fleet until 1956 and then saw further passenger service with J. Stewart of the A1 Service consortium in Ayrshire until 1959. It was also of interest because of its registration number RN 9000, the last commercial vehicle in the RN series before Preston switched to three-letter marks with ACK.

for smaller types of vehicle.

Another rather remarkable aspect of this was the retention of hand starting for Ribble's Cheetah models and at least some of the Tiger coaches of that era. Ribble's maintenance meant that a Cheetah would instantly come to life with one firm upward pull on the starting handle, at least when the engine was warm, but the 7.6-litre engine of a Tiger did call for quite a hefty heave. It may well have been Ribble influence that caused Leyland to quote electric starting as an extra on petrol single-deckers right up to 1939, even though virtually universal in other major fleets by then.

The proportion of oil-engined vehicles was growing quite rapidly however, as more new Titans and, from late 1938, Tiger buses so powered were added to the fleet. A pattern of standardising on either oil or petrol at individual depots was adopted and followed for several years, the general pattern being that the former served industrial or urban areas while petrol fleets were in country areas, such as those in and around the Lake District. By the early war period, Liverpool and Bootle were 100 per cent diesel, with petrol vehicles laid up as services were cut back. It has been said that the solitary ex-demonstrator AEC Regal coach KMG 593 was allocated to Liverpool for use on the Carlisle service to allow conformity to this. Morecambe and Lancaster were other examples of 'diesel' depots. Carlisle was also, for the most part, though the 20-seat Dennis Ace buses for the Bowness-on-Solway service were an exception. This general pattern continued into the early post-war period, though then fading as new vehicles, by then all diesel, began to arrive in larger numbers, and of course the equipment both at Frenchwood and in the depots altered to suit the changing situation.

However, during the war period this pattern was modified by the temporary adoption of a third fuel, producer gas. The Government was concerned at the threat to fuel availability from the ferocious German U-boat attacks on the tankers that brought the entire national supply in those days, and issued an edict in May 1942 that all bus operators were to convert 10 per cent of their fleets to producer gas operation, which relied on home-produced coke. Supply of producer gas trailers was arranged and operators' engineering departments required to convert the buses. Petrol vehicles were generally chosen as conversion was then relatively simple, and the saving of imported fuel would be greater than with the more efficient diesel.

Unfortunately, the gas buses were unreliable and suffered serious loss of power by comparison with petrol, normal practice being to convert the more generously powered six-cylinder models to try and compensate for this. Ribble conversions began early in 1943, though progress lagged well behind the delivery of trailer units. By July eight vehicles were in service, and this figure had only crept up to ten single-deckers, of which eight were Tiger TS6 coaches and two, presumably TS8, were diesel, when the scheme was abandoned by the Government in view of the improved war situation in September 1944. At that stage delivery of the full order of 95 trailers to meet the official requirement had recently been completed. Other notes on this episode appear on page 154.

The situation in the years after the 1939-45 war called for a special initiative. Ribble had been fortunate in beginning the war with an unusually modern fleet, as 852 new Leyland vehicles had been purchased between 1936 and 1941 (see tables on page 108 of Volume 1), helping it to maintain better standards through that period than many operators. By 1947, however, there were many vehicles reaching ten years old or more with body framing that had deteriorated quite seriously, partly due to the extended periods between repainting, always important on timber-framed body structures, as were usual in the Ribble fleet of the time. They would have been due to be sold off if it had been possible to follow the pre-war practice, though the chassis had lasted well and overhaul of these was relatively straightforward. Moreover, quite apart from delivery delays for new vehicles because of the huge backlog of demand, there was urgent need to put as many sound vehicles on the road as possible to meet the growth in demand for travel, both local and long-distance.

In order to cope with the extra work, the former Kendal Motor Bus Co. premises in Kendal and a former balloon hangar at Fazakerley, Liverpool were opened up as subsidiary body shops – see also pages 50 and 52 – but even so, it was clear that extensive body repairs to so large a fleet of vehicles was going to be very expensive as well as taking longer than could be justified. At that stage it was standard practice to carry out major body overhauls at mileages of 126,000, and within a few years the post-war fleet would also be requiring attention.

Accordingly a large-scale rebodying programme was put in hand, concentrating mainly on the Titan TD4 and TD5 double-deckers of 1935-39. It is understood that extra assistance in regard to chassis units was obtained from Leyland, to whom mechanical units stripped from the chassis were sent for overhaul, augmenting the work done by Ribble itself. By replacing most of the double-deck bodies, as well as a substantial proportion of those of the coaches (fuller details are given on pages 96-98), the body shop could devote extra attention to those bodies that were retained.

Geoff Bailey has worked out that by adding 229 rebodied and thoroughly overhauled vehicles in the period between 1947 and 1950 and 70 further vehicles (largely wartime double-deckers) that had been refurbished in 1951-52 to the 507 new buses and 184 new coaches placed in service between 1946 and 1952, the combined total of 990 new, rebodied or refurbished vehicles represented 84% of the total fleet of approximately 1,180 at that date. Certainly it is a fact that, even by 1950, this policy had given a very 'fresh' look to the fleet at a time when many undertakings were still struggling to regain anything approaching pre-war standards. What is more, the rebodied Titans in particular then went on to give good all-day service, generally for over double the lives that would have been expected of them when new, most surviving until 1957-61.

During that period, there was some relaxation of the general rule that overhauled bodywork was refitted to its original chassis, as more of the bodies that were retained needed extensive work and the time needed to carry this out varied. After circumstances settled down to a more normal pattern, a typical 'body off' complete overhaul would take about five weeks and this continued in the later years during which the procedure remained in use, though there was a further period of disruption around the early 'seventies, when there were severe shortages of spare parts.

Recollections of Frenchwood

Someone with special ability to recall Ribble's evolving overhaul methods is Ron Hopkins, who began his career as an apprentice bodybuilder in December 1938, becoming a bodybuilder in 1945, body shop foreman in 1965, body shop superintendent in 1970, and Works Manager of the entire Frenchwood workshops, then a new position, in September 1972. In his early days, almost all bodywork in the fleet was wood-framed, so the skills he needed at that stage in his career were primarily those of a carpenter, but he was always interested in buses and mechanical matters generally.

Working attitudes in the early days were far from easy – Ron recalls seeing Captain Betteridge, Chief Engineer in those days, running a stick across unsatisfactory paintwork and demanding that it be done again, and of men working unpaid at week-ends to complete jobs to the required standard. The livery, right up to the wartime period, remained unusually elaborate, not only retaining lining-out as was still quite common, but having small fleur-de-lys emblems at the corners, so the work involved in a repaint was considerable. Gradually, attitudes changed though the concept of doing the job properly did not, and Ron Hopkins speaks highly of Harry Tennant, who became Chief Engineer in 1949 and remained in the post until appointed NBC Regional Chief Engineer (Western Area), still based at Frenchwood Avenue, in the mid 'seventies – naturally, he still took a close interest in Ribble matters until he died in office a few years later.

During that period, in addition to the various standard Leyland types operated by Ribble and its subsidiaries, often after participation in their development, work was done on such projects as the full-fronted PD3 layout, the Atlantean 'Gay Hostess' double-deck coaches and perhaps most ambitious of all, the Bristol VRL coaches for Standerwick which set the pattern for more recent double-deck coaches in many respects.

Further out-of-the ordinary projects which stemmed from the Government's interest in alternative sources of power were the battery-electric version of the Leyland National produced in 1974, and the conversion to liquid petroleum gas of a Leyland Atlantean in 1980. The electric National conversion was carried out by Ribble, using a Bosch 120hp motor and seven tons of batteries, carried in a two-axle Dyson trailer – despite the use of up-to-date technology, the range before the batteries became discharged was only about 60-80 miles at best, falling in adverse conditions, and it was decided to use the vehicle on the Runcorn busway, where operating conditions were favourable and predictable, so its operation was transferred to Crosville.

The LPG Atlantean, No. 1470 of the ECW-bodied batch then being delivered, entered service from Carlisle depot in 1980, but though quieter than the standard version and 'cleaner' environmentally, it used fuel at almost twice the rate, giving 3.6mpg as compared to 7.4mpg for an otherwise identical diesel example on the same route over 18,000 miles. Refuelling was also complicated by elaborate safety requirements and the experiment was not continued further. Other experimental vehicles of that period included Leyland Nationals 386 with automatic gearbox, 406 with G2 type gearbox, and 407 adapted to carry wheelchairs, with lift at the centre exit. Atlantean/ECW 1514/5 were early applications of Transign electronic destination display. Bristol VRT 2029 was running with a Maxwell automatic gearbox in 1982.

Turning to engines, full advantage was taken of the long life attainable from the Leyland O.600 and O.680 engines, from which 250,000 miles between overhauls were expected without question and indeed enquiries would be made in any instance where this was not achieved – engines still performing well were allowed to continue in service, so the average was well above this and 400,000 or more was obtained in a number of cases.

The Leyland National's 510 engine with its non-detachable cylinder head was not as long-lived, as well as failing to achieve the declared aim that it would not need intermediate attention and could be treated as a 'throw-away' unit after a full service life. However, Frenchwood Avenue set about overcoming the type's shortcomings and meticulous care during overhaul and subsequent

These two photographs of Leyland design models date from the earlier months of 1956, and are evidently meant to show possibilities for 30ft double-deckers, to become legal from 1st July that year, illustrating how Ribble figured in Leyland's thinking at an early stage in the development of new models. The upper one, apart from its livery and Ribble fleetname, is an accurate representation of the Atlantean prototype which was displayed at the Commercial Motor Show later that year and, registered 281 ATC, made a series of demonstration visits, including to Ribble, as shown later.

The lower photograph, taken at or near the same date despite the registration plate reading 'LM 1957' rather than the '1956' of the Atlantean, shows a most intriguing design. The general layout, and in particular the set-back front axle, are remarkably similar to Midland Red's D9 type, of which the prototype did not appear until 1958, so had this Leyland design, even though not pursued, been studied by the designers of that model? The body design, with half cab having a wrap-round windscreen and very low bonnet line, would have given excellent forward vision for the driver, and the upper-deck front windows were also curved. The inscription 'Fuel Oil' on what might be taken for a radiator filler raises more questions – did this imply a front-mounted fuel tank, and if so, where was the engine to be? The provision of what seems to be a large opening bonnet panel seems to suggest it was at the front, but was it to be horizontal, perhaps? The style of side windows is nearer to Burlingham than MCW practice.

maintenance got the average mileage of such units up to 225,000, with 375,000 as the highest recorded from a Ribble-overhauled engine of this type, comparing with stories of 80,000 only being obtained elesewhere. However, it was much more troublesome to rebuild whenever the need did arise, and Ribble pressed Leyland to fit the O.680 to the National, carrying out the initial installation of this unit to No.755, confirming that it was practicable before Leyland adopted the L11 and turbo-charged TL11, both derived from the O.680, as the power units for the National 2.

Over the years, there were numerous instances of close cooperation between Leyland and Ribble, it being found that a period of testing of new or modified designs under operational service conditions was often more revealing and valuable as a guide to their practicality than testing by Leyland's experimental department under what inevitably were apt to be artificial conditions.

When mechanical units capable of much longer mileages without need for repair, and more durable metal-framed bodywork had been adopted, the period between the overhaul periods could be extended. Under the licensing system set up as a consequence of the Road Traffic Act of 1930, the Certificate of Fitness tended to control the overhaul pattern. It became standard practice throughout the industry to arrange for a major overhaul to coincide with expiry of the seven-year certificate given for a new vehicle. Commonly renewal for an overhauled vehicle would be valid for five years, but Ribble's overhauls were expected to allow the Ministry of Transport examiners to issue a six-year certificate, implying a standard of condition little short of that on a new vehicle. Apart from the obvious benefit of the injection of thoroughly overhauled buses on the overall condition of the fleet, further major attention would only be necessary if the vehicle was retained beyond 13 years – if need be, shorter-term certificates could be sought under the system then used by the Ministry of Transport.

In the final years within NBC, and following the change made in 1982 in the method of vehicle inspection, putting more emphasis on the annual inspection and making the Certificate of Initial Fitness (COIF) valid for the vehicle's life, Ribble adopted a system of major overhaul at six years and subsequent six-year intervals if still in the fleet. An intermediate body repair and repaint was laid down at two-year intervals. Coaches were to be painted annually, this being at least in part a consequence of the poor durability of the NBC white coach livery.

Backing up the major attention given by the central works, the garages provided servicing at more frequent intervals. In 1938, vehicles were given a two-day dock about every 10,000 miles. Fuel consumption was watched closely, each type of vehicle having a norm from which any major discrepancy was investigated and if need be, 'carburetter experts were sent over from the Frenchwood works'. In more recent times a cycle of weekly safety and, at twelve-week intervals, intermediate docks were used between the preparation for the annual certificate.

In general, if an engine or other major unit required attention of a kind needing dismantling, whether scheduled or due to a major fault arising, the depot engineer would report the situation to central works, arrange for it to be removed, and a replacement would be sent out the following day from Frenchwood works so as to allow the vehicle to be put back into service with no more than a couple of days or so out of use. This also allowed investigation of the fault and repair to be handled by staff who were experts in the particular field.

The administrative organisation to run this system is covered by the chart reproduced overleaf. The Chief

Engineer and Assistant Chief Engineer were in overall charge, with the Works Manager in charge of activities at Frenchwood Avenue works, administered via Body Shop and Mechanical Superintendents plus an Electrical Supervisor, this last including the fuel injection work under his responsibilities.

The four Area Engineers – Northern, Central, Eastern, and Southern – each covered about six main garages, plus dormy sheds in some cases, reporting to the Chief Engineer and each in charge of the Depot Engineers in his area. Other departments looked after services which, in some cases, touched on the responsibilities of other parts of the organisation, such as uniforms and commercial advertising, although they also included a Building Inspector with staff responsible for maintenance of this type. No doubt in today's climate, the cost-effectiveness of many of these posts would be subject to question as compared to putting work out to commercial suppliers or specialists, and of course recent developments in computers would reduce the clerical needs. Even so, the complete control of standards did give an assurance of work being done to a high standard, as with the engine overhauls mentioned above, thereby obtaining maximum life from such units, difficult to achieve by other means.

It was also possible for Ribble to be a leading participant in the work of improving bus design. The liaison with Leyland over many years has already been mentioned, but Ribble played a leading role within the BET and then NBC. The latter introduced a scheme for the costing of maintenance over the whole life of the vehicle, using methods akin to those of manufacturers when assessing warranty claims, but continuing until the vehicle went to the scrap heap. Ribble was an active participant, and one of the conclusions that emerged from this work was that the apparent savings of lightweight vehicles in first cost and fuel was apt to be outweighed by increased maintenance costs.

In the last decade or so, circumstances have altered greatly. Even before the end of the NBC era, the general trend was one of decline in the amount of work at Frenchwood. The introduction of minibuses meant that more of their maintenance could be done at operating garages. There was a general trend towards the separation of workshop facilities from the operating side, and Ribble Engineering Services was set up as a distinct entity within the company, in line with changing NBC policy, partly to provide means for establishing precise costs but also to encourage diversification to find outside customers for its skills and facilities. Alongside overhaul, painting and repair work for commercial vehicle operators, the design and manufacture of welfare ambulances was undertaken, and out-of-the-ordinary projects were the restoration of a 1938 SS Jaguar 100 sports car for a private customer and the reconstruction of two vintage single-decker buses.

The splitting of the fleet in the run-up to privatisation, resulting from the hiving-off of the newly-created North Western concern and the transfer of the northern section to Cumberland, had a major effect in cutting the fleet size down to 532 in 1987 and this process went further when Stagecoach transferred the remaining operations in Cumbria to the Cumberland company in June 1989. Later that year, it was announced that the engineering activities at Frenchwood Avenue were being closed and 88 staff made redundant, though sixteen were transferred to Blackburn and Lancaster. An era had ended.

Among its efforts to diversify, Ribble Engineering Services became a bodybuilder. The two PLSC Lions onto which it built new bodies became well-known and VY 957 is shown above. It had been new to York Corporation Motors in 1929 and the body shown is a replica of that built by C. H. Roe when the vehicle was new. In the lower picture, Ron Hopkins, the Works Manager, poses with a minibus body built on a Freight Rover Sherpa chassis. The destination display, with three-track route number, is reminiscent of Ribble practice in its own fleet. The vehicle was sign-written with the name of Gilbraith Commercials, the well-known local dealers of Chorley. A smaller, more utilitarian, body design also on Sherpa chassis was used for a batch of welfare minibus-type ambulances for Lancashire County Council social services department.

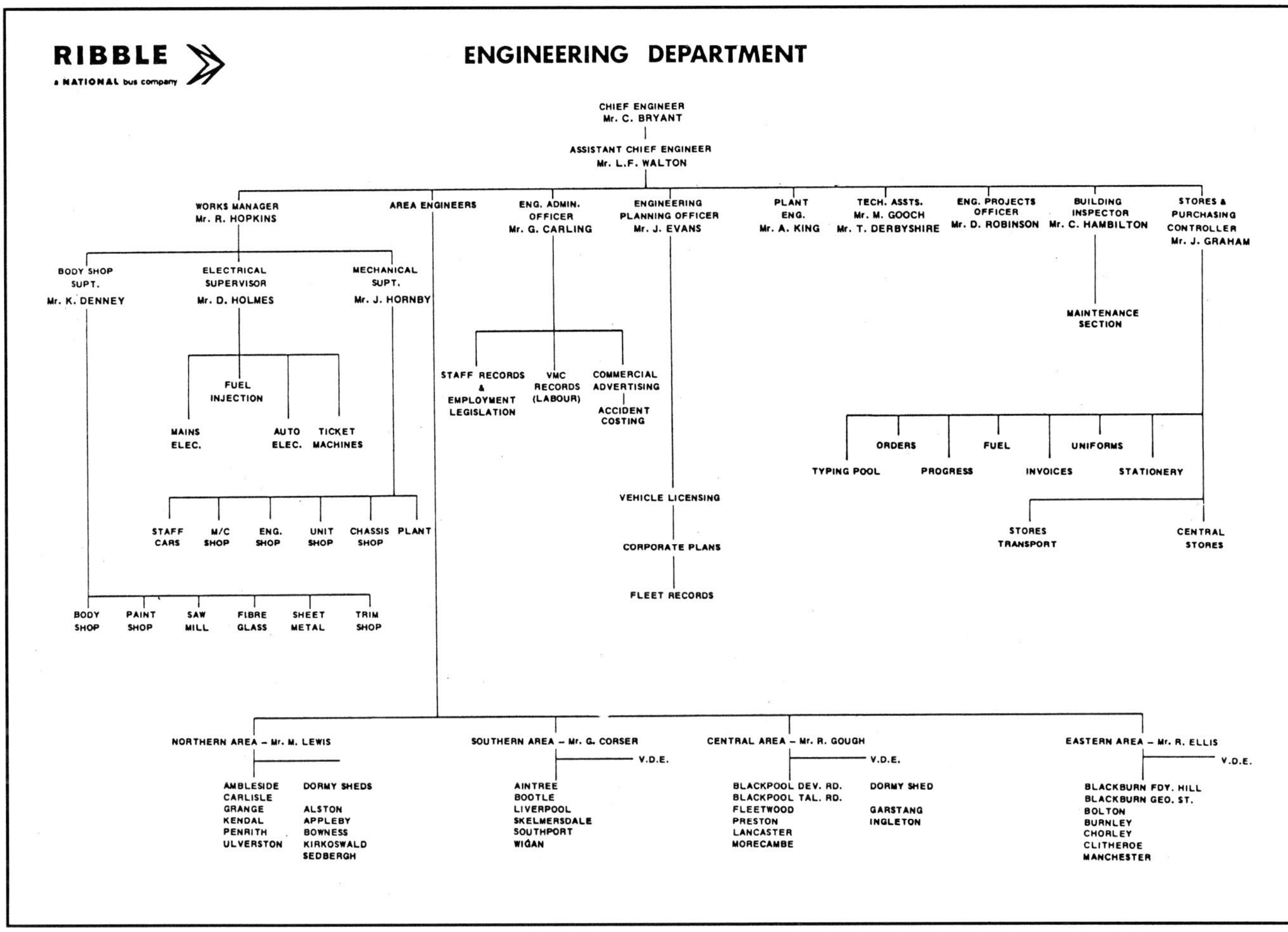

This chart indicates the engineering department organisation as it stood shortly before the dramatic changes of the mid 'eighties. Its rather bureaucratic nature was characteristic of the period, and somewhat similar structures applied in other large bus operating organisations, but the aim of retaining centralised control of a large operating area increased the tendency.

Titan PD3 1841, TCK 841, is seen below posed for the photographer after being painted into an overall advertising livery for Gilbraith, a local British Leyland Truck dealership. As Ribble moved back into private ownership the Management Team sold the Frenchwood Engineering Stores to this dealer to partly finance their takeover. The bus itself was painted into original colours about this time, and added to the company's 'preserved' fleet. Unfortunately, this did not last: Stagecoach ownership led to the bus being passed to Cumberland as a Driver Trainer and its registration mark being transferred to a coach.

HODSON'S CHOICE

Even before Ribble came into existence, the business which had been set up by James Hodson which was to become its nucleus had some noteworthy vehicles. One of the original fleet when operations began in 1910 was this Wolseley, which it has been suggested dated from 1904. Its design appears to support that period but the registration number, CK 611, implies a later date for its registration in the Preston area; early rules on the issue and transfer of registration numbers were much more flexible than applied from c1919.

These two views show the same vehicle, registered CK 447. The identity of the chassis make is unknown to the authors, but its layout, effectively forward-control, having what might be a radiator element at the side of the very short 'bonnet' with drop-down flap at the front, suggests unorthodox mechanical design, though the chain drive to the rear wheels was normal for early heavy vehicles. The body is mounted relatively low by the standards of 1910-13 or so, which seems the probable period. It has been reported that CK 447 was in use on an AEC 40hp, alleged to be new in 1909 (strictly speaking, impossible since the Associated Equipment Co Ltd was not formed until June 1912) that was licensed, apparently by Hodson, in the period up to December 1913 – even at that date, an AEC operating for anyone but the London General Omnibus Co or its associates was extremely rare and only the B-type, of bonneted layout and different in every visible respect to this vehicle, was in production. The number CK 447 was transferred that month to a Leyland 40hp which survived into Ribble ownership, as recorded on page 66, and it is possible that the body shown may have gone to that vehicle with the registration number, as was common practice at the time.

The smaller view, taken near the Old Oak Inn shows the vehicle with 'Hoghton, Higher Walton, Walton-le-Dale, Preston' displayed in the windows.

FLEET SUMMARY

Ribble and Leyland grew together and, over the years, there were many occasions when the latter's finishing shop was full of Ribble vehicles. In this scene in March 1931, an order for 52 Tiger TS3 saloons and 37 Titan TD1 double-deckers, all with Leyland-built bodywork, as usual for Ribble at that period, was going through. Note that all cab and emergency doors have been left open, probably to avoid the risk of damage to paintwork that may have been still tacky. The only interlopers were a TD1 for Thames Valley, which still favoured the open staircase, and beyond it one for Scout of Preston, 30 years later to become part of the Ribble empire.

The aim of the summary of Ribble's fleet of buses and coaches which appears on the following pages is to give an indication of the character of the fleet, along with the fleet numbers and other details. With a fleet of this size and complexity, particularly in the earlier years when expansion was often by acquisition of existing companies, it would be impossible to include full details of every individual vehicle. Readers are referred to the PSV Circle and Omnibus Society Fleet Histories for this information, including that of the often long and involved later careers of vehicles after they left Ribble service. Ex-Ribble buses were widely recognised as good buys because of their high standards of maintenance and for many years were to be found especially in Scottish fleets and those of independent operators in the north-east of England.

Ribble regarded the registration number as the primary form of identification during its earlier years, even though it began to issue its own numbers for chassis, using a C prefix, from 1920, and gradually this was elevated to the stage of becoming the fleet number. Even so, and despite being applied to the bonnet side in quite large characters, it was positioned so low as to be virtually hidden by the nearside mudguard on most vehicles until 1946, when it was decided to display it on the front and rear panels, the C prefix being dropped. Until 1950, the numbers ran in a continuous series, reaching 2777 by that date. A classified system was then adopted.

There were also 'B' numbers for bodies, which, understandably, were not the same as the C numbers, especially in the early years when body transfers were quite frequent. From about the mid-'twenties, they kept pace with the C number, but very confusingly, the figures were one less than the latter, a situation that continued right up to the war. Some vehicles had them displayed internally on the front or rear bulkhead, but this was less consistent, and they were dropped when the non-prefix version of the fleet numbers began to be used.

Until 1972, vehicles new to Ribble were almost always registered in the County Borough of Preston, in whose area its headquarters was based, receiving CK or RN numbers as appropriate. Very early numbers were often re-issued, thus appearing on quite different vehicles or sometimes moving with a transfer of body, but this generally ceased from about 1919. Preston was one of a minority of authorities that used a classified system, adopted in 1919, using CK 3001-5000 for commercial vehicles, including buses, from then until 1934, when the commercial vehicle series jumped to RN 7501, continuing to RN 9000 in 1940 – private cars had begun using RN numbers from 1 in 1928, and motor cycles RN 9001 up from 1935. As by far the largest user, Ribble took a very high proportion of the numbers in these series. From 1940, the three-letter system ran conventionally from ACK, then ARN, BCK, BRN etc until the suffix letter system began in 1964, Ribble's first example being the solitary Panther in the fleet ACK 774B.

For a brief period in 1972-74, Ribble buses appeared with Lancashire registration marks and then the introduction of the Local Vehicle Licensing Office system caused a much more confused system to apply. The Preston office was allocated a range of marks hitherto issued by other boroughs in the surrounding area in addition to the traditional Preston ones, while the ex-Lancashire marks were dispersed elsewhere.

Reference has been made to sets of Company Minute Books recently made available to the authors, and in a number of instances 'conventional wisdom' is challenged. It has, however, been presumed that the Ribble Minute Books reflect the true position rather than other versions generated over the years.

Initial fleet acquired from J. Hodson, June 1919

All but one of the ex-Hodson fleet were on Karrier chassis, in those days made just over the Pennines, in Huddersfield, and although the 1914-18 war limited operators' choice, this seems to have been the favoured choice. The exception, a Leyland dating back to 1913 and thus quite old by the standards of the time, was sold within three months of the take-over. This Karrier 50hp model had been acquired in November 1918, double-deck bodywork being usual in the fleet at the time – its registration, CK 471, had previously been on a brewer's wagon, also a Karrier. The fleet name is already quite close to the form used up to 1945.

FLEET No.*	REG'N	CHASSIS	BODY	TYPE	DATE NEW
-	CK 464	Karrier 30hp	-	O R	3/13
-	CK 447	Leyland 40hp	-	O33R	12/13
-	CK 489	Karrier 45hp	-	O R	11/15
-	CK 471,3087	Karrier 50hp	-	O36R	11/18,5/19

* Up to 1946, these had a C prefix, omitted in these lists.

AEC, Daimler and Vulcan buses of 1919-23

Like other operators in the BAT group, Ribble used ex-military AEC and Daimler Y-type chassis as the basis for most of its needs in the early post-war period, when they could be obtained cheaply. Although condition varied, they were of rugged design and the interchangeability of most components between the two makes helped in reconstructing sound vehicles – the Daimler tended to be favoured for bus work because of its quiet sleeve-valve engine. Bodywork was mixed, but many examples had saloon bodies built to BET standard pattern, at least one by the local firm Preston Motor Body Building Co but around 1921-2 often by Birch Bros, a major supplier to the group at the time.

In 1922, six Vulcan VSD and in 1923, one Vulcan 2-ton model, all with Northern Counties 20-seat bodywork, were purchased, the first of the very rare instances of Ribble buying new small buses until recent times. Examples of both Daimler and Vulcan buses are illustrated in Vol 1, page 101.

–	CK 3102-3	AEC YC	–	O43R	1919
–	CK 3104	AEC YC	–	B32	1919
–	CK 3144	AEC YC	–	O36R	1920
–	CK 3178–9	AEC YC	–	B32	1920
–	CK 3246-7	AEC YC	–	B26	1920
–	CK 3296-8, 3321	Daimler Y	–	various	1920
–	MA 1234-5	AEC YC	–	B32	*

MA 1234-5 were ex-BAT, new in 8/19 and understood to have been used to start the Preston branch of BAT in 12/19, their Cheshire registrations indicating the parentage of the Macclesfield Branch.

31/28/33-5 37/6/8/9	CK 3322-4/8/34, CK 3426/30/6/7	Daimler Y	–	various	1921

The above, of which six are known to have had Birch B28R bodies, plus CK 3298/3321, were given fleet Nos. 29 and 31-9. though not in sequence. The pattern in 1922-3 was rather tidier, though two Daimlers were acquired from BAT's Barrow branch.

40-44	CK 3444/8/62/6/7	Daimler Y	–	B28R	1922
47-51	CK 3474-5,3486-8	Vulcan VSD	N.Counties	B20R	1922
–	EO 576,2322	Daimler Y	–	Ch	c1920/2
52-54	CK 3489,3849-50	Daimler Y	–	B32	1923
55	CK 3348	Vulcan 2-ton	N.Counties	B20	1923
56-60	CK 3352/9,3502/4/7/6	Daimler Y	-	B	1923

The Leyland SG types, 1923-25

The first production type of Leyland buses for Ribble were SG7 models with 38-seat two-doorway bodywork. The vehicle shown was C72 (CK 3538), numerically the last of ten which followed the 39-seat prototype in 1923. The 'S' in the designation stood for Side-type, Leyland's phraseology for forward-control, early versions of which usually had full-fronted bodywork as shown.

The interior of the Leyland-built bodies on the SG buses was quite austere, with very 'basic' and tightly-spaced seats, though at least they were upholstered – contemporary trams often simply had wooden seats. This photograph is thought to show the interior of C84, the first of the half-cab examples dating from 1924, of which an external view is on page 102 of Volume 1.

There hadn't been a Leyland in the fleet between September 1919 and mid-1923, but a G7 demonstrator with 32-seat Leyland body registered by Ribble as CK 3510 in June of that year clearly impressed, even though it was not retained. Ribble was interested in larger passenger capacity and the equivalent forward-control SG7 offered seating for up to 39, a very high figure for a single-decker in those days, although partly achieved by tight spacing of the far from luxurious seats. The G and SG had much in common with what had become known as the RAF-type chassis, Leyland's interpretation of the military specification of the 1914-18 war, solid and reliable, though certainly not built for speed and still in essentials a goods model, with its high frame. Yet, as with later generations of Leylands, there was undoubted engineering quality – those who knew them well spoke of smooth idling of the very simple side-valve four-cylinder engine, as with succeeding generations of Leyland petrol engines.

Ribble began with thirteen of the SG7 in 1923-4, then moving to nine of the SGH7 with higher radiator. All had Leyland-built bodywork, as was to be usual for Ribble for a decade, and these early versions had full-fronted cabs. Ribble disliked this arrangement because of poor access to the engine and, when moving on to the SG9, basically similar but with larger engine, adopted the half cab, at that date still quite rare outside London – it may well have been Ribble's choice of the layout that influenced its general adoption by most major operators, certainly on Leylands and perhaps even generally, throughout Britain within the next year or two. Following the 21 SG9 came the final SG buses for the fleet, 38 of the SG11 which had a slightly shorter wheelbase – the stress on maximum seating capacity seems to have eased.

62	CK 3513	Leyland SG7	Leyland	FB39D	1923
63-72	CK 3517-8/30-2/34-8	Leyland SG7	Leyland	FB38D	1923
73-74	CK 3548-9	Leyland SG7	Leyland	FB38D	1924

75-83	CK 3566/58/9/67/76, 3581/79/7/80	Leyland SGH7	Leyland	FB38D	1924
84-88	CK 3591-5	Leyland SG9	Leyland	B38D	1924
89-98	CK 3602-11	Leyland SG9	Leyland	B36D	1924
99-100	CK 3616-7	Leyland SG9	Leyland	B36D	1924
101-104	CK 3624-7	Leyland SG9	Leyland	B35D	1925
105-106	CK 3635-6	Leyland SG11	Leyland	B35R	1925
107-124	CK 3637-54	Leyland SG11	Leyland	B36R	1925
128-142	CK 3660-74	Leyland SG11	Leyland	B36R	1925

Vehicles acquired from The Chorley Auto Co Ltd, April 1925

(three vehicles*)	Various	Leyland	Various		1919
143	TC 8273	Leyland G7	-	Ch32	6/24

*These are thought to have received the numbers 125-7.

Vehicles acquired from Kenyons, Coleman & Robinson (KCR), Blackburn, December 1925

KCR's number 14, seen in a Leyland official picture when new. There was a Leyland of this number, CB 3495, dating from December 1921, type unspecified but with Leyland 32-seat rear-entrance body, among those taken over by Ribble, in whose fleet it became 146. However, there is an element of doubt as to whether, by then, it was entirely the vehicle shown here as the chassis number quoted, 13236, appears to suggest manufacture in 1925. It seems possible that the body had been mounted on a later chassis.

(14 vehicles)	various	Leyland	various	various

Understood to have taken the fleet numbers 144-157, of which all but 144/5, 150/2 are confirmed. All had CB or CW registrations, with nominal dates between 1919 and 1925, though most were the subject of rebuilds by KCR of one kind or other, often carried out to Leyland specification.

The Leyland Lion PLSC types, 1926-28

The Lion PLSC was the most important member of a new passenger range, all given names and with push-rod overhead-valve four-cylinder engines, introduced by Leyland at the end of 1925. They abandoned the idea of high straight frames common to goods models, as hitherto usual, in line with a growing trend, and the original PLSC1 was a relatively compact vehicle seating up to 31 passengers in standard form, shorter and altogether more nimble than the SG as well as having the benefit of pneumatic tyres, then beginning to become available for vehicles of this size. At about that time, there was a hope, unfulfilled at that stage, that relatively light buses of this size would be allowed to run at slightly less restrictive speeds than the ridiculous 12mph then specified by the law, and this may have influenced the choice of size for the PLSC1.

Leyland's standard body for the new Lion retained the upright outline of earlier types, even though noticeably lower-built and, particularly in hindsight, this gives an impression of a rather 'stodgy' vehicle. Yet it had much more comfortable seats than its predecessors and the 5.1-litre engine remained sweet-running at speed, capable of bowling along at 36mph or so with much less fuss than most contemporaries, even though the continuous whine from the double-reduction rear axle was also a characteristic.

Ribble was beginning to expand its fleet much more rapidly at this time, and 84 of the PLSC1 were placed in service in 1926-7. Then the longer but otherwise virtually unchanged PLSC3 became available, and 108 of these were added to the fleet, all with standard bodies but for the final two, thought to have been ordered by Lancashire & Westmorland. The seating capacity of Ribble's PLSC3 buses was 32 rather than the 35 commonly found for the type, a sign of a trend towards offering passengers more generous leg-room that was to remain a Ribble characteristic for many years – it is said that some at least of the PLSC1 were reduced to 28-seat in line with this policy.

With 182 Leyland Lion PLSC purchased new by Ribble on the road by the end of 1928 and withdrawals not occurring until 1935-38, the model was the first to be seen in quite large numbers all over the company's territory at its full extent. This scene of Grand National traffic in March 1930 happens to show C310 (CK 3840), the first example of the PLSC3 type sometimes known as the Long Lion to enter the fleet in mid-1927. This bus, and the next, retained the 31-seat capacity of their predecessors before the switch to 32. Just visible on the left is C540 (CK 4003), of the final batch of standard examples delivered in 1928. The row of small hinged roof vents was a common but effective way of providing ventilation on saloon buses of that period. Ribble's 3in. destination allowed use of a 'universal' blind but tested would-be passengers' eyesight.

158-167	CK 3702-11	Leyland Lion PLSC1	Leyland	B31F	1926
170-179	CK 3733-42	Leyland Lion PLSC1	Leyland	B31F	1926
180-181	CK 3756-7	Leyland Lion PLSC1	Leyland	B31F	1926
222-229	CK 3764-71	Leyland Lion PLSC1	Leyland	B31F	1926
256-272	CK 3780-96	Leyland Lion PLSC1	Leyland	B31F	1926
273-275	CK 3797-9	Leyland Lion PLSC1	Leyland	B31F	1927
276-309	CK 3806-39	Leyland Lion PLSC1	Leyland	B31F	1927
310-311	CK 3840/7	Leyland Lion PLSC3	Leyland	B31F	1927
312-345	CK 3848-81	Leyland Lion PLSC3	Leyland	B32F	1927
456-465	CK 3914-23	Leyland Lion PLSC3	Leyland	B32F	1928
506-565	CK 3969-4028	Leyland Lion PLSC3	Leyland	B32F	1928
566-567	CK 4033-34	Leyland Lion PLSC3	Massey	B32F	1928

Vehicles acquired from J. S. Bretherton, Ormskirk, February 1926

168	TC 7959	Leyland A13	-	B26F	5/24
169	TD 1729	Leyland A13	Leyland	B26F	4/25

Vehicles acquired from Lancashire Industrial Motors (Pendle Motor Services), Blackburn, September 1926

(40 vehicles)	various	various	various	various

This was a very mixed fleet, including a variety of Leyland, Daimler, AEC and Karrier models as well as a Chevrolet, largely with CB registrations, filling the Ribble fleet numbers 182-221, although not all individually confirmed. Among the later vehicles were five AEC 413, three AEC 507 and a final pair of Leyland PLSC1 with rear-entrance Leyland bodies, the last mentioned, CB 6456-7, becoming Ribble 219-220 and surviving to 1935-6.

Vehicles acquired from The Pilot Motors Ltd, Preston, October 1926

(25 vehicles)	various	various	various	various

Mainly Leylands, ranging from RAF-type to a trio of rear-entrance PLSC1 (CK 3726/32/53, which became Ribble 236/7/40. These ran until 1936/7). There was also a Vulcan and two Maudslay dating from 1925/6, at least one of which was of the ML3 type of modern design for the period. An SG7, CK3357, is illustrated on p29 of Volume 1.

Vehicles acquired from Collingwood Motors (Liverpool) Ltd, July 1927

346-349	KB various	Daimler CJK or CK	-	Ch29	1920

The above were not operated by Ribble, being sold off almost immediately.

Vehicles acquired from T. E. Smith (Pilgrim Motors), Elswick, July 1927

350-357	various	various	various	various	various
358	TE 826	Leyland Lion PLSC1	Leyland	B31F	6/27

The above included six Vulcans, a Dodge and a Leyland C7, the last-mentioned illustrated on page 13 of Volume 1.

Vehicles acquired from Skipton Motor Co Ltd, Skipton, August 1927

359	CX 8241	Karrier ZX	-	20	1926
360	WW 415	Karrier ZX	-	B20	3/27

Vehicles acquired from W. Webster, Wigan, November 1927

361-364	various	Leyland various	-	various	various
365-367	EK 4572/4/6	Leyland Lion PLSC1	Leyland	B32R	1926
368	EK 5947	Leyland Lion PLSC1	Leyland	B32F	7/27

The early Leylands above, dating from 1920-24, included an S5 and an SG9. 367 did not enter service until 3/27.

Vehicles acquired from Lancashire and Westmorland Motor Services Ltd, Lancaster, December 1927

As explained more fully on page 13 of Volume 1, this fleet was itself the result of several take-overs, though its main origin was the setting-up of Westmorland Motor Services Ltd in 1925 as a subsidiary of Cumberland Motor Services Ltd, founded by the Meageen family but part of the BAT group from 1921. Expanding southwards, it was renamed as above in 1926 but then BAT decided it would be logical to absorb it into Ribble. Westmorland had begun operations with a fleet of AEC 411 buses (which became Ribble 415-22) before switching to the PLSC (423-9/38-41), but the vehicles transferred also included a mixed bag of older vehicles, notable among which were the Lake District Road Traffic Co Ltd fleet of Thornycrofts (401-7/9-11). Other groups of vehicles came from Fahy's of Lancaster and the Lancaster & District Tramways Co (in both cases numbered among the early Leylands), Hodgson & Barnes of Preston (433-7) and Rutter of Kendal (two Thornycroft and three Guy)

369-392	various	Leyland various	various	various	various
393-394	various	Tilling-Stevens	-	various	various
395-397	various	Daimler CK	-	B26	various
398-399	-	-	-	-	
400-411	various	Thornycroft various	various	various	various
412-413	EC 5768-9	Guy BA	-	B20	1924
414	EC 5883	Guy BB	-	B30	1924
415-416	EC 6442/52	AEC Renown 411	-	B30	1925

This Leyland of Lancaster & District Tramways & Fahys Ltd might have survived into Ribble ownership via Lancashire & Westmorland, not necessarily with the body shown. This might well have been older than the chassis, thought to have dated from around 1921, though its identity is not known. There was an open-top double-decker in the fleet as taken over, TC 9011, believed to have become Ribble 386, but that was on a 1924 Leyland RAF-type chassis, having a taller radiator and bonnet. Clearly the long title created problems for the signwriter!!

One of the AEC 411-type buses purchased by Westmorland Motor Services Ltd when it began operations in 1925; eight of the model passed to Ribble. This one, No.12, displays clear evidence of having bodywork by Strachan & Brown, then one of AEC's main body suppliers, in the form of the distinctive transfer at the front end of the waistrail, but quite similar bodywork was built on others of the type in the Westmorland fleet by Massey Bros. The 411, introduced with the model name Renown in March 1925, was a relatively light design with four-cylinder 5.1-ltre engine, much the same as used in the NS double-decker.

417-419	EC 6586-8	AEC Renown 411	-	B30	1925
420-422	RM 1519-21	AEC Renown 411	-	B30	7/25
423-424	TD 4706/60	Leyland Lion PLSC1	Leyland	B31R	2/26
425-426	TD 5192,5562	Leyland Lion PLSC1	Leyland	B31R	1926
427-428	TD 5808,5960	Leyland Lion PLSC1	Leyland	B31R	4/26
429	TD 6434	Leyland Lion PLSC1	Leyland	B31R	6/26
430-431	NL 3235,4114	Daimler Y	-	-	1922
432	-	-	-	-	
433-435	various	Leyland various	various	various	various
436-437	CK 3723/0	Guy O	Massey	B20	3/26
438-439	TE 1206-7	Leyland Lion PLSC1	Leyland	B31R	7/27
440-441	TE 1709-10	Leyland Lion PLSC1	Leyland	B31R	9/27
442	TC 8438	Leyland RAF G7	Leyland	B32	6/24

443-447 (thought to have been cars or possibly taxis)

The older Leylands included at least seven RAF types (in addition to 442), of which one was an open-top double-decker; two SG7 and an SGH7, all three with Leyland 40-seat Leyland bodywork, plus a 36-seat SG9, and various smaller types such as a pair of Z5 with 20-seat Leyland bodies. The Thornycrofts were largely of the J-type, that maker's main model built for the War Department in the 1914-18 war and continued into the 'twenties, but also included an X and two of the small A1 dating from 1925.

Vehicles acquired from J. E. Loynds and C. F. Higgins (Belford Bus Service), Darwen, December 1927

448-453	various	Vulcan VWBL	-	B32	1927

The Ribble Minute Book of the day records that five other vehicles were taken over. No identities are revealed, but they were probably Karriers.

Leyland Tiger, Titan and Lion LT-type models 1928-31

The Leyland Tiger TS1 single-decker, along with the corresponding Titan TD1 double-decker of similar mechanical design, was introduced at the 1927 Commercial Motor Show. Both were of low build and had a new 6.8-litre six-cylinder overhead-camshaft petrol engine known as the T-type which was to form the basis of a whole family of engines used in full-sized Leyland models up to 1942. The TS1 chassis had a 17ft 6in wheelbase and was intended to have an overall length of 27ft 6in, but at that date a maximum of 26ft was more generally accepted in Britain, and few of the TS1 were delivered before the TS2, having the same wheelbase but a shorter rear overhang, was introduced.

The first batch of 40 Leyland Tigers supplied to Ribble early in 1928 was the first large fleet of this lively model for any operator. The low-built Leyland body showed influence of American taste in its design and though soon to look very utilitarian, offered more practical comfort for all-weather use on long distance services than the canvas-topped coach designs of the day. The short rear overhang allowed no room for the usual side window behind the rear entrance doorway. Luggage was carried internally at the rear, the rear window being provided with bars for this reason. The vehicle shown, C470 (CK 3928), was one of nineteen sold to Western SMT in 1936-7.

The Lion LT1 of 1929 had a distinctive rather squat version of the Leyland radiator of the time, but the standard Leyland body for the model was very similar to the contemporary version for the Tiger. Ribble ordered 25 with front-entance layout, of which C593 (CK 4075) is seen here negotiating varied types of traffic in Preston in August of that year. The solid-tyred LMS railway lorry may have been a Thornycroft, judging by the style of rear wheel, though usually the front wheels were similar. Ribble's LT1 batch was sold off in 1939, many for further passenger service.

One of the very early TS1 demonstrators, registered TE 635, was painted in Ribble livery though not purchased, but Ribble was the first operator to put a large fleet of the new model into service, when 40 were delivered beginning in the spring of 1928, taking the numbers 466-505 between the final batches of Lion PLSC models. Some records indicate that these were TS1 models, but they were of the 'short-tailed' pattern and seem to have been listed as TS2 by Ribble. At that date, the concept of the coach was still emerging from the charabanc idea of a vehicle with a fabric top. The Leyland bodywork on this first batch of Ribble Tigers, though to what would later be thought of as 'bus' specification, apart from the internal luggage rack at the rear, was regarded as high-class 'saloon', offering higher standards of refinement than many cars of the day. The vehicles were used on early long-distance routes.

A further 31 followed in 1929, very similar but of front-entrance layout with luggage rack on the roof and with more spacious seating for 26, reseated to 30 in 1934 for bus duties. The 1930 TS2 deliveries included both bus versions seating 30 from new and more of the 26-seat 'coach' version. Meanwhile, Ribble's first Titans were delivered in 1929, these having the initial standard Leyland lowbridge open-stair body of the model, supplied to numerous company fleets at the time. It was realised that their capabilities made double-deck operation of suitable inter-urban routes a practicality. Larger fleets followed in 1930-31, these having the closed-stair version of the body.

To replace the PLSC, Leyland introduced the Lion LT1 in 1929, this having a four-cylinder engine of the same 5.1-litre size as its predecessor, but to the same overhead-camshaft design as the six-cylinder T-type engines. The initial chassis was of simpler design than the Tiger, having an affinity with the contemporary Badger goods model, and Ribble took 25 that year, to which were added seven more that had been ordered by taken-over businesses, all with front-entrance 30-seat bodies similar to those on the TS2 model.

Leyland decided to rationalise its single-deck range in the spring of 1930, introducing the Lion LT2 for bodywork of 26ft overall length, which conformed to the Tiger model in general design, apart from the four-cylinder engine, but with a shorter 16ft 6in wheelbase. Ribble's first examples were also among the first to have a new pattern of Leyland bodywork, of more rounded outline. This was also used for the new Tiger TS3 model, having the same main dimensions as the LT2. Ribble's intake of new single-deckers switched to the LT2, and later in the year the TS3, both in 30-seat bus form, though in 1931 the entire Tiger intake of 52 TS3 were to the 26-seat long-distance specification.

In general, the 1928-9 vehicles were sold off in 1936-39 and most of the 1930 ones in 1938-9, often for further use as buses. A start had been made on similar disposal of the 1931 single deckers in 1939 but the outbreak of war that year disrupted the pattern, causing some of the TS3 batch to be taken for War Department use in 1940 ,while most of the TD1 and some of the LT2 of that year remained in service until 1945-8. Five TD1 of 1930-31 were rebodied and re-engined in 1943-4 (see later section).

466-505	CK 3924-63	Leyland Tiger TS2	Leyland	C29R	1928
575-578	CK 4057-60	Leyland Titan TD1	Leyland	L27/24RO	1929
579-603	CK 4061-85	Leyland Lion LT1	Leyland	B30F	1929
604-634	CK 4086-4116	Leyland Tiger TS2	Leyland	C26F	1929
669-670	TE 6375-6	Leyland Titan TD1	Leyland	L27/24RO	1929
671	TE 6998	Leyland Titan TD1	Leyland	L27/24RO	1929
672-677	CK 4124-9	Leyland Titan TD1	Leyland	L27/24RO	1929
706-712	CK 4136-42	Leyland Lion LT1	Leyland	B30F	1929
713-722	CK 4148-57	Leyland Titan TD1	Leyland	L27/24RO	1929
723-742	CK 4187-4206	Leyland Tiger TS2	Leyland	B30F	1930
743-762	CK 4207-26	Leyland Titan TD1	Leyland	L24/24R	1930
763-772	CK 4233-42	Leyland Titan TD1	Leyland	L24/24R	1930
773-784	CK 4243-54	Leyland Lion LT2	Leyland	B30F	1930
801-810	CK 4281-90	Leyland Lion LT2	Leyland	B30F	1930
811-830	CK 4261-80	Leyland Titan TD1	Leyland	L24/24R	1930
831-853	CK 4291-4313	Leyland Tiger TS2	Leyland	B30F	1930
854-875	CK 4314-35	Leyland Tiger TS2	Leyland	C26F	1930
924-929	CK 4339-44	Leyland Tiger TS3	Leyland	B30F	1930
930-932	TF 1553-5	Leyland Tiger TS3	Leyland	B30F	1930
1012-4	CK 4365-7	Leyland Lion LT2	Leyland	B35F	1930
1046-82	CK 4403-39	Leyland Titan TD1	Leyland	L24/24R	1931
1083-1134	CK 4440-91	Leyland Tiger TS3	Leyland	C26F	1931
1135-98	CK 4492-4555	Leyland Lion LT2	Leyland	B30F	1931

669-71 were allocated to County until 12/30; 706-9 were ordered by Armstrong & Siddle, Penrith; 710-12 were ordered by County, Lancaster; 924-32 and 1012-4 were ordered by Furness Omnibus Co.

The interior of Leyland's bodywork had become much more 'civilised' by 1930 than it had been six years earlier, this view of the interior of a late example of the Tiger TS2 with 'square' body dating from May of that year. The vehicle was C838 (CK 4298) and the view shows the body number B837, out of step with the C number by one, as was to continue throughout the 'thirties. The Leyland maker's plate had the date built stamped on it, a characteristic touch of honesty that was to embarrass some operators in later years. The translucent Ribble sign was designed to help intending pasengers identify their bus in a period when there were many other operators' vehicles on the road. The side windows were of the full-drop type, spring-loaded towards the closed position but held open by a friction pad device controlled by the small ring at sill level. They gradually tended to close during the course of a few miles.

The capability of the Titan TD1 not only in carrying more passengers than a single-decker but in offering adequate comfort and performance for longer country routes led to the purchase of a total of 50 in 1930, all with the closed-stair version of the standard Leyland lowbridge body. Seen here in May of that year is C752 (CK 4216) on the Blackburn-Wigan route, just after passing the Hoghton Arms.

The introduction of the Lion LT2 in the spring of 1930 almost coincided with that of the 'rounded' style of Leyland body, the early version of which had quite a pronounced downward sweep of the front end of the roof. Seen here in what seems to have been a posed picture in Tithebarn Street bus station, Preston is C807 (CK 4287) not when new as might be thought from its condition but in May 1933.

The final batch of 37 Titan TD1 models were delivered in 1931, and although generally similar to the 1930 batch. with standard 48-seat Leyland lowbridge bodywork, some, at least, took on a little of the look of the following TD2 version, with large-section front tyres, quite common on late examples of the TD1. The front mudguard was reshaped to suit, losing much of the reverse curve at the rear that had been so characteristic of most Leyland bus designs of the period from 1928. Seen here is C1080 (CK 4437), one of the last of the batch, in an August 1931 Leyland photograph – it remained in service until 1947.

The final manifestation of the long-distance saloon body, based on the bus version but with more spacious seating and a roof luggage rack, were the 52 examples on Tiger TS3 chassis delivered in 1931, C1117 (CK 4474) being seen here. The front end of this body style now had a horizontal roof line rather than the 'drooping' style of the 1930 LT2 again photographed at Tithebarn Street, Preston. Note how Ribble's characteristic lamp used to illuminate a destination board, if carried, obscured the display from this angle. Like many of this batch, it was sold in 1940 and saw service with a firm of contractors and the Royal Ordnance Factory, Swynnerton. The poster for the Palladium visible beyond the front mudguard advertises 'Sally in Our Alley', featuring 'Our Gracie' – it was unneccesary to spell out Gracie Fields in full in those days, especially in Lancashire.

Vehicles acquired from W. Solloway (Eccleston Motor Co), August 1928

568-571	various	various	various	various	various

The above comprised a Vulcan VSD, a Maudslay ML4 and two Leylands, of which an A13 was soon sold with the others but a PLSC1, TD 6739, Ribble 570, was operated until 1936.

Vehicles acquired from Waterloo & Crosby Motor Services Ltd, Seaforth, January 1928

572-574	various	various	various	B26	various

Waterloo & Crosby came under Ribble control in January 1928, but these three vehicles, two Burford D models and a Halley, were transferred to Ribble later in the year. The fleet was absorbed in July 1930 (see 1015-24).

Vehicles acquired from County Motors (Lancaster) Ltd, February 1929

This company was operated as a subsidiary, but using Ribble fleet numbers, until December 1930. During that period a number of existing Ribble vehicles, mainly Leyland of various types, were transferred to County, including 148-50/2/3/7, 388, 678-81/5 and 895-9. As mentioned above, three TD1 buses ordered by Ribble, 669-71, were allocated from new to County.

635-642	various	Guy BB	-	various	various
643-647	various	Guy B	-	various	various
648-651	various	Guy BA	-	20	various
652-655	various	Thornycroft Boadicea	-	B32	6/24
656-658	various	Thornycroft J	various	O45 or 50	1924

659	BT 7269	Leyland Z5	-	30	5/24
660-662	various	various	-	various	various
663-666	various	Leyland various	various	various	various
667-668	various	various	-	various	various

The Guy BB buses seated 30 or 31 and dated from 1926-7, the Guy B were 24 or 26 seat buses of 1923-26. The Thornycroft Boadicea buses were new to Morecambe Motors (who were shareholders in County) and the J-type double-deckers came from a London independent operator, R. G. Monro, via the LGOC. The makes listed as various comprised one each of Dennis, Tilling-Stevens, Pagefield, Fiat and Overland.

Vehicles acquired from Armstrong & Siddle Motor Services Ltd, Penrith, April 1929

678	RM 5466	Leyland Lion PLSC3	Leyland	B32R	1928
679-680	RM 4555/4	Leyland Lion PLSC3	Leyland	B32R	1927
681	HH 4209	Leyland Lioness PLC1	Leyland	B26F	1928
682-684	RM 5066/35/4	Albion PM28	-	B32R	5/28
685-688	RM various	Albion various	-	various	various
689-691	various	Reo	-	24	various
692-694	various	Daimler Y	-	various	various
695-704	various	various	-	various	various

One of the Albions is illustrated on page 18 of Volume 1. The vehicles numbered 695-704 comprised a Thornycroft X of 1921; three Guy 20-seaters, one of BA type; three Daimler of 1921-5, a CC, a Y and an 8-seat car; and single examples of Dennis, Minerva, Dodge and Bean. In addition, four Leyland Lion LT1 on order were taken directly into stock as 706-9. The Ribble Minute Book gives the takeover date as 1st April but the vehicles were not absorbed until September (see page 14).

Vehicles acquired from Ideal Omnibus Services (Liverpool) Ltd, December 1929

785-787	WW 6434/2/3	Leyland Lion PLSC3	Leyland	B35F	7/28
788-789	KD 3481-2	Leyland Lion PLSC3	Leyland	B32F	1928
790/2	TE 5809/74	Leyland Lion PLSC3	Leyland	B35F	1928
791/3	TE 8298,8062	Leyland Lion LT1	Leyland	B35F	6/29
794-795	TE 8299,8301	Leyland Lion LT1	Leyland	B35F	6/29
796-797	TE 8300,8297	Leyland Lion LT1	Leyland	B35F	6/29

785-7 were new to G. H. Kilburn, Heckmondwike, passing to Rymer's Ideal, Liverpool, to whom 788-90/2 were new.

Vehicles acquired from S. P. and T. Adair, Carlisle, December 1929

798	HH 4668	Gilford 166 OT	Wycombe	B32R	3/29
799-800	HH 4097,3073	Dennis	-	B20, B19	various

The above were not used by Ribble, though 798, acquired by Merseyside, later reappeared in the fleet as 1249.

While the big intake of new Leylands was taking place in 1928-31, acquisitions with independent businesses brought many further additions to the fleet. Amongst these were 24 from Kendal Motor Bus Co, tabulated overleaf, of which No.17 (EC 6916), new in 1926, was the first of five Leyland Lion PLSC1 models almost identical to Ribble's examples. This was retained in the fleet alongside them, in this case becoming C910 and running until 1935. Kendal had turned to Thornycroft latterly, and its last new buses were a pair of the BC Forward six-cylinder model with Northern Counties bodywork, dating from April 1929. Shown below (right) is No. 30, which was registered as EC 8757, becoming Ribble C922 – it ran until 1934.

Vehicles acquired from Kendal Motor Bus Co, Kendal, April 1930

900	EC 5761	Leyland C7	Leyland	B32	1924
901	EH 5731	AEC 201	-	B20	9/24
902-909	EC various	Leyland various	various	various	various
910-911	EC 6916-7	Leyland Lion PLSC1	Leyland	B31F	4/26
912	EC 7025	Leyland Lion PLSC1	Leyland	B31F	6/26
913-916	EC various	Leyland various	various	various	various
917-918	EC 7623-4	Leyland Lion PLSC1	Leyland	B31F	4/27
919	EC 7735	Leyland Lion PLSC1	Leyland	B31F	6/27
920-921	EC 8251,8331	Thornycroft UB	N.Counties	B32F	1928
922-923	EC 8757-8	Thornycroft BC	N.Counties	B32F	4/29

Part of the Kendal Motor Bus fleet is illustrated in Vol 1, page 24. The older Leylands included several C7 and a Leveret 20-seat bus.

Vehicles acquired from Majestic and Empress, Preston, April 1930

The above was a partnership of Preston and Longridge Motor Co Ltd (Empress), the former owners of 883-7, and Matthew Wade (Majestic), who owned 888-99.

883-885	CK 3802-4	Leyland Lion PLSC1	Leyland	B31R	1926
886-887	CK 3885/96	Leyland Lion PLSC1	Leyland	B31R	1927
888-891	CK 3901-4	Leyland Lion PLSC1	Leyland	B31R	9/27
892/4	EH 8539,8506	Leyland Lion PLSC1	Leyland	B31F	1926
893	CK 4046	Leyland Lion PLSC3	Leyland	B32R	8/28
895-897	CK 4178-80	Leyland Lion LT1	Leyland	B31R	8/29
898-899	CK 4185,4232	Leyland Lion LT1	Leyland	B30R,B31R	1929

The most modern vehicles taken over from Majestic of Preston included CK 4178, a Leyland Lion LT1 with the rear-entrance version of the standard Leyland body of the time. It is seen ready for delivery on a sunny morning in August 1929. Note the 'Preston No.' lettering at the rear, ready to receive the number allocated by the Borough Council under the then local licensing system. It became Ribble C895 the following April and ran until 1939. Like many ex-Ribble buses, all the ex-Majestic LT1s found new homes in County Durham, this one, and C899, passing to F. Lockey of West Auckland in 1940 remaining in use until 1951.

Most of the more modern vehicles in the Furness fleet were standard Leyland products, but this Lioness PLC1, TE 1140, placed in service in July 1927, had been fitted with a special body by Hall Lewis, the London firm which was the predecessor of Park Royal. It ran on the Barrow-Manchester service started that month, which proved a failure. The interior layout included tables between the seats, an advanced concept for the time, and much more elaborate than anything Ribble then operated. It became Ribble C949, but was sold at an unknown date in the early 'thirties, passing to J. Browning of Whitburn, running briefly for SMT in 1935-6 before being sold again to Gorman of Coatbridge.

Vehicles acquired from the Furness Omnibus Co Ltd, Dalton-in-Furness, May 1930

933-936	various	various	-	various	various
937	TD 6270	Leyland Leveret LA	Leyland	B20F	5/26
938-939	various	various	-	various	various
940	TD 6477	Leyland Leveret LA	Leyland	B20F	6/26
941-942	TD 6683-4	Leyland Leveret LA	Leyland	B20F	6/26
943-944	TD 6822-3	Leyland Leveret LA	Leyland	B20F	6/26
945-946	TD 7523-4	Leyland Leveret LA	Leyland	B20f	8/26
947	TD 9219	Leyland Lion PLSC1	Leyland	B31F	3/27
948	TE 153	ADC 417	-	32	6/27
949	TE 1140	Leyland Lioness PLC1	Hall Lewis	C24D	7/27
950	MP 9318	GMC T20	-	20	1928
951-952	TE 2897/6	Leyland Lion PLSC1	Leyland	B31F	2/28
953-956	TE 2898-2901	Leyland Lion PLSC1	Leyland	B31F	2/28
957-959	various	ADC 416	-	B32	1928
960	TE 4563	Leyland Lion PLSC3	Leyland	B36F	6/28
961-962	TE 5418/7	Leyland Lion PLSC1	Leyland	B31F	9/28
963	CB 8329	GMC T20	-	B20	8/28
964/6	TE 8688/7	Leyland Lion LT1	Leyland	B35F	7/29
965/7-8	TE 8685/4/6	Leyland Tiger TS2	Leyland	B30F	7/29

The vehicle types listed above as 'various' comprised three AEC 26-seat buses, a 202 and two 414 models; a Daimler CJK 26-seater; and two 14-seat buses, a Chevrolet and an Overland. In addition, nine Leyland Tiger TS3 and three Lion LT2 buses on order were taken directly into Ribble stock as 924-32 and 1012-4 (q.v.). Two Furness vehicles are illustrated on page 25 of Volume1.

Vehicles acquired from Rishton & Antley Motor Co Ltd, Accrington, September 1930

This company came under Ribble control in March 1930, being operated as a subsidiary at first. Immediately, Claremont Omnibus Services, Burnley, was taken over by Rishton & Antley, and the ex-Claremont vehicles, mostly only a few months old and retaining Claremont fleetnames, were given the Ribble fleet numbers 876-882. The remainder of the Rishton & Antley fleet were given Ribble numbers when the business was absorbed in September.

876	CW 6365	Leyland Lion PLSC1	Leyland	B31R	1/26
877-879	CW 7833/6/7	Leyland Tiger TS2	Leyland	B30F	9/29
880-882	CW 7834/5/8	Leyland Tiger TS2	Leyland	B30F	9/29
969,971	CW 2839,2938	Maudslay C4, A	-	B26D	1920
970	TC 9653	Leyland S4	Massey	B32F	1924
972	CB 2002	Daimler Y	-	Ch26	1920
973-977	various	Maudslay various	-	various	various
978-982	TD various	Maudslay ML4	-	B30	1926
983	CW 6922	Leyland Lion PLSC1	Leyland	B31R	8/26
984-991	various	Maudslay various	-	various	1927
992-994	various	Leyland Lion PLSC1	Leyland	B31R	1927
995-1001	various	Maudslay various	-	various	various
1002	KW 4409	Leyland Lion PLSC3	Leyland	B35F	7/28
1003	TE 4028	Leyland Lion PLSC3	Leyland	B35F	5/28
1004	CW 8069	Leyland Lion PLSC1	Leyland	B31R	3/28
1005	KW 4432	Leyland Lion PLSC3	Leyland	B35F	7/28
1006-7	TE 7220-1	Leyland Lion PLSC3	Leyland	B35F	1929
1008-9	XI 4577,4430	Crossley		Ch14	1925
1010-1	various	Maudslay CP, C3	-	various	various

Of the above, 970/2/83/92-4 and 1002-5 were ex-Calder Motor Co Ltd, Great Harwood in October 1929. The fleet included a total of fourteen Maudslay ML4, ML4A or ML4B.

Vehicles acquired from Waterloo & Crosby Motor Services Ltd, Seaforth, July 1930

1015-22	TD various	AEC NS 409	LGOC	H26/26RO	1926
1023-4	TE 1401,1091	AEC NS 409	LGOC	H56RO	1927

Waterloo & Crosby had been run as a Ribble subsidiary since 1928, when three earlier vehicles transferred had become Ribble 572-4. One of the NS buses is shown on page 21 of Volume 1.

Vehicles acquired from H. Croisdale (Brunshaw Motors), Burnley, October 1930

1025/7	various	Leyland C	Leyland	B	various
1026/8	CW 6366,6987	Leyland Lion PLSC1	Leyland	B31R	1926
1029	UC 7191	Leyland Lion PLSC3	-	-	2/28
1030	CW 8441	Leyland C7	Leyland	B28R	5/27
1031-2	CW 9387,9473	Leyland Tiger TS2	Leyland	B30F	1929

1030 had been new to Manxland Bus Services, registered MN 4932, but was re-registered as above on sale to Croisdale in 6/28.

Vehicles acquired from Freeman's Silver Star Service, Chorley, November 1930

The oldest vehicle taken over from Freeman's was this Leyland SG11, seen here when new in October 1925 and basically similar to those supplied to Ribble. Pneumatic tyres were a recent development at the time, but oil side lamps were a conservative feature. Registered TD 3798, it became Ribble C1033 but was sold off almost immediately. Also noteworthy among the ex-Freeman buses was the only double-decker, TE 2943, which was older than any of the Titans bought new by Ribble, with chassis number 70014, nominally the 14th of the type, having begun life as a Leyland demonstrator in February 1928. It had evidently acquired a new radiator of the latest type when photographed in Freeman livery on sale in September 1929. Note the illuminated star over the destination box and the translucent Freeman's sign in the bulkhead window, copied from the Ribble type – identity was important in the competitive days of 1929, just as 65 years later. It ran as Ribble C1040 until 1937, when it was among the first Titans sold, beginning a further complex life, with two spells in the fleet of W. Alexander & Sons Ltd, and a few years with an independent operator, Grieg of Inverness, in between. It was finally withdrawn in 1940.

1033-4	various	Leyland various	Leyland	various	various
1035-6	TE 713,1246	Leyland Lion PLSC3	Leyland	B36	1927
1037	CX 9905	Karrier KL	-	B39	1927
1038-9	VH 1077,1176	Karrier various	-	B32	various
1040	TE 2943	Leyland Titan TD1	Leyland	L27/24RO	2/28
1041	EK 6472	Dennis G	-	B20	1928
1042	TE 6829	Leyland Lion PLSC3	Leyland	B35F	3/29
1043	TE 6830	Guy	-	B20	4/29
1044-5	TE 8290-1	Leyland Tiger TS2	Massey	B35F	1929

1038 was a WL6 and 1039 is thought to have been a CL6 and thus also a six-wheeler – all three Karriers were registered in Huddersfield, presumably by Karrier. 1040 had been a demonstrator, acquired in 9/29.

Vehicles acquired from Lawrence Motor Services Ltd, Fleetwood, January 1931

1205	UT 225	Chevrolet X	-	B14F	2/27
1206-7	TD 6837,8866	Leyland Lion PLSC1	Leyland	B—F	various
1208-10	TE various	Vulcan 3XB	-	B20	2/28
1211/3	various	Leyland Lion PLSC1	Leyland	B—F	1928
1212	TE 4602	Dennis G	-	B20	6/28
1214	TE 6741	Leyland Lion PLSC1	Leyland	B31F	3/29
1215-7	various	Vulcan 3XS	-	B20	various

A photograph of 1206 when new appears on page 26 of Volume 1.

Vehicles acquired from Merseyside Touring Co, Liverpool, 1931

This operator became a Ribble subsidiary in February 1930, continuing to function as a separate business until absorbed in September 1931. In the interim, there was some inter-action between the two undertakings, eight AEC of types 411 and 413, together with a Gilford, that had been taken over with other businesses by Ribble being transferred to Merseyside in 1930. These returned to the main fleet with new numbers 1249, 1328-34/43 on absorbtion (albeit briefly), except for the Gilford. Six Leyland Lion LT2 coaches newly delivered to Merseyside between March and June 1930 ran as such for that season only and were transferred to Ribble in April 1931, receiving fleet numbers 1199-1204. They entered service between May-September 1931, but with Leyland bus bodies believed to have been transferred from KF 4721-6 Tiger TS3, newly delivered to Merseyside but which entered service in May 1931 with the coach bodies from the LT2 chassis, to become Ribble 1278-83 on absorbtion. The numbering indicates that it had not been planned to take further ex-Merseyside vehicles beyond that numbered 1283 into Ribble stock, for those acquired from Carlisle independents following the tramway replacement deal in that city (see page 26 of Volume 1) began at 1284. However, the urgent need for more buses suited to Ribble's new commitments led to briefly extended lives for those which became 1328-44. They are understood to have been sold within a few months, along with other oddments, including 1237, the remarkable Tilling-Stevens petrol-electric six-wheel double-decker, which later became a van. Many of the TillingStevens B10A2 and Bristol B types survived with Ribble until 1935.

The Merseyside Touring Co effectively introduced Ribble to the idea of the coach as understood in later years, as well as running extensive tours, excursions and express services (including that to Weston-super-Mare and Ilfracombe shown in the destination and side route board here). Bristol chassis, produced by a concern which in those days had no connection with the major bus combines, were favoured by a number of independent operators as a basis for coach bodywork, and Merseyside contributed six of the B-type, with its 6-litre four-cylinder engine, to Ribble's fleet. This one, No.39 (KD 9412), which became Ribble C1274, had Burlingham 26-seat bodywork and was new in June 1930 – others of the same batch had similar bodywork by Massey. It ran for MacShane of Liverpool after sale by Ribble in 1935, but is understood to have been damaged in an air raid before withdrawal in 1941.

Not many pictures survive of ex-independent vehicles in Ribble livery, especially on other than Leyland chassis. This scene on Southport promenade in about 1932 was photographed by D. R. Randall, and shows KD 9402, a Tilling-Stevens Express B10A vehicle which by then was Ribble 1272. It had been Merseyside 26 when new in March 1930. The body is reported originally to have been a 26-seat coach (as were all of the B10A vehicles KD 9401-8, which became Ribble 1265-72, though not in order). In this case the original body was by Massey, but it seems that a different bus body had now been fitted. The Express B10A was the most numerous type in the Merseyside fleet, 36 being taken over by Ribble.

1199-1204	KF 411-6	Leyland Lion LT2	Leyland	B30F	1930
1218-9	various	Tilling-Stevens B10A2	-	B	1928
1220-3	EM 2263-6	Tilling-Stevens B10A2	Vickers	B32F	3/29
1224/6	EM 2300-1	Tilling-Stevens B10A2	Massey	B32F	1929
1225	EM 2268	Tilling-Stevens B10A2	Vickers	B32	3/29
1226-36	EM various	Tilling-Stevens B10A2	Vickers	B32	1929
1237	EM 2422	Tilling-Stevens TS15A	Massey	H64D	1929
1238-45	various	Tilling-Stevens B10A2	Massey	B32F	1929
1246	EM 2303	Bristol B	Bristol	B32R	1929
1247	EM 2330	Bristol B	N.Counties	B32R	6/29
1248	HW 6638	Bristol B	Bristol	32	8/29
1249	HH 4668	Gilford 166OT	Wycombe	B32	3/29
1250	FR 2252	Daimler CJK22	-	Ch28	1920
1251	FR 4270	Leyland S6	-	Ch33	6/21
1252	KA 9480	Tilling-Stevens	-	C26	1927
1253-4	KD 3147,3444	GMC	-	C	1928
1255-9	KD various	Tilling-Stevens B10B	-	C	various
1260	HW 3864	Bristol B	Bristol	C24F	1/29
1261	HW 6049	Bristol B	London Lorries	C26F	7/29
1262-3	various	Tilling-Stevens B10B	-	various	6/29
1264	EM 2302	Tilling-Stevens B10A2	Massey	B32F	5/29
1265-72	KD various	Tilling-Stevens B10A	-	C	1930
1273/77	KD 9410-1	Bristol B	Massey	C26F	1930
1274/6	KD 9412/09	Bristol B	Burlingham	C26F	1930
1278-81	KF 4723-6	Leyland Tiger TS3	-	C26F	5/31
1282-3	KF 4721-2	Leyland Tiger TS3	-	C26F	5/31
1328-34	various	AEC 411 & 413	various	B30-32	various
1335	GD 3453	Republic	-	26	6/26
1336-41	various	Minerva	-	various	various
1342	KD 3020	Laffley	-	24	1928
1343	EC 6588	AEC 411	-	B30	1925
1344-5	various	Minerva	-	B32	various
1346	EM 2267	Pagefield LFC	N.Counties	B32R	3/29
1347-9	various	GMC various	-	various	1929

Of the above, 1335-42/4/5 came from Nor-West Bus Services Ltd which was taken over by Merseyside about 1st January 1930. It ran as a subsidiary for some months.

Vehicles acquired from Carlisle city operators, November 1931

The principal operator whose vehicles were taken into Ribble stock at this time was Carlisle & District Motor Services Ltd, but buses from other independents also taken over were numbered in among them to give at least some semblence of order. Thus White Star Motors Ltd was the source of 1287/8/90, 1311/3/57/22; G. Bristow supplied 1286/97 and 1312; F. Waugh 1298, 1314/8: H. Hayton 1323 and R. Vickers 1327.

1284-90	various	Albion various	-	various	various
1291-4	various	Daimler CF6	various	B32	various
1295-7	HH various	Albion PMA28	-	B32R	1930
1298	HH 5150	Albion	-	B24	3/31
1299-1300	HH 5412-3	Daimler CF6	N.Counties	B32R	1930
1301-6	HH 5480-5	Albion PMA28	-	B30R	1931
1307-13	HH various	Albion various	-	various	various
1314-27	various	various	-	various	various

The vehicles numbered 1314-27 comprised a Morris, four Beardmore, five Guy, a Saurer, a Bean, a Dennis GL and a Chevrolet U, mostly of small capacity though 1315 was a Guy FBB 32-seat bus. Three small Albions (1287/8/90) and a Beardmore (1316), all from White Star, were retained until 1935 for the weight-restricted Bowness-on-Solway route. Two Carlisle & District Albion PH24, thought to be those that became 1308-9, are illustrated on page 26 of Volume 1.

Vehicles acquired from E. & I. Wright, Cumwhinton, November 1931

1350-1	various	Guy OND	-	B20	various

Vehicles acquired from H. Lace, Kirkoswald, December 1931

1358-62	various	various	-	various	various

These comprised three Albion and a Guy BB, all seating 26, and a Chevrolet LQ 14-seater, taking fleet numbers after the TD2 batch, for which numbers had been booked.

Leyland Titan TD2 double-deckers, 1932

The TD2 was, in effect, a heavier-duty version of the TD1, with a larger-capacity, 7.6-litre, version of what was basically the same six-cylinder petrol engine. Other engineering modifications were incorporated, but with appearance and dimensions of both chassis and the standard body only altered in detail. After several years when vehicles, both new and those acquired with taken-over businesses, had been entering the fleet in hundreds, the small intake of just six buses reflected the modernity of much of the fleet. Some rationalisation following the string of acquired businesses ensued, and may also have been influenced by the depression then particularly hitting Lancashire's industries, plus ça change!

1352-7	CK 4627-32	Leyland Titan TD2	Leyland	L24/24R	3/32

Leyland Tiger TS6 coaches, 1933

These 36 vehicles represented Ribble's first venture in the purchase of true coaches as by then generally understood, and doubtless influenced by the section of the Merseyside enterprise based on the use of such vehicles. The TS6 was a new model completed in prototype form by January that year, with more compact front end design and a deeper radiator which modernised the appearance considerably, and Leyland, also breaking into new ground, produced an elegant rear-entrance coach body design for it. The prototype, though painted in Ribble colours, was not purchased, becoming AAL 486 of a Nottinghamshire operator, Leah Bros. The Ribble batch, delivered between April and July, was split equally between Leyland bodywork, similar, though not quite identical, to the prototype, and a version by English Electric. All had the 7.6-litre petrol engine as built, though a new type of gearbox introduced the different sound, with 'musical' third gear, to remain standard on Leylands until 1942. One vehicle, 1372, ran with an oil engine for three months in the autumn of 1934, but Ribble decided to continue with petrol engines for coaches. Most were used for war service of one type or another and although five returned to Ribble, only 1376/95 re-entered passenger service in 1949, with 1938 bodies, being renumbered 1459/62. Several ran on producer gas in 1941-2.

1363-80	CK 4717-34	Leyland Tiger TS6	Leyland	C31R	1933
1381-98	CK 4735-52	Leyland Tiger TS6	English Electric	C26R	1933

Leyland Titan TD3 double-deckers, 1934

The TD3 was the Titan equivalent to the TS6, but these vehicles were diesel engined from new, a pattern followed on all subsequent double-deckers in the fleet. Leyland's first production oil engine, derived from the six-cylinder T-type petrol unit in design, was of 8.1-litre capacity, but was enlarged to 8.6-litre capacity at just about the date, June-July 1934, these were built. They had lowbridge bodies by English Electric, which at that time had a large bus and tram bodybuilding works in Preston, to a style not unlike the Leyland 'piano-front' type of earlier Titans, but with sloping upper-deck front windows. They remained in service until 1947-9.

1399-1410	CK 4869-80	Leyland Titan TD3	English Electric	L26/26R	1934

The 36 Leyland Tiger TS6 coaches of 1933 represented the beginning of a new era for Ribble in more ways than one. They were the company'a first true coaches to be purchased new and the first of a new generation of Leyland chassis, setting the pattern of front-end layout and radiator style that was to remain standard for the heavy-duty additions to the fleet until 1942, The bodywork on eighteen was by Leyland to a particularly attractive new design with wide window bays, of which the first example, C1363 (CK 4717), is seen above shortly before entering service in April of that year. There was a faint echo of the previous Leyland saloon in the arched window outline, though the overall effect was much more modern-looking. The English Electric bodywork on the balance of the order, represented by C1383 (CK 4737), was also impressive, even if lacking quite the styling flair of the Leyland-built version, and was laid out in more spacious pattern within, having Ribble's traditional 26-seat capacity rather than the 31 of the Leyland-built version. Both were far more luxurious internally than their predecessors.

The revised chassis appearance was matched by technical advance in the case of the twelve Titan TD3 models added to the fleet in 1934, which were Ribble's first oil-engined buses. The body design remained conservative. By that date, Leyland had put its new metal-framed double-deck body into production, but Ribble chose to give the order to English Electric. These bodies were of a style which differed only slightly from that of the familiar Leyland design of TD1 days – some very similar bodies were also supplied to Preston Corporation. The batch was allocated to Liverpool, which for some years was to be Ribble's centre for the operation of oil-engined vehicles, remaining there for most if not all of their lives. C1404 (CK 4874) is seen in one of a series of photographs taken by A. L. Witham at the Thornton terminus of the L5 route in 1941. It was to be one of the last to remain in service, being withdrawn in 1949 and scrapped by Ribble itself.

Dennis Ace 20-seat buses, 1934 and 1936

The delivery of six Dennis Ace 20-seat buses doutless caused some chagrin to Leyland, but the 'Flying Pig', as the model tended to be called because of its appearance, was a very practical model, well suited to a route with a tight weight limit. Seen here before delivery from English Electric's premises is C1415 (CK 4885) – a rather surprising feature on a bus intended for a route of about ten miles was a roof-mounted luggage carrier. These were Ribble's last deliveries with CK registration marks, though not the last in service, being outlasted by the five rebodied TD1s.

These were purchased for the Bowness-on-Solway route from Carlisle, with a weight-restricted bridge. A Ribble minute indicates that it had been planned to use Leyland's small Cub model of the time, but the reason for the change is a matter for speculation, Ribble perhaps wishing to remind Leyland of its freedom to go elsewhere for its vehicles, though the Ace, with a simple 3.8-litre four-cylinder petrol engine, may have had lower weight on its side. English Electric bodied the batch of six delivered in July-August 1934, but the extra bus bought in June 1936 had a generally similar body by Dennis. It is visible in the background of a picture on page 45 of Volume 1.

1411-6	CK 4881-6	Dennis Ace	English Electric	B20F	1934
1657	RN 7858	Dennis Ace	Dennis	B20F	1936

Vehicles acquired from Kenyons, Coleman & Robinson Ltd, Blackburn, June 1934.

This 1932 AEC Regal, had Harrington bodywork of a standard type built in some numbers by that concern for various fleets. It is seen when new to KCR, becoming Ribble C1417 and was kept in service until 1939. The Regal was comparable to the Tiger in general character and capabilities. Both this vehicle and C1418 were sold to Andrews (Clifton Greys) of Bristol in 1940 and were rebodied by Duple in 1946, passing to Wessex in 1948 and remained in service until 1959.

This was the second KCR take-over, bringing with it two modern AEC coaches, which were retained until 1939.

1417	BV 1739	AEC Regal	Harrington	C32R	8/32
1418	BV 2159	AEC Regal	Duple	C32R	3/33

Leyland Lion LT7 buses, 1935-6

The LT series of Lion models had reached the LT7 by 1935, retaining a four-cylinder version of the T-type engine, but modernised in a rather similar way to the Tiger, though taking advantage of the shorter engine to give more passenger space. As if to emphasise this, there was a particularly slim radiator shell. Ribble had added no new full-sized single-deck buses to the fleet since 1931, but still had only modest needs because of the downgrading of the former long-distance early Tiger saloons. The LT7 in petrol form was chosen, five with Leyland's recently introduced metal-framed body in 1935, and four with English Electric bodywork in 1936. It seems that three more of the Leyland-bodied version were ordered and intended to be 1491-3, but these were not delivered, the numbers remaining unfilled. Those delivered were to be the last Lion models supplied to Ribble. Note the switch to the RN registration series. The four 1936 buses received 1938 Duple coach bodies in 1948-9.

1477	RN 7583	Leyland Lion LT7	Leyland	B36F	8/35
1478-81	RN 7661-4	Leyland Lion LT7	Leyland	B36F	8/35
1482-5	RN 7665-8	Leyland Lion LT7	English Electric	B36F	3/36

Although the numbers were small, the bodywork on the Lion LT7 buses of 1935-6 was significant. The five with Leyland bodies were to be the last single-deck examples so bodied to join the Ribble fleet until the Royal Tigers of 1951. This early metal-framed design from Leyland was not very successful, the single-deck version possibly even less so than the double-deck. Its design was standardised and did not make any concession to operators' ideas – the Ribble front destination box looked a little lost on the large panel provided, for example. Seen here before delivery in July 1935 is C1478 – its identity would not have been visible with the registration number yet to be applied had the number not been positioned incorrectly high on the bonnet side. The four English Electric bodies were to a design not repeated, though some details hinted at what was to follow, such as the shaping of the cab window above the bonnet. On the other hand, the inset entrance door, similar to previous Ribble standard practice, was soon to be dropped in favour of the sliding type as used on the Leyland body. The last vehicle, C1485, is shown before delivery.

Leyland Tiger TS7 coaches, 1935-7

A major renewal and expansion of the coach fleet was begun in March 1935 with the delivery of the first of an order for 50 vehicles on the TS7 chassis, generally similar to the TS6, but with hydraulic operation of the vacuum-assisted brakes. The bodies were built by English Electric to a new Ribble design specified by the then Chief Engineer, Captain Betteridge.These were the first of the family of designs which was to include single- and double-deck buses becoming a Ribble standard until 1939. They reverted to front-entrance layout and had a seating capacity of 31, adopting the half-canopy style of front-end then becoming popular for coaches. Delivery continued until March 1936, but twelve of the order (1455-66) were diverted to Standerwick, now under Ribble control, they are recorded here because of their numbering. One vehicle (1452) is understood to have had a pre-delivery accident and the body, retaining the same fleet number after repair, put on a later chassis, the original having been diverted to receive a body from a later batch and registered accordingly.

A major step in the creation of the distinctive 'Ribble look' which characterised the fleet in the late 'thirties was the introduction of the standard coach design in its original form as built by English Electric on 50 Leyland Tiger TS7 chassis in 1935-6. Those for Ribble's own fleet were originally painted in a crimson and cream livery, as shown on the left of the smaller view, but the twelve allocated to Standerwick were in what was an almost exactly 'reversed' style, as shown by the main view of FV 5740, which was allocated Ribble number C1464, though this was not carried. It seems that the resulting appearance was thought preferable, and subsequent Ribble coaches adopted a generally similar style, though the downswept relief colour was applied differently.

The Duple version of the Ribble coach design for the 50 Tiger TS7 built in 1936 was virtually identical to that built by English Electric, save for the mofified livery and consequential revision to the rear mudguard and moulding layout. These TS7 coaches were delightful vehicles in which to travel, with quiet smooth-running engines – it was easy to think the engine had stopped when it was idling – and an illegal 60mph or so was available. Alan Townsin has a vivid memory of one exhilarating wartime journey in particular when a driver took full advantage of a traffic-free A6 between Preston and Lancaster to more than make up for a very late departure. Here, C1500 (RN 7750) is seen at Lower Mosley Street, Manchester, when new enough still to show the Duple bodybuilder's transfer on the skirt strip just behind the front mudguard.

At the beginning of 1936 delivery had begun of a further 50 TS7 coaches with almost identical bodywork, but built by Duple, in those days based in Hendon and a leading coach body specialist. The most obvious difference was the reversed livery, later applied retrospectively to the English Electric batch. In 1937, a further ten were ordered plus seventeen more intended for Standerwick but these chassis were diverted to Ribble's own fleet as part of a body-swap exercise in which they received 1936 Duple bodies, while the new ones went on to 1936 chassis transferred to Standerwick. Almost all these vehicles survived the war years, unlike coaches in many fleets where requisitions often made substantial inroads into stock. From 1948, a more complex pattern of rebodying and body transfers affecting some of these vehicles took place, as described later, though many ran in virtually original form until the early 'fifties.

1419-21	RN 7586/8/7	Leyland Tiger TS7	English Electric	C31F	3/35
1422-36	RN 7589-7603	Leyland Tiger TS7	English Electric	C31F	6/35
1437-51	RN 7604-18	Leyland Tiger TS7	English Electric	C31F	1936
1452	RN 7857	Leyland Tiger TS7	English Electric	C31F	3/36
1453-4	RN 7620-1	Leyland Tiger TS7	English Electric	C31F	3/36
1455-66	FV 5731-42	Leyland Tiger TS7	English Electric	C31F	1936
1467-8	RN 7635-6	Leyland Tiger TS7	English Electric	C31F	1936
1494-1543	RN 7744-93	Leyland Tiger TS7	Duple	C31F	1936
1647-56	RN 7991-8000	Leyland Tiger TS7	Duple	C31F	1937
1745-59	FV 8027-41	Leyland Tiger TS7	Duple	C31F	1937
1770-1	FV 8558-9	Leyland Tiger TS7	Duple	C31F	5/37

Leyland Titan TD4 double-deckers, 1935-37

The TD4 was equivalent to the TS7, but as mentioned above, Ribble had adopted the oil engine for double-deckers, so these had 8.6litre units from new. The company's policy on bodywork was going through a period of transition. From 1934, Leyland had switched to a new metal-framed design which Ribble treated with caution, taking a solitary double-deck example on a TD4 in 1935 but staying with English Electric bodies, similar to the 1934 type, for the other four of the type that year. In 1936, the split was ten more of the same Leyland vee-front type

The first production version of Leyland double-deck metal-framed body proved to be prone to rapid corrosion of the framing. Ribble's cautious attitude to it may well have reflected some knowledge of this, with the first single example, C1490 (RN 7673) not delivered until August 1935, well over a year after production began. It is seen, below left, in October of that year. Ten more delivered the following March were similar apart from the addition of a route number box to the left of the route box.

For 1936, the double-deck body order was divided, each builder producing its own version of Ribble's requirement. It seems that Burlingham worked on the basis of a new front-end, quite close to the subsequent standard, grafted on to what looked very like the old-style Leyland timber-framed body. Seen below at the Nags Head Hotel, Thornton, terminus of the L5 route in 1941 is C1605 (RN 7872), which had been new in September 1936.

Roe simply took its newly-introduced curved-profile style and built it in six-bay form, suggesting that this latter was in response to Ribble's wishes, as Roe standardised on five-bay layout. The resulting vehicles were of modern-looking outline but, for whatever reason, Ribble took no further Roe bodies until the utility era. Three of them, C1612, 1609 and 1610 (RN 7967, 7864 and 7965) are seen to the right of this view at the L5 terminus at the Nags Head, together with C1618 (RN 7961) with Eastern Counties body on the left. Noteworthy in these wartime pictures of five-year-old buses is the good condition – Ribble sought to maintain its standards , though admittedly the material and labour shortages had yet to have their full effect in 1941.

Eastern Counties offered perhaps the most elaborate of the 1936 interpretations of Ribble's double-deck requirements, and could perhaps be said to have set the pattern for what followed in the general outline and in such details as the radiused lower corners of all windows, with the larger radius at front and rear bulkheads on the lower deck. The shaped windscreen, peculiar to these buses (and not found on other ECOC or ECW Titans of the period) was not repeated, and indeed Lowestoft did not get further Ribble double-deck orders at that time, though bodying numerous Cheetah single-deckers. This view of C1616 (RN 7875), again at the Nags Head head in 1941, reveals a distinct touch of typical Lowestoft styling at the front of the upper deck.

and eight each from Burlingham, Eastern Counties and Roe. Burlingham, based in Blackpool, had been primarily a coach bodybuilder but was emerging into bus work; Eastern Counties, part of the same TBAT operating group as Ribble, though with a majority Tilling shareholding, had a bodybuilding works in Lowestoft growing into a major supplier to the group, while Roe was based in Leeds, already supplying several BET-associated companies. Burlingham established itself as one of Ribble's major suppliers, taking half the 1937 order for 24 TD4 double-deckers, the others being built to the same outline by Brush, of Loughborough. The latter was long established as a major BET supplier and also set for a run of regular orders from Ribble. In the event, the TD4 chassis outlasted almost all the bodies from all four sources though, had there been no war, it seems likely that the vehicles would have been sold off before rebodying became necessary. They were at least eleven years old when this occurred.

1486-9	RN 7669-72	Leyland Titan TD4	English Electric	L27/26R	1935
1490	RN 7673	Leyland Titan TD4	Leyland	L27/26R	8/35
1588-97	RN 7794-7803	Leyland Titan TD4	Leyland	L27/26R	3/36
1598-1605	RN 7865-72	Leyland Titan TD4	Burlingham	L27/26R	1936
1606-9	RN 7861-4	Leyland Titan TD4	Roe	L27/26R	1936
1610-3	RN 7965-8	Leyland Titan TD4	Roe	L27/26R	9/36
1614-7	RN 7873-6	Leyland Titan TD4	ECOC	L27/26R	1936
1618-21	RN 7961-4	Leyland Titan TD4	ECOC	L27/26R	9/36
1721-32	RN 8082-93	Leyland Titan TD4	Burlingham	L27/26R	1937
1733-44	RN 8094-8105	Leyland Titan TD4	Brush	L27/26R	3/37

By the time the orders for 1937 delivery were placed, Ribble had decided upon its preferred double-deck style. This might be described as largely as the 1936 Eastern Counties bodies, but with five bays between bulkheads. The relatively shallow rectangular windscreen typical of the company's single-deckers of the period, was inclined at an angle slightly less than the upper-deck front windows, though a little more than the panel immediately above. The profile was to remain typical of Ribble double-deckers for many years. A well-proportioned vehicle resulted, with much the same appearance from both Burlingham (see p110 of Volume 1) or, as in the case of C1736 (RN 8097) seen here, Brush. The latter built upper decks separately, and heavier beading was used at the joint, with a noticeable upward curve across the front panel. A noteworthy feature was that all the opening windows on the upper deck were on the nearside.

Vehicles acquired from James Pearson & Sons, Liverpool, May 1935

Few vehicles from acquired businesses were taken into stock by this period, but exceptions were made of largely modern coach fleets, as in this case. Tiger TS4 1471 was noteworthy as having an oil engine on take-over, this having been fitted in January 1934, and it ran as such with Ribble for one season, but a petrol engine was fitted when it was transferred to Standerwick in March 1936.

1469-70	KF 4123-4	Leyland Tiger TS1	London Lorries	C32R	3/31
1471-2	LV 2311,2400	Leyland Tiger TS4	Duple	various	1933
1473	LV 8318	Leyland Tiger TS6	Duple	C28F	5/34
1474-5	AKB 601,371	Leyland Tiger TS7	Duple	C various	1935
1476	AKB 900	Leyland Tiger TS6	Duple	C29F	2/35

Leyland Cheetah buses and coaches 1936-41

The style for Ribble's single-deck buses of the late 'thirties was set by the first batch of 25 Cheetah models with bus bodywork. Eastern Counties had secured the body contract and the initial vehicle, 1622 (RN 7877), is seen here before delivery in May 1936. As with the double-deckers from the same bodybuilder, there seems to have been some influence in both directions between Frenchwood Avenue and Lowestoft, even though the Ribble designs remained unique. The Cheetah buses adopted the half-canopy front-end, giving a look of uniformity with the company's coaches. In this case the influence may have come from North Western, which used a similar front-end for its buses from early 1935. The Ribble design retained the relatively low build of earlier generations of Leyland-bodied buses and this, coupled with particularly neat detail design, gave them a distinctive look. These initial vehicles had sliding roofs, just visible in this view – their quiet running and spacious internal layout made excellent buses for scenic routes.

The Leyland Cheetah was introduced towards the end of 1935 as a light single-deck chassis, using mechanical components shared with the smaller Cub range but with appearance, including the short bonnet and ultra-slim radiator, very similar to the contemporary Lion LT7, though the style of wheels and hubs gave a clear indication of the Cub affinities. It was offered with 4.7-litre six-cylinder engine available in petrol or diesel form, The model designations began at LZ1, but Ribble chose the full-length LZ2, and later equivalent LZ2A and LZ5 in petrol versions for both coach and bus work from 1936, the latter becoming rare for full-sized vehicles in a major fleet by that date, and also took care to keep the weight within Leyland's recommendations. This proved wise, for though the petrol version used more fuel, it was comparable in reliabilty to the heavier models (the diesel seems to have been one of Leyland's few failures) and was very smooth running.

The bus version, with a Ribble body design sharing the half-canopy styling of the coaches, tended to be used largely in rural areas, the first batch (and some of the later ones) having sliding-roof bodywork. With seats for 30, very generously spaced, they were almost ideal for scenic Lake District routes. The 31-seat coach bodies were very similar to the Tiger version, and tended to be used on the medium-distance routes.

Eastern Counties built the first 25 buses; a further ten later in 1936 from the same factory were by Eastern Coach Works, which had been set up to take over the bodybuilding side of the business. The 1937 bus orders went to Brush (15) and Burlingham (26) before reverting to ECW for a remarkable total of 121 in 1938 and then swinging back to Burlingham (30) and Brush (10) in 1939. Later batches had slightly arched windows reminiscent of the 1930 Leyland style.

Brush built all the coaches, delivery of the initial 40 of which spanned the spring and summer of 1936 being followed by twelve the next winter, ten later in 1937 and a final order for ten to a modified design with curved-waist styling, nine being delivered in July 1939.One, possibly held back for the 1939 Show (cancelled due to the war), did not enter service until 1941. What was evidently its planned fleet number, 2281, was left blank. The 1939 batch of Cheetah buses were converted to diesel in the early post-war years, using 6.2-litre engines of what had been an experimental batch installed in new Tiger buses in 1939. Most of the model completed their service with Ribble much as built. Withdrawals of the earlier Cheetah buses began in 1948 but quite a number of both buses and coaches remained in service until the early 'fifties, some of those with diesel engines running until 1954.

1548-87	RN 7805-43	Leyland Cheetah LZ2	Brush	C31F	1936
1622-45	RN 7877-7900	Leyland Cheetah LZ2	ECOC	B30F	1936
1646	RN 7960	Leyland Cheetah LZ2	ECOC	B30F	1936
1670-79	RN 7979-84	Leyland Cheetah LZ2	ECW	B30F	1936
1658-69	RN 7969-78	Leyland Cheetah LZ2	Brush	C31F	various
1680-94	RN 8041-55	Leyland Cheetah LZ2	Burlingham	B30F	1937
1695-1720	RN 8056-81	Leyland Cheetah LZ2	Brush	B30F	1937
1760-69	RN 8106-15	Leyland Cheetah LZ2	Brush	C31F	1937
1807-56	RN 8191-8240	Leyland Cheetah LZ2A	ECW	B30F	1938
1857-1900	RN 8251-94	Leyland Cheetah LZ2A	ECW	B30F	1938
1974-2000	RN 8404-30	Leyland Cheetah LZ2A	ECW	B30F	9/38
2094-2123	RN 8659-88	Leyland Cheetah LZ5	Burlingham	B32F	1939
2124-33	RN 8689-98	Leyland Cheetah LZ5	Brush	B32F	1939
2272-80	RN 8837-45	Leyland Cheetah LZ5	Brush	C31F	7/39
2379	RN 8927	Leyland Cheetah LZ5	Brush	C31F	4/41

Leyland used this picture of a scene in Tithebarn Street bus station, Preston in April 1937 in an advertisement announcing the receipt of a repeat order for Cheetah chassis for Ribble. It shows C1582 (RN 7838), one of the first batch of LZ2 coaches, dating from March 1936, calling in when on the X60 Manchester-Blackpool service, very much the type of fairly short-distance express route on which the coach version of the Cheetah was often used. The 31-seat bodywork, built by Brush, was almost identical to that of the Tiger coaches except that the step in profile at the base of the windscreen was less pronounced. The unladen weight, 4tons 16cwt 3qr, was remarkably low even by the standards of those days of great skill in keeping weight down and about 1½ tons less than that of a similar-looking Tiger coach. Two Titan TD1 double-deckers are visible behind.

Brush also built two batches of the bus bodies on Cheetah chassis, fifteen in 1937 and ten in 1939, C1711 (RN 8072) being seen here before delivery in May 1937. There were various minor differences in design among Ribble bus bodies during this period, more related to the date of construction than bodybuilder. The cab roof became more level than the original 1936 version shown opposite, and there were slight differences in the cab side window and rearmost window outlines as well as other details – see also the 1938 ECW version as shown on page 109 of Volume 1. The 1939 version had the slightly arched side windows shown by the Tiger TS8 bus also illustrated on that page.

The 1939 version of the Ribble coach body adopted the curved waistline which had become fashionable, though the remainder of the body was largely unaltered – the curved roof line was now followed by the upper edge of the windows. The vehicle shown in the Brush official photograph was C2275 (RN 8840), one of the nine similar coaches dating from July 1939. The interior view is representative of Ribble coaches on either Cheetah or Tiger chassis of the 1935-39 period – as was almost universal on coaches of the time, a sliding roof was fitted.

Leyland Titan TD5 double-deckers, 1937-39

The Leyland TD5 buses were almost identical to the later TD4 deliveries, with Burlingham or Brush bodies to what had become the Ribble standard pattern. The example shown is C1780 (RN 8164), with Burlingham body, which dated from February 1938 and is seen at Thornton in 1941, the wartime white paint neatly drawing attention to the different style of front dumb-iron which made identification of TD5 from TD4 so easy. The translucent Ribble sign had been abandoned but the display of L5 in the bulkhead window is noteworthy. This vehicle shows the 'plain' between-decks cream band which up to then identified the Burlingham-built version, but in 1939 it seems that the version with upswept top edge marked by beading, hitherto associated with Brush, was adopted for Burlingham deliveries. This suggests that Ribble may have requested the adoption of the Brush form of construction.

The TD5 differed only in minor respects from the TD4, though readily identifiable by the squared-up front dumb-irons which formed neater radiator mountings. Ribble carried on with the pattern established with the TD4, splitting body orders between Brush and Burlingham, both to the same 'Betteridge' outline. Brush began with eleven examples (delivered ahead of their Burlingham counterparts) in December 1937, followed by totals of 22 in 1938 and 24 in 1939. Burlingham bodied 32 in 1938 and 24 in 1939. As with the TD4 batches, a high proportion were rebodied in 1948-50.

1772-88	RN 8156-72	Leyland Titan TD5	Burlingham	L27/26R	1938
1789-99	RN 8173-83	Leyland Titan TD5	Brush	L27/26R	1937
1800-06	RN 8184-90	Leyland Titan TD5	Brush	L27/26R	1938
1901-15	RN 8295-8309	Leyland Titan TD5	Burlingham	L27/26R	1938
1916-30	RN 8310-24	Leyland Titan TD5	Brush	L27/26R	1938
2036-59	RN 8601-24	Leyland Titan TD5	Burlingham	L27/26R	1939
2060-83	RN 8625-48	Leyland Titan TD5	Brush	L27/26R	1939

Leyland Tiger TS8 buses and coaches, 1938-40

The TS8 was the single-deck equivalent of the TD5, and for the first time since 1931 Ribble added some Tiger buses to its fleet with basically the same mechanical specification as contemporary Titans. These TS8 buses were also the first oil-engined single-deckers purchased as such for the fleet, the standard engine being the 8.6-litre unit as fitted to the TD4 and TD5. Bodywork on all but the final batches was similar to that on the Cheetah buses, though seating capacity varied and many were later reseated to accomodate 34 passengers. The initial order was for nine each from Brush and Burlingham, delivered in 1938.

In 1939 some 129 were supplied, split 89 Burlingham and 40 Brush. These were also notable for a large-scale experiment, in which 79 vehicles, thought to be 2178-2231 and 2247-2271, were fitted with a new Leyland 6.2-litre six-cylinder oil engine known as the L-type. This was not put into volume production, but formed the basis for the later 7.4-litre unit standardised after the war, sharing its 'cackling' engine note, markedly different from the smooth roar of the 8.6. In fact these vehicles were re-engined with the 7.4 in 1945-6, the 6.2-litre units being transferred to Cheetah buses. Many of these 6.2-litre TS8 buses operated in the area around Chorley, the TS8 buses generally being found in the more urban parts of the territory, from Carlisle in the north to the Liverpool area in the south. The TS8 remained in production into the early wartime period alongside the 'next generation' Titan TD7. Ribble's final batches, delivered in 1940-1, had bodywork which though of

The reappearance of new Tiger buses in the fleet was achieved by putting bodywork almost identical to that of the contemporary Cheetah on the current TS8 chassis, these being Ribble's first oil-engined single-deckers. Seen here is one of the first batch, C1960 (RN 8390), with Brush bodywork, when new in August 1938. These were 35-seat vehicles, the odd number resulting from one single longitudinal seat placed over the nearside rear wheelarch. The 1939 batch were similar but seated 32, all facing forward, and had slightly arched side windows (see page 109 of Volume 1).

The interiors of Ribble buses of the late 'thirties were very distinctive and had that hard-to-define welcoming characteristic often lacking in more recent times. The moquette, with red rose floral design appropriate for a Lancashire-based company, used for the upholstery was also applied to the seat backs and the tubular seat frames were stove-enamelled in crimson. The polished wood waistrail trim had an unusual ribbed section and the bevelled-edge mirror on the bulkhead was almost coach-like in effect. The round Clayton heater was a very common fitment on company buses in those days, even though heaters on private cars were almost unknown. The parcel racks were rather shallow, which created problems if a passenger boarded with anything bulky. The seats towards the rear were raised slightly to minimise wheel-arch intrusion, the vehicle shown being Brush-bodied Tiger C1960.

similar outline to the earlier examples, had a broader slightly downswept waist panel. The type continued to be a familiar sight, often on the same duties, until replaced by underfloor-engined models in the early 'fifties.

The TS8 coaches continued Ribble's coach policy by having petrol engines as built. At that time, Leyland was introducing a new design of petrol unit with push-rod valve gear instead of the overhead camshaft, and it is known that some, at least of Ribble's TS8 coaches, as well as TS7 number 1745, were so fitted. The numbers built were fewer than for the previous model, there being 25 having Duple bodies in 1938 and a final nine, bodied by Burlingham to the contemporary Ribble standard, in 1939. In the post-war reconstruction programme, these TS8 were the first to be selected for rebodying by Duple and also received 7.4-litre diesel engines.

1931-55	RN 8361-85	Leyland Tiger TS8	Duple	C31F	1938
1956-64	RN 8386-94	Leyland Tiger TS8	Brush	B35F	1938
1965-73	RN 8395-8403	Leyland Tiger TS8	Burlingham	B35F	1938
2134-42	RN 8699-8707	Leyland Tiger TS8	Burlingham	C31F	7/39
2143-2231	RN 8708-96	Leyland Tiger TS8	Burlingham	B32F	1939
2232-71	RN 8797-8836	Leyland Tiger TS8	Brush	B32F	1939
2348-63	ACK 150-165	Leyland Tiger TS8	Burlingham	B32F	1940
2364-71	ACK 166-173	Leyland Tiger TS8	Brush	B32F	1940
2372-78	ACK 174-180	Leyland Tiger TS8	Brush	B32F	1941

The Tiger coach body was also given the curved waist restyling, though it retained the more pronounced step below the windscreen and thus retained much the same frontal appearance as the version first seen in 1935. The example shown is C2141 (RN 8706), one of the final batch of nine delivered in July 1939 and notewothy as being the first Burlingham-bodied coaches for Ribble – this bodybuilder was primarily a coach constructor but Ribble's introduction to the firm had been as a bus builder.

The final batch of Tiger TS8 buses, delivered in 1940-41, introduced a new body design variant, even though they were basically similar to their predecessors. The combination of slightly curved roof line with straight side windows was rather reminsiscent of the 1935-7 coaches, but there was also a new form of waistband, flat rather than slightly rounded in section as hitherto, and with drooping lower edge ending in a point under the rearmost side window before reverting to normal depth across the rear. In addition, the rear dome was now crimson, like the remainder of the roof, instead of white as on previous single-deck buses, and the rear mudguards were also of 'swept' shape. Whether it was an improvement aesthetically is perhaps a matter of opinion, but the idea was not pursued further. Seen here is C2375 (ACK 177), with Brush body, one of the last few to enter service, in 1941. The Burlingham version was similar, though not quite identical in minor details. Note that the full pre-war livery, complete with elaborate lining out, was still being applied.

Vehicles acquired from Arthur Christy (Bolton) Ltd, April 1938

The Christy fleet as it stood soon after the five 1936 Tiger TS7 coaches (which later became Ribble 2023-7) had entered service – they are seen at the left of the line, which also shows the 1935 deliveries (2020-1) and, on the right, two 1934 TS6/Duple coaches which were sold before the Ribble take-over. A Bolton Corporation double-decker is visible in the background. (See also page 43 of Volume 1.)

The Christy concern had followed a policy of running an up-to-date fleet and the modern Duple-bodied Tigers readily fitted into Ribble stock, although of different body style. One, WH 6577. was to have a remarkable career, rebodied and re-engined in 1950, surviving in service until 1961.

2020-1	WH 6577-8	Leyland Tiger TS6	Duple	C32F	6/35
2022	WH 6477	Leyland Tiger TS6	Duple	C32F	6/35
2023-7	WH 7575-9	Leyland Tiger TS7	Duple	C32F	5/36
2028-30	WH 8777-9	Leyland Tiger TS7	Duple	C32F	4/37

Vehicles acquired from F. Snaylam, Bolton, May 1938

This was a more mixed fleet and it is rather surprising that all were taken into stock at that date. The Albions and Regal 2034 remained in Ribble's fleet until 1948.

2031	WH 3787	Leyland Tiger TS4	Spicer	C32R	3/32
2032	WH 5380	Albion Valiant PV70	Spicer	C28R	4/34
2033	WH 6430	Albion Victor PK115	Burlingham	C26R	3/35
2034	WH 7684	AEC Regal	Watson	C32C	5/36
2035	WH 8650	AEC Regal	Watson	C32F	3/37

Leyland Titan TD7 double-deckers, 1940-42

Above, C2338 (RN 8994) shows the deep windscreen characteristic of this generation of Leyland body, which initially may have been accepted because of the war.
Top left. The Brush bodies were to Ribble's pre-war standard, though 2318 (ACK 140) is seen in later livery deleting the upper waistband in this May 1952 photograph; it had also received the post-war style of destination box.
Centre left. One of 2381-7, showing the shallow sliding windows and, just visible, the destination box, both to Alexander specification.
Bottom left. The 2388-90 batch had East Lancashire bodywork.

Leyland introduced a new version of the Titan, the TD7, in the autumn of 1939, retaining the 8.6-litre engine and general appearance of the TD5, but with quite a number of new features, including a flexible engine mounting. Ribble took delivery of 59, of which 40 had Leyland metal-framed bodywork to a design which had been introduced just after Ribble took delivery of its previous Leyland-bodied Titans, in 1936. The remaining nineteen had Brush bodywork to Ribble's usual pattern and it is significant that all of these were among the first of the model to be withdrawn in 1952. All the Leyland bodies (three of them transferred to 1942 chassis) survived to 1955-6, and their better-lasting qualities, which would have become clear after a few years' service, may well have influenced the choice of Leyland bodywork for much of the post-war Titan fleet.

In 1942, bus supply was under Government control, and Ribble received ten more TD7 from the so-called 'unfrozen' stock released after a period when bus production had virtually ceased. Seven had Leyland bodywork that had been intended for W. Alexander & Sons and with that concern's style of destination display and opening windows, the remaining three having bodywork by East Lancashire Coachbuilders. These latter also proved less durable and in 1952 were transferred to three TD7 chassis dating from 1940 which were then sold off, the 1942 chassis receiving the Leyland bodies from them and surviving with the rest until 1955-6.

2289-2308	RN 8964-83	Leyland Titan TD7	Leyland	L27/26R	1940
2309-27	ACK 131-149	Leyland Titan TD7	Brush	L27/26R	1940
2328-44	RN 8984-9000	Leyland Titan TD7	Leyland	L27/26R	1940
2345-7	ACK 127-129	Leyland Titan TD7	Leyland	L27/26R	1940
2381-7	ACK 578-584	Leyland Titan TD7	Leyland	L27/26R	1942
2388	ACK 526	Leyland Titan TD7	East Lancs	L27/26R	1942
2389-90	ACK 562-563	Leyland Titan TD7	East Lancs	L27/26R	1942

Ex-demonstration vehicle acquired from AEC

This AEC photograph of KMG 593 dates from the spring of 1939 and thus can be taken to show the vehicle as built, the chassis to standard oil-engined Regal specification of the time, with no bonnet louvres – petrol-engined chassis, tending to run hotter, still had louvred bonnet panels. Clearly, Burlingham's instructions had been to build the body to Ribble specification down to the smallest details, and the trouble taken indicates some determination to impress, as it would have been less readily saleable on the open market, had Ribble declined to buy it. Allocated to Liverpool, it was to remain a regular performer on the Carlisle service until transfer to Standerwick in 1948.

Ribble did not make a practice of buying former demonstration vehicles, even when produced to a specification to suit its requirements. An exception was made for this AEC Regal, first registered in April 1939 and fitted with a Burlingham coach body to Ribble standard design. AEC records show it to have had a standard A173-type 7.7-litre oil engine and, initially, a D124 four-speed gearbox but an experimental overdrive D139B gearbox was fitted later, the D139 being an experimental synchromesh unit, usually four-speed, being tested by various operators around 1939. Initially, the fleet number 2289 (from May 1940 occupied by the first of the batch of TD7 models) was allocated, evidently at some date in 1939, but its more permanent numbering as 2380 in May 1940 may have coincided with the decision to add it to the fleet on a permanent basis, perhaps after completion of a one-year period of trial, as not uncommon with AEC. It was in service with Ribble until transfer to Standerwick in 1948, by whom it was withdrawn in 1953.

2380	KMG 593	AEC Regal	Burlingham	C31F	4/39

'Utility' buses, 1943-45

From 1942, new bus production came under Government control and operators put in applications for their preferred make from the very limited choice available, though with no guarantee of receiving what was requested and virtually no influence over the make of body, which was a matter of allocation. Double-decker production was concentrated mainly on the Guy Arab, an updated version of a model built in small

The Guy Arab was the dominant wartime utility model in Ribble's fleet, as usually the case with major operators. The severely limited availabilty of vehicles of all kinds is conveyed by the continuing use of the ACK registration number series, which remained current from December 1939 to October 1945. This bus was one of a batch of five with Roe bodywork dating from October 1944, the photograph being taken as a 'before' picture to compare with one of a similar vehicle after the rebuilding and updating exercise carried out in 1951-52.

The utility buses were put into service in grey livery, commonly used in wartime as supplies of pigment for normal colours became scarce, though Ribble managed to avoid its use for the bulk of the fleet. Seen below is C2409 (ACK 755), one of the pair of Daimler CWA6 models with Duple bodywork delivered in September 1943. The offset destination display was a consequence of the limitation to one box then in force, Ribble opting to take its usual 3in screen – the blank space was later used for a number display. The 'British Buses' slogan 'Active on the Home Front' was part of a national advertising campaign run jointly by company operators.

numbers from 1933 and available with Gardner 5LW five-cylinder engine of 7.0 litres or, in very limited numbers, the 6LW six-cylinder 8.4-litre unit. Daimler wartime chassis began to be delivered in 1943, initially the CWG5, also with 5LW but having the fluid flywheel and preselective gearbox then standard on that make of chassis. Later in 1943, Daimler switched to the CWA6, with AEC 7.7-litre engine. None of these, save marginally for the AEC engine, were familiar to Ribble, but the numbering suggests that initially the Daimler chassis may have been preferred as slightly less of an unknown quantity, basically similar COG5 chassis being already in service in many municipal fleets. As it turned out, the first four Guy Arab arrived first, these being of the type with extended bonnet which became known as the Arab II, followed by the entire 1943 allocation of Daimlers, comprising the four CWG5 and two CWA6 – six more CWA6 following in 1944. Otherwise, Ribble's 'utility' bus deliveries were of Guy Arab II models, totalling 46, including seven of the 6LW type. Northern Counties proved to be the principal supplier of bodies, with Roe as runner-up, but that was simply because those concerns were among the main builders required to produce lowbridge bodies on Guy chassis over that period. Eight Arab chassis were noteworthy as having full-height 'highbridge' bodies by Park Royal. These were the first centre-gangway double-deckers in the fleet since the ex-Waterloo & Crosby NS-types, being allocated to Carlisle City services and setting a precedent for wider use of highbridge buses post war. The entire fleet of utility buses was involved in a rehabilitation programme in later years.

2391-4	ACK 724-727	Daimler CWG5	Brush	L27/28R	9/43
2395-8	ACK 745-748	Guy Arab II 5LW	N.Counties	L27/28R	8/43
2399-2404	ACK 764-769	Guy Arab II 5LW	N.Counties	L27/28R	1943
2405	ACK 770	Guy Arab II 6LW	N.Counties	L27/28R	1943
2406-7	ACK 756-757	Guy Arab II 5LW	Duple	L27/28R	1943
2408-9	ACK 754-755	Daimler CWA6	Duple	L27/28R	9/43
2410-5	ACK 793-798	Guy Arab II 5LW	N.Counties	L27/28R	3/44
2416-21	ACK 799-804	Guy Arab II 6LW	N.Counties	L27/28R	1944
2422-27	ACK 776-781	Daimler CWA6	Brush	L27/28R	5/44
2428-30	ACK 818-820	Guy Arab II 5LW	Roe	L27/28R	7/44
2431-38	ACK 821-828	Guy Arab II 5LW	Park Royal	H30/26R	6/44
2439-43	ACK 829-833	Guy Arab II 5LW	Roe	L27/28R	9/44
2444-8	ACK 871-875	Guy Arab II 5LW	Roe	L27/28R	1945

Leyland Titan PD1 double-deck buses, 1946-47

The visual impression of Ribble's first post-war buses conveyed an air of continuity, for Burlingham had adopted the late pre-war Ribble outline as the basis for its standard double-decker design, modernised in glazing details and with top sliding windows as standard in conformity with a widespread trend. There was an important change in the adoption of highbridge layout, reflecting a change in management thinking for routes, particularly those of urban nature, where headroom allowed such buses to be used. There were only 21 such buses, almost immediately outnumbered by 68 similar bodies on reconditioned TD4 and TD5 chassis. This bodybuilder's picture of 2462 (ARN 196) shows how advertisements were sometimes applied in a manner retaining the main colour as background. Examples of Leyland and Brush bodied PD1 buses are to be seen on pages 114-5 of Volume 1.

Leyland introduced a new passenger range for the immediate post-war period, the basic models being the Titan PD1 double-decker and Tiger PS1 single-decker. Their design was almost completely new, even though generally conventional for the period. The engine was a 7.4-litre six-cylinder diesel unit whose ancestry could be traced back to the 6.2-litre L-type unit fitted to some of Ribble's TS8 buses of 1939 but which the war prevented from going into production.

Ribble's early post-war new vehicle intake was quite modest in size by comparison with those of the late 'thirties, entirely confined to double-deckers and, unlike those of many other fleets, did not begin to appear until over a year after the war ended. The first order was for 21 PD1 models delivered between November 1946 and January 1947. They had Burlingham bodywork of outline which echoed the pre-war Ribble standard but of highbridge layout, following on from the batch of wartime Guy buses of this pattern. Ten more highbridge buses appeared in May 1947 but these had Leyland bodywork and were on the PD1A chassis, which incorporated Metalastik shackle pins. The biggest group, delivered from August 1947 onwards, was one of 38 PD1A with lowbridge bodywork by Brush, built to a design which structurally had much in common with wartime designs even though having quite well-rounded front and rear profiles. Ribble was unusual in deciding to modify some of its PD1 buses by fitting the larger O.600 engine. The Burlingham bodied batch was so altered in 1948/9, running thus until just before sale in 1958. Some 22 of the Brush batch were rebodied in 1955, as described later.

2449-66	ARN 183-200	Leyland Titan PD1	Burlingham	H30/26R	1946
2467-9	ARN 201-203	Leyland Titan PD1	Burlingham	H30/26R	1/47
2470-9	BCK 413-422	Leyland Titan PD1A	Leyland	H30/26R	5/47
2480-2517	BCK 423-460	Leyland Titan PD1A	Brush	L27/26R	1947

'White Lady' double-deckers on Leyland Titan PD1/3 chassis

Quite extensive effort was put into making the 'White Lady' double-deckers look coach-like, even though internally they differed only slightly from typical lowbridge buses of the time. The use of semi-circular ends to the upper-deck side windows produced an odd appearance from certain angles, as captured in this official view of the first of the batch, 2518 (BRN 261) before entering service in June 1948. Raising the rear platform to saloon floor level allowed space for a small locker with horizontally hinged access flap at the rear, and there were luggage racks internally over the rear wheel arches but overall luggage capacity was modest for a 49-seat vehicle intended largely to carry holidaymakers to and from the Lancashire coast resorts. The Ribble Chief Engineer of the day, A. S. Woodgate, oversaw the design work.

The demand for express travel over relatively short distances from industrial towns in Lancashire to coastal resorts, notably Blackpool, grew immensely in the post-war years. Duplication of such services by double-deckers was common and the idea of vehicles built to cater for this need was a logical consequence. In essentials, the 'White Lady' vehicles were barely more than lowbridge buses made to look more glamorous by the provision of full-fronted cabs with 'modern'-style grille and a special livery, though they did have the benefit of 8ft width, by then permissible instead of 7ft 6in, on approved routes. The North Western Traffic Commissioners took a more liberal view on this than most and Ribble was among the operators which took advantage to improve passenger comfort.

The chassis for the batch of 30 built in 1948-9 was the PD1/3 8ft version of the standard PD1 and Burlingham built the bodywork, a 'dolled-up' version of its standard design of the time, though platform doors were then still a rarity on double-deckers. Within, the seating was no more than marginally more comfortable than bus versions except that the seats over the rear wheel arches were replaced by luggage racks. The original grille was rather reminiscent of that on Leyland goods models of the time, but restricted air flow too much and a version with horizontal strips was fitted. In later years, these vehicles were repainted in bus livery and lower-deck seating increased to 26 by replacing the luggage racks.

2518-42	BRN 261-285	Leyland Titan PD1/3	Burlingham	L27/22RD	1948
2543-7	BRN 286-290	Leyland Titan PD1/3	Burlingham	L27/22RD	1949

Leyland Tiger PS1 coaches, 1948-49

The small fleet of Tiger PS1 coaches delivered between June 1948 and September 1949 had standard Burlingham bodywork, some having painted rather than chromium-plated radiators, as was normal with Leyland chassis in the early post-war period. The first one was originally numbered 2548 but is seen here in Liverpool when renumbered 701 and thus marking the beginning of the coach series established by the new numbering scheme introduced from September 1950.

Ribble purchased only fourteen new single-deck coaches in the early post-war years, a very small number in relation to the existing fleet. This cautious approach was related to knowledge of the plans for an underfloor-engined model and a wish to wait for that to become available before putting a major replacement programme in hand. The model chosen was the Leyland PS1/1, with drop rear frame to accomodate a rear luggage boot, and the Burlingham bodywork was to the maker's standard design being built for numerous fleets at the time. Ribble continued its policy of restricting the seating capacity to 31 rather than the more usual 33 of the time, in the interests of comfort. They remained in service until 1959. One is illustrated on page 114 of Volume 1.

2548-54	BRN 850-856	Leyland Tiger PS1/1	Burlingham	C31F	6/48
2555-61	BRN 857-863	Leyland Tiger PS1/1	Burlingham	C31F	1949

Leyland Titan PD2/3 double-deck buses, 1948-50

The PD2 was by far the most important element in Ribble's intake of new buses during the early post-war years, with 227 examples placed in service between 1948 and 1950. All were 8ft wide, and the characteristic look of Leyland's body design as adapted for this width, with pronounced inward taper towards the front which retained windscreen and other panels of the 7ft 6in version, is emphasised in the view (top right) of the first example, 2566, undergoing tilt testing before delivery in August 1948. Note that the destination display had two separate apertures at that stage, as on earlier post-war deliveries, though the 'hexagonal' form was adopted for later examples, and retrospectively at overhaul.

The highbridge buses, known to staff as Capetowns, diverted from South Africa, lost their original destination displays and some of their opening windows (see page 48 of Volume 1) on overhaul, as shown by 2625 in Liverpool, above, and 2635 was delivered with the standard hexagonal Ribble display.

The final Brush bodies supplied to Ribble had rubber glazing but had obvious affinities to the 1947 version on PD1 chassis, 2684 being shown, right.

The Leyland PD2, outwardly similar to the PD1 but with new 9.8-litre O.600 engine, flexibly mounted, and synchromesh gearbox, was put into production in 1947. The new engine proved very successful from the beginning but the gearbox was less so at first and Ribble was among quite a number of operators which took the PD2 model with PD1-type constant-mesh gearbox, an option which received no publicity at the time, for some of its earlier deliveries of the type, which began in August 1948. A number of vehicles were fitted with a gearbox having syncromesh on 3rd & 4th gears only. It is believed 2719-21 were amongst these. The 8ft-wide PD2/3 model was adopted as standard, largely with Leyland bodywork, of lowbridge type for the main batches of 50 in 1948 and two of 50 each in 1950, though the 42 highbridge examples (2618-47/9-60) of December 1948 to April 1949 formed part of an order intended for Cape Town but diverted to British operators and readily identifiable as such by the generous provision of half-drop windows. Three lowbridge buses (2719-21) had been built for Scout, in those days quite independent of Ribble, but had been added to Ribble's intake in exchange for three PS1/Burlingham coaches. Burlingham bodied one example (2648) with a half-cab bus version of the 'White Lady' body, sometimes nicknamed the 'Red Lady', for its stand at the 1948 Commercial Motor Show, but that remained a one-off. Brush built a revised version of its 1947 PD1 lowbridge batch on 31 PD2/3 delivered between September 1949 and March 1950. The final batch of Leyland lowbridge examples had platform doors and began the 1301-up series for double-deck buses under the new numbering scheme of September 1950. Withdrawals began with the Brush and Burlingham examples in 1960, the Leyland-bodied buses mostly running until 1962-5 and often remaining in passenger service with new owners for some time after sale.

2566-2615	CCK 341-390	Leyland Titan PD2/3	Leyland	L27/26R	1948
2618-47	CCK 606-635	Leyland Titan PD2/3	Leyland	H30/26R	various
2648	CCK 636	Leyland Titan PD2/3	Burlingham	L27/26R	1948
2649-60	CCK 821-832	Leyland Titan PD2/3	Leyland	H30/26R	1949
2661-89	CCK 637-665	Leyland Titan PD2/3	Brush	L27/26R	various
2690-1	CCK 667-668	Leyland Titan PD2/3	Brush	L27/26R	3/50
2719-21	CRN 218-220	Leyland Titan PD2/3	Leyland	L27/26R	6/49
2728-77	CRN 821-870	Leyland Titan PD2/3	Leyland	L27/26R	1950
1301-50	DRN 241-290	Leyland Titan PD2/3	Leyland	L27/26RD	1950

Coaches transferred from Standerwick, 1948

Seven coaches from a batch of twelve (1455-66) that had been included in the 50 Tiger TS7 with English Electric bodies of 1935-6 but were allocated to Standerwick when new were transferred 'back' to Ribble in 1948, taking up their original numbers. Also transferred were two TS6 originally owned by Wright Bros of Burnley, and these were given two others of the same batch of fleet numbers.

1455-8	FV 5731-4	Leyland Tiger TS7	English Electric	C31F	1935
1461/3	FV 5737/9	Leyland Tiger TS7	English Electric	C31F	1936
1466	FV 5742	Leyland Tiger TS7	English Electric	C31F	1936
1460/4	HG 2759/8	Leyland Tiger TS6	English Electric	C31R	5/34

Rebodying and engine changes – double-deckers 1943-52

Above left
Most of the Titan TD1 buses dating from 1930 had been withdrawn in 1938-9 but 747 (CK 4211) was the oldest of three survivors which, together with two of the 1931 batch, received new Northern Coachbuilders utility 53-seat lowbridge bodies in 1943 – all five also received 8.6-litre oil engines. It is seen in Penrith in 1949, still working its regular duty on the the Carlisle service.

Above right
The largest rebodying exercise was the fitting of Burlingham 56-seat highbridge bodies to 68 Titan TD4 and TD5 chassis in 1947. 1590 (RN 7796), a 1936 TD4 chassis, is seen in later years – it was to remain in service until 1958.

Left
ECW was the supplier of new lowbridge bodies in 1948, including that on TD5 1772 (RN 8156) seen here at Whalley on the Burnley-Clitheroe route; it remained in service until 1959.

Generally, Ribble had not made a practice of replacing or transferring bodywork to update older vehicles during the pre-1939 period, unlike some neighbouring companies. The situation began to alter under wartime conditions, when, in 1943-44, five Leyland Titan TD1 models dating from 1930-31 were given new bodywork to utility standard by Northern Coachbuilders – one of the firms given the task of building on reconditioned rather than new chassis. They were also given Leyland 8.6-litre oil engines and it seems to have been realised that the resulting buses, if austere in appearance, could be treated almost as if new, remaining in service until 1950, often on inter-urban services. The vehicles in question were 747, 764, 818, 1047 and 1065.

The next major step was the rebodying of 68 Titan chassis from the 1936-38 period with new highbridge Burlingham bodies similar to those on new PD1 chassis, in 1947. The vehicles in question were 54 TD4 models, including all but two of those new in 1936 (1588-98, 1600-4/6-21) and all but two of the 1937 buses (1722/4-44), plus fourteen TD5; three of 1937 (1789/95/6) and eleven of 1938 (1775/8/86-8, 1901/9/15/8/24/6). They took over urban duties, notably at Carlisle, where most of the city services were operated by them.

Eastern Coach Works was building new bodies on pre-war Titan chassis for several operators in 1948 and Ribble took 25 lowbridge, all on TD5, that year (1790/2/3/7-9 dating from 1937 and 1772/3/81, 1800/2-6, 1903/7/12/7/9/20/2/3/5/8 of the 1938 batches).

In 1949, ECW no longer being able to build for concerns outside the British Transport Commission to which it by then belonged, Alexander came into the picture. This concern, originally the bodybuilding department of the large operating company of that name, had been excluded from sale to the BTC and was beginning to expand its market as a separate business. It had built bodies with close resemblance to Leyland products and there was evidence of this in the 25 lowbridge bodies built for Ribble that year on four TD4, the oldest chassis included in this

The oldest of the buses given 8ft-wide Alexander bodies in 1950 was a TD4 dating from 1936, retaining its original number 1599 until 1958, when the delivery of new PD3 models receiving fleet numbers in the double-deck series by then in use made it necessary to renumber it 2782, as seen here, running thus until withdrawn in 1961.

The rebuilding of most of the bodies on wartime Guy and Daimler buses to Ribble's requirements by Bond went further in removing obvious 'utility' features than most operators attempted, even though the lack of curvature across the front of the upper deck still rather gave the game away. Seen here is 2413 (ACK 796), a Guy with Northern Counties lowbridge body dating from 1944. Another noteworthy feature was the repositioning of the radiator to eliminate the familiar projecting 'snout' effect of the Arab II model as built and giving the appearance, as shown here, of an Arab I model of 1942-3, though in fact Ribble had no examples of this type.

programme (1487-90, dating from 1935), and 21 on TD5 (1801 and 1910 dating from 1938, and 2038/41/4/50/3/7/8/61/6/7/71/3/4/7-82 of those dating from 1939).

In 1950, a final 30 Alexander bodies for pre-war Titans were supplied, but these were 8ft-wide, the chassis being slightly modified to suit. They went on two TD4 (1599 and 1605, dating from 1936) and 28 TD5 (1791 dating from 1937; 1777/9/80/2/5, 1904/6/8/11/3/4/6/21/30 of 1938, and 2036/7/9/40/3/6-8/54/9/65, 2070/2 of 1939).

A total of 148 of the 176 TD4 and TD5 buses in the fleet had thus been rebodied, making a contribution to the modernisation of the fleet not far short in numbers of that made by the 196 new PD2 buses over much the same period. Most then continued in service until 1957-61, confirming the durability of the chassis – in five cases Burlingham bodies of the 1947 delivery were transferred from TD4 to TD5 chassis hitherto unrebodied in 1952/3, taking their fleet numbers with them. It seems that all but five of these vehicles retained their 8.6-litre engines, but 1780, 1906/14, 2040/74 received 7.4 units and this also applied to unrebodied 1774/6/83, 2045/52.

The final stage of the rehabilitation process for pre-war or wartime double-deckers involved the Guy and Daimler utility buses dating from 1943-5. Some minor work had been done in adding extra opening windows, etc but most of the bodies were in poor condition by 1951-2 and it was decided to rebuild or replace the bodies on all 58. Of these, 42, covering all combinations of chassis and body, were sent to S. H. Bond Ltd of Wythenshawe, Manchester, for body rebuild, this including the rounding of rear domes and fitment of sliding windows. The remaining sixteen (Daimlers 2391-3, 2422/5/6 and Guys 2404/11/2/4/31-4/6/7) were fitted with Metro-Cammell highbridge bodies dating from 1937-40, from Wallasey Corporation Leyland Titans, a body type well-known for durability. The Leyland chassis were used as a source of spares. In the event, the lives of the utilities were not greatly extended by either course of action. The 5LW-powered Guy buses, remaining unpopular with drivers because of their poor performance, were withdrawn in 1954-6. See Volume 1, page 46 for other illustrations.

Rebodying and engine changes – single-deck coaches and buses, 1946-50

At the end of the war, the 6.2-litre experimental engines in 79 of the 1939 TS8 buses were replaced by 7.4-litre units and some of the displaced engines used to replace petrol units in the 40 Cheetah buses dating from 1939 (2094-2133) during the 1946-48 period.

The emphasis tended to be on coaches, so far as rebodying was concerned and, although not carried out on the same scale as with double-deckers, the impact was proportionately greater, as so few new coaches were added to the fleet over the same period. For a couple of years or so, the likeliest type of vehicle to appear on many scheduled long-distance express duties would be one of the 54 rebodied Tigers. The first group to be dealt with were the TS8 coaches of 1938 (numbers 1931-55) and 1939 (2134-42), a total of 34 vehicles. They had 7.4-litre diesel engines fitted in place of the petrol units, some since 1946 – though doubtless an improvement in efficiency, this was hardly one from the passenger's viewpoint, as not only the noise level but also its harsh tone were much inferior not only to the petrol version but, rather ironically, even the 8.6-litre oil engine retained in the rebodied double-deckers. The new bodies, with 31-seat capacity in line with Ribble's usual policy, were by Duple and to that firm's curvaceous post-war standard style, which looked well in Ribble coach livery.

For 1950, it was decided to make 20 more basically similar conversions with new Duple bodies and 7.4-litre engines, but the relaxation in dimensions whch came into force that year meant that 8ft-wide coaches could be used more freely, so the new bodies were to this width. This was quite unusual among rebodied coaches and reflects the extent of Ribble's commitment to this feature for the improved comfort it allowed. It was necessary to use earlier chassis this time, nineteen being TS7 models, of which eleven came from the batch with Betteridge-style Duple bodies dating from 1936 (1494/5/7/9. 1502/4/7/9/15/8/40) and one from a 1937 batch (1650). Seven more came from part of the English Electric-bodied batch of 1935-6 which had been allocated to Standerwick from new but which were transferred to Ribble in 1948, taking up the Ribble fleet numbers they had been allocated when new (1455-8/61/3/6) but which had given way to Standerwick numbers when that concern began its own scheme in 1936. The other body from this batch went on to an even more remarkable chassis, 2020, which was one of the vehicles taken over from Arthur Christy in 1938. It was a TS6 model, though first registered in June 1935 and thus slightly

Among the coaches given new 8ft-wide Duple bodywork and 7.4-litre diesel engines in 1950 were the seven Tiger TS7 models, originally with English Electric bodywork, transferred from Standerwick in 1948, including FV 5734. This had then reverted to the Ribble fleet number 1458 as originally allocated when new in April 1935 though not carried because of their delivery to Standerwick. In the new numbering scheme of 1950, it became 752, as seen here in Morecambe, with passengers boarding for a working to Bradford on the X88 service.

Some of the displaced coach bodies were remounted on former bus chassis, as in this case. ACK 174 had begun life as one of the last batch of Tiger TS8 32-seat buses, 2372, placed in service in 1941. In 1951, it was one of fifteen of the type ftted with older Duple coach bodies, this one dating from 1936. In 1951 it became 1172, as shown here. They were painted in an approximation of bus livery, creating an effect not unlike that of the 1935 coaches when new and were generally referred to as 'week-end coaches'.

newer than the ex-Standerwick 1455-8, and it seems quite likely that the differences in specification, notably in the brake system, between the TS6 and TS7 might have been eliminated during the course of reconditioning for rebodying.

As a follow-on to these events, most of the 25 Duple and nine Burlingham bodies removed from 1938-39 TS8 coaches were fitted to earlier chassis during the winter of 1948-49. Of these, 22 were TS7 and six TS6 coaches, some ex-Pearson, but they are also believed to have included the four Lion LT7 buses of 1936 (1482-5), though it is not known what work may have been done to the chassis in this case. The vehicles in question ran for two or three more years. Ten of the 1938-39 coach bodies then went on to ex-bus TS8 chassis of 1939 in 1950-51, and in 1951, fifteen of the 1940-41 batch of TS8 buses with ACK registrations received Duple coach bodies, seven of 1938 and eight from 1936. These formed a pool of 'week-end coaches' painted red, also including 25 remaining Cheetah coaches, for which there were plans for diesel conversions, though RN 7824, which survives, is still petrol.

A rather more elaborate exercise was the rebuilding and 'modernising' of twelve Duple coach bodies of 1936-38 that also went on to 1939 TS8 chassis that had been buses in 1950-52. They were restyled externally with detail features reminiscent of the White Lady double-deckers, see page 119 of Volume 1. The common factor behind all of this work was a short-term need for the provision of enough coaches pending the arrival of the planned new fleet of underfloor-engined models.

A more limited programme of producing single-deck buses of rather similar character was also carried out. Some 27 Tiger TS7 models were given new Burlingham 35-seat bus bodies of the bodybuilder's standard pattern of the period and, in most cases, 7.4-litre engines in 1949. Of these, sixteen were drawn from the 1935-6 batches of TS7 coaches (1420/30/6/40/1/5-9/52-4/67/8, 1524) but the remainder had been purchased from other BET companies, a new departure for Ribble and one that was not repeated for many years. Two came from Yorkshire Woollen District in July 1948 and were then numbered 2616-7, but did not enter service as such and were given the new numbers 2692-3 when rebodied and placed in service in 1949. They had been joined by 2694-5 from the same source and 2705-11, which had come from Devon General.

2692-3	HD 5802/12	Leyland Tiger TS7	Burlingham	B35F	1935
2694-5	HD 6308-11	Leyland Tiger TS7	Burlingham	B35F	1937
2705	BDV 1	Leyland Tiger TS7	Burlingham	B35F	1936
2706	CTA 110	Leyland Tiger TS7	Burlingham	B35F	1937
2707-9	BDV 2/5/7	Leyland Tiger TS7	Burlingham	B35F	1936
2710-11	BDV 6/3	Leyland Tiger TS7	Burlingham	B35F	1936

The former TS7 coaches from Ribble's own fleet now rebodied as buses were given the fleet numbers 2696-2704 and 2712-2718.

The nearest approach to new single-deckers to be found in some Ribble areas in the earlier post-war period were the Tiger TS7 chassis fitted with new Burlingham 35-seat bus bodies and 7.4-litre diesel engines in 1949. As delivered they were in a livery which was based on the pre-war bus style, with white window surrounds. This preserved example, seen in Halifax in 1987, recaptures the resulting appearance very effectively. RN 7588 had begun life as one of the English Electric-bodied coaches of 1935, numbered 1420, and when rebodied in 1949 was renumbered 2700, as if a 'new' vehicle. In 1951 it became 209. Similar vehicles were produced by rebodying some second-hand TS7 chassis, though those from the Yorkshire Woollen District fleet, which already had 8.6-litre engines, retained them. RN 7588 is now in the custody of the South Lancashire Transport Society.

Sentinel STC4 buses, 1949-50

Quite unlike any vehicle in the existing fleet, the Sentinel-Beadle integral single-decker of 1949 had more than a little in common with some of today's midibuses in general proportions, though its four-cylinder engine was in a mid-underfloor position. This is the prototype of the Ribble batch, 2722 (CRN 211).

Ribble's management was enthusiastically interested in the concept of the underfloor-engined single-decker. When Sentinel, in co-operation with Beadle, beat the larger British manufacturers, including Leyland, to the mark by exhibiting a prototype vehicle at the 1948 Commercial Motor Show, the Company promptly placed an order. The initial model was a 27ft 6in by 7ft 6in example seating 40 passengers. The lightweight integral structure was designed, and on Ribble's first example, built by Beadle, the Dartford-based bodybuilder, which had pioneered a similar design used in various forms by Tilling companies.

Sentinel, based at Shrewsbury and long known for its steam wagons with 'underfloor' engine position, had developed a diesel lorry of similar layout, with a horizontal four-cylinder engine, and this provided the basis of the mechanical units for the bus, designated SB on the prototype but STC4/40 in generally unchanged production form. Ribble made a point of running its first example on the 109 service past Leyland's works, but in fact it was not trouble-free and Ribble engineers helped in development before the rest were delivered. The batch was transferred to Carlisle, and ran until 1962-3. This was certainly a full lifespan.

2722	CRN 211	Sentinel SB	Beadle	B40F	5/49
2723-7	CRN 212-216	Sentinel STC4/40	Sentinel	B40F	1950

Leyland Tiger PS2/5 buses, 1950

The only batch of new front-engined single-deck buses added to Ribble's fleet after the 1939-45 war comprised 20 Leyland Tiger PS2/5 chassis with Burlingham bodies very like those built for the re-engined TS7 chassis the previous year, save for being 8ft wide. They were rather surprising in two respects. One was their existence at all when clearly the hope was to adopt the underfloor layout within a year or so – delivery began in March 1950. The other was the choice of the PS2, which was the single-deck equivalent of the PD2, with O.600 engine. In theory, it had been current since 1947 but in practice the PS1 had remained the normal production model, only quite small numbers of PS2 being produced for home-market customers. Ribble's requirement for 8ft width, not a production option with the PS1, may have been a factor, as well as the evident preference for the larger engine. They remained in service until 1962-3, although some subsequently served as Recovery Vehicles for many years.

2778-97	CRN 978-997	Leyland Tiger PS2/5	Burlingham	B35F	1950

'White Lady' double-deckers on Leyland Titan PD2/3 chassis, 1950-51

These were in essence a continuation of the 1948-49 White Lady vehicles for the shorter express duties, but on PD2/3 chassis. The body order went to East Lancashire, the only such instance for Ribble except for the three 'unfrozen' TD7 buses of 1942. They were built to a very similar style, though with four bays between bulkheads, a feature that had become quite fashionable on double-deckers but one that did not otherwise find favour in Ribble's fleet. They were delivered in 1950-51 and remained in service until 1961, not altered in livery though latterly quite often used on bus duties.

1231-50	DCK 202-221	Leyland Titan PD2/3	East Lancs L27/22RD	various

The Tiger PS2/5 buses with Burlingham bodywork of 1950 were bordering on the old-fashioned even when new, and were the heaviest front-engined single-deckers in the fleet, at 7tons 1cwt. The sliding entrance door was an uncommon feature on this body design – 2793 (CRN 993) is seen before delivery.

Though benefiting from being on PD2 chassis, the second batch of 'White Lady' coaches looked little changed, apart from the four-bay layout – the modified grille style had been applied to the earlier buses retrospectively. They received numbers in the new system, 1246 (DCK 217) being seen here.

Renumbering scheme of September 1950

With no surviving vehicles having numbers below 1419, and increasing complexity due to the large-scale rebodying involving former coaches becoming buses and vice versa, it was decided to introduce a classified system, as follows:-

201-700 were to be single-deck buses
701-1200 were to be single-deck coaches
1201-1300 were to be double-deck coaches
1301 upwards were reserved for double-deck buses

In practice, the renumbering was only partial, existing double-deckers retaining their old numbers running up to 2777, as did other types expected to be withdrawn in the next year or two. In 1956, rebodied TD4 double-deckers 1487-90 were renumbered 2778-81 to clear the way for a new double-deck batch spreading into the old numbers, and the same happened in 1958 when 1599 and 1605 became 2782-3.

Those renumbered are summarised as follows.

New Numbers	Old Numbers	Chassis type	Comments
Single-deck buses			
201-227	2692-2718	Leyland Tiger TS7	Rebodied
228-247	2778-2797	Leyland Tiger PS2	
278-283	2722-2727	Sentinel STC4	
Single-deck coaches			
701-714	2548-2561	Leyland Tiger PS1	
715-739	1931-1955	Leyland Tiger TS8	Rebodied
740-748	2134-2142	Leyland Tiger TS8	Rebodied
749-767	various	Leyland Tiger TS7	Rebodied (8ft)
768	2020	Leyland Tiger TS6	Rebodied (8ft)
769-780	various	Leyland Tiger TS8	'Modernised' body
1151-75	various	Leyland Tiger TS8	Transferred bodies
1176-1200	various	Leyland Cheetah	Coaches
Double-deck coaches			
1201-30	2518-47	Leyland Titan PD1/3	'White Lady' coaches

Leyland-MCW Olympic single-deckers, 1951

There was a touch of BET Federation ideas in the styling of the Leyland-MCW Olympic, though it did not conform to that orgnisation's design in a strict sense, and in any case Ribble was not one of the companies which took Federation-style buses in those days. Seen here in Penrith not very long after entering service in April 1951 is 273 (DRN 137). It had arrived after making the climb over Kirkstone Pass on the summer-only route from Windermere.

The switch to underfloor-engined single-deckers materialised in 1951 and for several years the emphasis turned to such vehicles for most of Ribble's new vehicle needs. The first fruit of Leyland's development work in this field was the Olympic, a joint exercise with the Metropolitan-Cammell Weymann concern, the latter being responsible for the integral structure to which the Leyland mechanical units, including a horizontal version of the O.600 engine and a synchromesh gearbox, were attached. It was largely intended for export but a 'home range' was included. The thirty Ribble examples were of type HR44, built at the Weymann factory, the figures denoting the seating capacity, made possible by its 30ft length, permissible on a two-axle single-decker from 1950. The first vehicle, 248, was exhibited at the 1950 Commercial Motor Show. They remained in service to 1963-68, some having been converted for one-man operation in 1965. Whilst initially allocated to the then south of Ribble territory, they were quickly displaced to the rural north by incoming Royal Tigers. It was said that their bodies were not compatible with the 'setts' of south and east Lancashire roads.

248-277	DRN 112-141	Leyland Olympic HR44	Weymann	B44F	1951

Sentinel STC6 buses, 1951

The renumbering of the first batch of Sentinels so that they followed the Olympics despite being older brought them together with the second batch of fourteen of the same make. These were to the new dimensions and had six-cylinder 9.1-litre engines, though Sentinel remained faithful to the Ricardo indirect injection system once favoured by several British diesel engine makers but which had given way to direct

The six-cylinder Sentinel STC6 had a body design derived from the four-cylinder version, but extended to 30ft by 8ft dimensions and mildly restyled at the front. They were to remain a familiar sight on Carlisle area services until the early 'sixties. Their prime use was on rural journeys, particularly after Denton Holme Bridge was lowered around 1954, allowing all city services to be double-deck operated. Seen here amid the red sandstone buildings so typical of the area is 293 (DRN 350) on the C4 to Longsowerby.

injection as used in one form or other on all of Ribble's oil-engined buses from the beginning. As it turned out, Ribble was the only major operator to give Sentinel a bulk order for its buses, but these STC6 models, based at Carlisle together with the earlier STC4 types, served until 1962-3.

284-297	DRN 341-354	Sentinel STC6	Sentinel	B44F	1951

Leyland Royal Tiger coaches, 1951-54

Despite the early essays into integral construction, it was the Royal Tiger, with similar underfloor engine and other units to those of the Olympic but in a conventional chassis, that was chosen by Ribble for a major modernisation of its single-deck fleet. Coaches were the first priority,

The Royal Tiger was to be the most typical Ribble vehicle on coach and single-deck bus duties from 1951 until the early 'sixties. A prototype coach had been shown at the 1950 Commercial Motor Show, but the first vehicle for Ribble, 781 (DRN 703), seen here after completion by Leyland's body shop in February 1951, set the production standard not only for the rest of the batch but for deliveries to other operators. The styling largely broke with the previous trend to smooth curves, and although curved glass was used for some of the front-end glazing, the effect was quite angular, though certainly bold. Having placed 120 in service before the end of the year, the effect on Ribble's 'presence' was quite dramatic. The front 'apron' was later replaced by plain panels.

Within, the Leyland coach body of the Royal Tiger set good standards of comfort, using coach seats based on metal frames with bus-style grab rails. The model was quiet-running and gave a better standard of ride than earlier types. It was a new experience for passengers on a 'big' coach to find the driver seated with them inside the saloon, and the positioning of the entrance behind the first three rows of seats meant that the front nearside seat was a favourite for 'small boys' of all ages. However, it soon became apparent that powerful demisters were essential on such a layout.

and the initial batch comprised 120 of the new model, complete with a new metal-framed coach body that was the first venture into coach bodybuilding by Leyland since the days of the TS6. A remarkable vote of confidence. The total order was for 246 Royal Tigers, including sixteen coaches for Standerwick and 110 buses, forming the main strength of the fleet in these categories until the early 'sixties. Ribble had been involved in the development work, especially of the 41-seat body, for which a mock-up in Ribble livery had been produced. Delivery began in March 1951, many being in service by the summer, and was completed later in the year. A further 25 similar coaches were delivered in mid-1953, these proving to be the last vehicles for Ribble to have Leyland bodywork.

The designations of the model were based on PSU1, with suffix numbers to indicate variations, the original home-market coach version with vacuum brakes being PSU1/15. These vehicles proved generally very successful, offering good standards of comfort and were sturdily built if heavy. The only significant weakness was in the way in which drivers found it easy to expect too much of the brakes, at least partly because of the relaxed performance. Withdrawal began in 1962, the last surviving to 1967.

For touring duty, fifteen further PSU1/15 chassis were fitted with the curvaceous Burlingham Seagull bodywork, having luxurious seating for 32 passengers and entering service in mid-1953. The final Royal Tiger delivery was of five more touring coaches with the Seagull body, beginning in May 1954 but, significantly, these were on PSU1/16 chassis with air-pressure brakes. In 1961-2 these touring coaches were reseated to accomodate 41 passengers; they were withdrawn in 1966.

781-840	DRN 703-762	Leyland PSU1/15	Leyland	C41C	1951
841-900	ECK 121-180	Leyland PSU1/15	Leyland	C41C	1951
901-925	FCK 401-425	Leyland PSU1/15	Leyland	C41C	1953
926-940	FCK 426-440	Leyland PSU1/15	Burlingham	C32C	1953
941-945	FRN 675-679	Leyland PSU1/16	Burlingham	C32C	1954

Leyland Royal Tiger buses, 1952

The Leyland bus body produced for the Royal Tiger chassis had a utilitarian appearance, with a shallow roof, almost vertical front and an odd-looking small window just behind the entrance doors which almost had the look of being unrelated in design to the rest of the body. In practical terms, the vehicle was sturdy and reliable, though weighing more than many double-deckers then in the fleet – the figure quoted on the side of 337 (ECK 600) being 7tons 11cwt 2qtr; it was Leyland practice to weigh buses individually at that time.

The emphasis switched to the Royal Tiger bus in 1952, though the first example of the 110 ordered arrived in December 1951, delivery being completed in just about the year. These vehicles were on the PSU1/13 chassis, with auxiliaries differently arranged to the coach version. Leyland's body, the first single-deck design since 1939, was rather utilitarian in appearance but, like the coach, of sturdy construction. Many were converted for one-man operation in 1958-65. They remained in the fleet until 1963-67.

298-357	ECK 561-620	Leyland PSU1/13	Leyland	B44F	1952
358-407	ERN 681-730	Leyland PSU1/13	Leyland	B44F	1952

Leyland Titan PD2/12 double-deckers, 1952

The last examples of a long line of lowbridge double-deckers on Titan chassis of succeeding types to emerge from Leyland's body shops for the Ribble fleet at intervals since 1929 were the 30 supplied during the latter part of 1952. Apart from taking advantage of the 27ft length limit, the Farington body for PD2/12 chassis incorporated the revised style of glazing shown. There was a growing feeling of dissatisfaction with the lowbridge concept, with a view that the 30ft underfloor-engined single-decker might replace it, though even a 53-seat capacity was still an appreciable increase on 44. Seen here is 1357 (ECK 927) the combination of dimensions and specification, including platform doors, had pushed the weight in this instance up to 7tons 19cwt 3qr.

These 30 vehicles were to be the only double-deckers added to the fleet between 1951 and 1955, a contrast to the period from 1933 to 1950, when some had been purchased every year except for 1941. Leyland had modified the PD2 chassis to suit the increase in maximum length from 26ft to 27ft permitted from 1950, the PD2/12 being of 27ft by 8ft dimensions. The Leyland body was revised in design and given the Farington name, these being the last Ribble Titans to have Leyland bodywork. Apart from one example withdrawn in 1964, they remained in service until 1966-7.

1351-80	ECK 921-950	Leyland PD2/12	Leyland	L27/26RD	1952

Leyland Tiger Cub buses, 1953-54

Ribble's strategy in putting the first of its Sentinel underfloor-engined buses on route 109 to keep Leyland on its toes had the desired effect, and by 1953 it was possible for Leyland's second such model to be put on the route. Here 408 (ERN 776), the first of the batch of 50 Tiger Cub buses for Ribble is seen running through Leyland town – the street gives the impression of a small, quiet town, though within Leyland's works upwards of 5,000 chassis per year were being built. The Saunders-Roe body was of a very distinctive rounded style and quite well regarded in practical terms. The firm went out of business soon after the last example was delivered, due mainly to problems within the parent aircraft company.

There was renewed interest in lightweight vehicles from 1952, particularly in regard to underfloor-engined single-deckers, of which early production designs had proved heavy. Leyland introduced its Tiger Cub model, type PSUC1/1, at the Commercial Motor Show that year. It had a lighter chassis, with a horizontal version of the 5.76-litre O.350 six-cylinder engine which had been introduced in vertical form for the Comet goods range. It had a gearbox derived from the PD1 design but had air-pressure brakes, a feature that was gaining growing acceptance. Two demonstrators were built, both with weight around 5½ tons, about 2 tons less that a typical Royal Tiger. One had an MCW body and the other was by Saunders-Roe, a concern with aircraft origins which had turned to bus bodybuilding in 1946 and had built up a considerable business, sometimes using the shortened Saro version of its name. Ribble favoured the Saunders-Roe design and one of the Show exhibits was the first of a batch of 50, though it was on a pre-production chassis and was transferred to a production one before delivery, entering service in January 1953. Almost a year went by before the next was delivered, but the order was then completed in the spring of 1954. Eight carried weight saving even further in having single rear wheels as delivered, this being possible within the weight rating of the tyres fitted, but the idea was not pursued, adhesion under slippery conditions being impaired. They proved quite successful vehicles, though the small engine was noticeably 'busier' than the relaxed O.600. The batch was converted for one-man operation in 1958-9 and remained in service until 1967-9.

408	ERN 776	Leyland PSUC1/1	Saro	B44F	1/53
409-457	FCK 841-889	Leyland PSUC1/1	Saro	B44F	1954

Leyland Tiger Cub coaches, 1954-58

A coach version of the Tiger Cub chassis, the PSUC1/2, was introduced in 1953 and Ribble chose this as the basis of its coach needs in the mid to late 'fifties, though the quantities were not as great as the Royal Tigers. The first batch of fifteen carried Burlingham Seagull bodywork quite similar to those on the heavier chassis being delivered at about the same time in 1954, though seating 41 from new. In 1956, 26 more were delivered, this time on chassis with two-speed rear axles giving a wider spread of overall gear ratios. In this instance the Seagull bodies were of the front-entrance layout and ten were of 36-seat capacity for touring work, five (977-81) being allocated to Auty's Tours Ltd of Bury, an independent operator which had just been taken over, but which was run as a subsidiary until 1959. In addition, 982-6, though owned by Ribble and in standard livery, carried Auty's fleetnames. The final batch of 32 appeared in 1958, these having a simplified design of body, still of the basic Seagull outline but with bus-style glazing and flat-glass windscreen. They were fitted with 5-speed Albion gearboxes and single-speed rear axles. The Tiger Cub coaches ran until 1965-68.

946-960	GCK 281-295	Leyland PSUC1/2	Burlingham	C41C	1954
961-976	JRN 27-42	Leyland PSUC1/2T	Burlingham	C41F	1956
977-986	JCK 889-898	Leyland PSUC1/2T	Burlingham	C36F	1956
987-1018	LCK 701-732	Leyland PSUC1/2	Burlingham	C41F	1958

The Burlingham Seagull body as built for Ribble gradually evolved, early Tiger Cub coaches, such as 949 (GCK 284) of 1954, below left, being very like the styles as built on Royal Tiger chassis, apart from the larger destination display. The final 1958 version, of which 1008 (LCK 722) is seen, below right, about to leave Blackpool for Liverpool on the X24 en route to its ultimate destination, Cheltenham, lost something of the original subtlety in the revised glazing arrangements.

Leyland Titan PD2 double-deckers, 1955-56

The ubiquitous MCW Orion metal -framed body appeared in Ribble's fleet in 1955, when 50 examples on Titan PD2/13 air-braked chassis were delivered. The Orion had been strongly publicised as a lightweight design but the Ribble examples, built by Metro-Cammell, were in a medium-range category with unladen weight of 7tons 9cwt 2qr for the version without platform doors, such as 1413 (HCK 473), seen in Carlisle not long after entering service. In 1956, Burlingham re-entered the supply of double-deck bodywork to Ribble for the first time since the building of the first 'White Lady' coach versions in 1948-9, having introduced a metal-framed design. Seen here ready for delivery in June 1956 is 1434 (JCK 509), one of the 40 with platform doors.

Double-deckers came back into the picture in the mid 'fifties, and indeed, apart from coaches, Ribble's intake of new vehicles was entirely of this category from 1955 until 1962. Highbridge bodywork on PD2 chassis was chosen for the 1955-56 orders, though with Leyland's decision to cease passenger vehicle body construction, a new source had to be found. A large proportion of former Leyland body customers switched to MCW, which became the 'obvious' supplier, partly because its Orion double-deck body design was in tune with, and indeed had helped to foster, the interest in lightweight bodywork. Additionally there was a friendly relationship between the two firms because of the Olympic integral model, perhaps amounting to tacit encouragement for body orders to go in that direction.

The 1955 order was for 50 vehicles with 61-seat capacity, the body order going to Metropolitan-Cammell, the Birmingham-based part of the MCW organisation, 25 having platform doors and 25 without them. They conformed to the Orion outline but were not of lightweight construction. The chassis were of type PD2/13, which had air-pressure brakes but was otherwise similar to the PD2/12. The 1956 order reverted to the PD2/12, suggesting that the vacuum brake version was, after all, found preferable at that stage for the type of duty for which they were intended, possibly because drivers new to air brakes were apt to apply them unduly sharply. This time Burlingham got the major part of the order, building 45 bodies to its contemporary metal-framed design, of similar outline to earlier generations but with revised glazing, all but five with platform doors. Metro-Cammell built 25 more of the same style as in 1955, without doors.

1381	HCK 461	Leyland PD2/13	Met.Camm.	H33/28RD	1955
1382-85	HCK 463-466	Leyland PD2/13	Met.Camm.	H33/28RD	1955
1386-1405	HRN 26-45	Leyland PD2/13	Met.Camm.	H33/28RD	1955
1406	HCK 462	Leyland PD2/13	Met.Camm.	H33/28R	1955
1407-25	HCK 467-485	Leyland PD2/13	Met.Camm.	H33/28R	1955
1426-30	HRN 21-25	Leyland PD2/13	Met.Camm.	H33/28R	1955
1431-70	JCK 506-545	Leyland PD2/12	Burlingham	H33/28RD	1956
1471-75	JCK 546-550	Leyland PD2/12	Burlingham	H33/28R	1956
1476-1500	JRN 43-67	Leyland PD2/12	Met.Camm.	H33/28R	1956

Rebuilding and rebodying of PD1A double-deckers, 1955

The Brush bodywork on the 1947 batch of lowbridge Leyland Titan PD1A double-deckers had deteriorated quite badly by 1955, suffering from the rot in poor-quality timber framing common on vehicles of the period. It was decided to rebody 22 of the 38 (numbers 2480/2-5/7/9/91-5/8/9, 2501/4/7-9/13/4/7), but the exercise was taken further than in earlier ventures of this kind. The chassis were rebuilt with new 8ft axles and other units to suit the new Burlingham lowbridge bodies of this width, producing vehicles which looked almost indistinguishable from new. At first they retained their 7.4-litre engines, but when the 1946 PD1 buses which had been re-engined with O.600 units were withdrawn in 1958, the larger engines, plus two others found the following year from stock, were installed in all but one (2517) of the 1955 rebuilds, producing buses which Ribble listed as PD2/3 subsequently. They remained in service until 1965-6 whereas the unrebodied examples of the batch were withdrawn in 1958. 'Before and after' illustrations are on page 115 of Volume 1. The unrebodied buses were rebuilt, however, receiving rubber glazing in the process.

Leyland Titan PD3/4 double-deckers, 1957-59

In 1956, the maximum permitted length for two-axle double-deckers was increased from 27ft to 30ft, and Leyland introduced the PD3 version

Ribble's first 30ft-long double-deckers broke new ground in several respects, brought together in what was widely agreed as one of the most elegant vehicles of the period. It was derived from Burlingham's standard products, but with a full-width cab and grille design developed by Ribble, the latter more 'Leylandish' than Leyland's own concealed-radiator styles. Deleting the glazing from the nearside bulkhead window opening was intended to improve the driver's ability to supervise loading but increased the internal noise level. As so often the case with Ribble's double-deckers in those days, they were liable to be pressed into duty on the shorter express services, and here 1551 (KCK 912) waits in Blackpool with blind set for Liverpool on the X81.

of the Titan to suit, mechanically similar in most respects to the PD2 but to the new length. Ribble decided to move the entrance forward so that it could be more readily supervised by the driver, though at that date there was no prospect of the conductor being eliminated, it being considered that he or she was becoming increasingly unable to supervise passengers boarding or alighting when collecting fares on so large a vehicle. Taking this idea a little further, elimination of the glazing of the front bulkhead was seen as an advantage, this being possible if the cab was full-fronted. It is significant that a White Lady double-decker was used as a mock-up for styling purposes, and that a grille outline inspired by Leyland practice was adopted when Leyland's own products were tending to abandon the traditional outline. A large sliding entrance door was power-operated.

Burlingham was given the body contract for an initial batch of 69, the first three vehicles being delivered in September 1957. The chassis were of type PD3/4, with synchromesh gearbox and air-pressure brakes, the latter feature now regarded as standard for additions to Ribble's fleet. A particularly well-proportioned vehicle resulted, with just enough of the traditional Ribble/Burlingham outline to give a sense of continuity of 'house style'. A further 36 followed and delivery continued without a break, being completed in October 1958. Illuminated exterior advertisement panels were in favour at the time and 27 of the type were so fitted. Air suspension was another new concept and number 1600 was so fitted on both axles, possibly to gain experience for the subsequent use of the system on the 'Gay Hostess' Atlantean coaches. The vehicles remained in service until 1971-75.

1501-19	KCK 847-865	Leyland PD3/4	Burlingham	H41/31F	1957
1520-69	KCK 866-930	Leyland PD3/4	Burlingham	H41/31F	1958
1570-1605	LCK 733-768	Leyland PD3/4	Burlingham	H41/31F	1958

Leyland Atlantean PDR1/1 double-deck coaches, 1959-62

Ribble pioneering at its best! The Leyland Atlantean rear-engined double-decker, with entrance ahead of the front axle, had been put into production in 1958, after a series of experimental vehicles had been built. It had the O.600 engine mounted transversely at the rear and driving through a Pneumo-cyclic gearbox, in principle much as used for many years on buses by Daimler and AEC. Leyland adopted the idea as a production option from 1954, when it was redesigned to operate directly, eliminating any need for a clutch or equivalent pedal. At that stage Ribble, like most company operators, had preferred to stay with conventional gearboxes, but the rear engine position made use of the latter

From a visual point of view, it was perhaps unfortunate that Ribble's next venture in the development of a double-deck coach was destined to be based on the standard MCW body produced for the early Atlantean, so lacking in the subtlety of contours of the Burlingham-bodied PD3. Weymann, charged with the job of making it look like a coach without being allowed to alter the shape, did its best, using a touch of the styling of its Fanfare single-deck coach of the period. This picture of the first vehicle, 1251 (MCK 812) is noteworthy in being taken on 30th June 1959, at Aintree, with driver Sid Patterson, of Preston depot at the wheel, during the course of a tour of inspection made by the Directors. It had an O.600 engine and the power-to-weight ratio would have been inferior to that of a PD1 White Lady, so it is not surprising that performance, especially on hills, was found unsatisfactory until an O.680 was installed.

The Gay Hostess title related to the idea of providing a refreshment service on the Atlantean coaches – here a hostess offers sandwiches and takes orders for tea, coffee or soft drinks on the upper deck, while in the other view, the lower-deck seating is seen – quite comfortable, but hardly giving the most inspired view forward. The left view was taken on the first public outing, a non-stop duplicate on a Preston-Southport stage carriage service (100) during the school holidays in the summer of 1959. The Hostess is a Preston garage conductress. It is believed that the passengers were given a free ride.

impractical. Another key feature was the low-built chassis frame, designed to be greatly stiffened by the body structure which, though separate, played a more direct role in the vehicle's overall strength than hitherto usual. The model was designed primarily as a large-capacity bus, but Ribble's first example, based on one of the earliest chassis, was a double-deck coach, taking the idea much further than the 'White Lady' concept, and intended for use on much longer-distance services, notably to London. An advanced feature was the fitment of air suspension to the front axle, similar to that on the L1 Leopard and Titan PD3 No. 1600. This used a parabolic steel link to locate the axle to the chassis on the same centres as conventionally sprung versions. As a result of the confined space, a pair of small horizontal shock absorbers was squeezed in. This became the achilles heel of the vehicle for the inadequate damping led to a roller coaster ride on all but the best roads of the day. The same system, much refined, was to serve with considerable success on the Stockholm Atlantean order and through to the end of Tiger production in 1992.

This was another instance of close association with MCW, which designed the rather austere-looking body with which the model was introduced. Construction was shared between the Metro-Cammell and Weymann works, generally without significant difference in design, and the body shell of this first vehicle, like those of Ribble's first Atlantean buses described below, was built by Metro-Cammell in Birmingham. However, Weymann's Addlestone workforce had more experience of coach bodybuilding and that factory was considered a more appropriate choice for its completion, as well as building the later bodies of the type. The structure and basic appearance was unaltered, though the external mouldings and livery style were slightly reminiscent of the Weymann Fanfare coach of the time. Within, in addition to comfortable seating for 50 passengers and space for luggage at the rear of the lower deck, there was a toilet compartment and a servery for hot and cold drinks and light refreshments, served to passengers by airliner-style hostesses. Although toilet compartments had been quite common on Standerwick and other London service vehicles, the overall concept was quite new, and the name given to the type – 'Gay Hostess' – was an apt description when the adjective did not have the meaning commonly ascribed to it nowadays. The first completed vehicle weighed only just under 10 tons unladen, so performance with the O.600 engine was rather limited, especially on hills. After its first public outing, shown in the accompanying pictures, the vehicle is known to have been used during August, September and October of 1959 on both the Blackpool-London service (three round trips up to 3rd September) and Manchester-Glasgow express services. The first journeys on the latter, crewed by David Meredith, amongst others, took place before 8th September and subsequently this team worked several more. The fitment of an O.680 engine of 11.1 litres capacity and associated regearing to be capable of a maximum speed of 64mph took place at Frenchwood Works between 16th September and 6th October. This specification subsequently became standard for the production examples. As part of the on-going refinement, after returning from Glasgow on the first night journey on 10/11th October, 1251 was taken back into Frenchwood Works. Unfortunately during this time no one emptied the toilet . . .

The vehicle's next outing, about two weeks later, was to the official opening of the M1 motorway – a 24 hour duty. The return from London was on a cold winter's night and the upper-deck heating had failed but the hardy official group aboard preferred the rigours of freezing upstairs to the company of swarms of bluebottles and others in the rear of the warm lower saloon. An early lesson in double-deck coach operation! Re-entry into the main fleet was in November 1959.

A production run of fourteen more, with entirely Weymann-built bodies to the same design entered service with Ribble the following summer, but ten and the prototype were transferred to Standerwick ownership in 1963 to join 22 supplied direct to that fleet in 1960-61, the other four going to Scout, by then also a Ribble subsidiary. They ran until 1970-71, running up to 400 miles per day and thus built up very large mileages, a few running for Ribble again for the final year. Also in 1962, an additional 20 broadly similar vehicles were built for Ribble, but to a rather less elaborate specification, without the servery and seating 59 passengers, as a second generation 'White Lady' fleet for use on the shorter express routes, running until 1976-7

1251	NCK 812	Leyland PDR1/1	MCW	H34/16F	1959
1252-65	NRN 601-614	Leyland PDR1/1	Weymann	H34/16F	1960
1266-85	RRN 415-434	Leyland PDR1/1	Weymann	H39/20F	1962

Weymann's livery improved the appearance of the standard MCW bodyshell out of all recognition and produced vehicles instantly recognisable to all who used the M1 motorway. When the Gay Hostess vehicles left the Ribble and Standerwick fleets for further service Teesside Municipal Transport was one operator to take several. In the lower picture Teesside A61, formerly Standerwick 26 is seen waiting to depart for Stockton. Despite the steamed up windows the high-backed coach seats can just be seen and the change in appearance from the revised destination layout will also be noticed, (compare with page 105).

Leyland Atlantean PDR1/1 double-deck buses, 1959-62

The bus version of the Atlantean, in this case with bodywork entirely supplied by Metro-Cammell, entered the fleet in the same month, November 1959, as the first 'Gay Hostess' coach version, but the fleet built up more rapidly – within a year there were 95. Of these, the first 50 were of full-height 'highbridge' type, with seats for 78 passengers, this capacity, the largest on offer in any British bus at the time, being one of the Atlantean's main selling points. Where lower overall height was required, the model was offered with centre gangway along most of the upper deck but the traditional sunken side gangway towards the rear where the lower deck floor was raised to clear the rear axle. There were 25 of this lowbridge version, delivered in the summer of 1960, and then 20 more highbridge in October-November.

The early Atlantean was apt to be troublesome, particularly in regard to overheating and transmission problems, sufficiently so for Ribble to revert to the PD3 for a time, restricting its further PDR1/1 bus purchases to five lowbridge examples in 1961 and fourteen in 1962. Even so, Ribble grappled with the model's problems and also began a series of conversions to one-man operation of suitable double-deckers with No.1617 in March 1969. Only a few of the earlier examples were so converted but all the 1801-14 batch were done, largely in 1971-2. It is noteworthy that although withdrawals began on a small scale in 1971 and in rather larger numbers in 1972-3, quite a number ran until 1976 and a few remained in the fleet for 20 years.

1606-31	NCK 347-372	Leyland PDR1/1	Met.Camm.	H44/34F	1959/60
1632-55	NCK 621-644	Leyland PDR1/1	Met.Camm.	H44/34R	1960
1656-80	NRN 556-580	Leyland PDR1/1	Met.Camm.	L39/33F	1960
1681-1700	NRN 581-600	Leyland PDR1/1	Met.Camm.	H44/34R	1960
1701-05	PCK 334-338	Leyland PDR1/1	Met.Camm.	L39/33F	1961
1801-14	RRN 401-414	Leyland PDR1/1	Met.Camm.	L39/33F	1962

Some of the early Atlanteans had relatively short lives but there were also noteworthy exceptions. Most of those delivered in 1959 had gone, with seemingly little regret, by 1972, but 1617 (NCK 358), one of the first to enter service, was to survive to 1978, having become Ribble's first 'one-man' double-decker in March 1969, operating in the Lancaster area as seen above left. The lowbridge version only required the awkward offset-ganway layout for the rearmost three rows of seats on the upper deck but there was dissatifaction with the idea, causing the company to seek other solutions. The example shown, 1704 (PCK 337), dating from March 1961, was withdrawn in 1973, though finding further service with the Kowloon Motor Bus Co of Hong Kong – by contrast, the fifteen examples of the same type dating from 1962 remained in Ribble service until 1981-2.

Leyland Titan PD3/5 double-deckers, 1961-63

The return to the Titan PD3 for Ribble's main intake of double-deckers in 1961-3 must have been rather an embarassment to Leyland, but Ribble decided that, overall, the earlier model was a better bet for a few further years. The Metro-Cammell interpretation of Ribble's body style readily revealed its Orion origins, especially the look of the upper deck, as shown in this view of 1781 (RCK 926) of the 1962 batch. Note that the illuminated advertisement panel had not found a commercial user; as elsewhere, the idea did not prove the money spinner that had been expected.

The reappearance of the PD3 in Ribble new vehicle deliveries was a clear sign of the extent of disillusionment with the early Atlantean. Even so, it is noteworthy that the Pnuemo-cyclic gearbox was considered desirable and included in the specification for these final new examples of the Titan for the fleet. Burlingham, by then taken over by Duple, was no longer building double-deck bodywork, so responsibility for this was transferred to Metro-Cammell. The structure and basic outline was to that concern's standard, lacking the graceful lines of the Burlingham but superficially similar by virtue of having a similar full-fronted cab and deeper skirt panels than usually found on MCW bodies of the period. The first 50 were built between April and July 1961, followed by 45 in the spring of 1962 and a final 36 in May-June 1963. Withdrawals began in 1972 but quite a number ran until 1981 – the MCW body was more durable than some of its rather crude detailing suggested. The buses built in 1961 had centrifugal clutches when new but were later converted to a fluid flywheel specification to give quiter running. Later batches were thus equipped from new. Only the 1963 batch were built to the then newly authorised width of 2.5 metres (8ft 2½ins).

1706-55	PCK 347-396	Leyland PD3/5	Met.Camm.	H41/31F	1961
1756-1800	RCK 901-945	Leyland PD3/5	Met.Camm.	H41/31F	1962
1815-50	TCK 815-850	Leyland PD3/5	Met.Camm.	H41/31F	1963

Leyland Leopard L2T coaches, 1961

In 1959, with little publicity, Leyland had introduced a new single-deck model called the Leopard, at first in effect a Tiger Cub with the O.600 engine and synchromesh gearbox. It had obvious appeal as a coach, and Ribble's first examples were 35 on L2T chassis with two-speed axles. At that time, the BET group was becoming more inclined to order bodywork centrally and yet to be willing to place orders with any of a number of approved suppliers. Thus the bodywork on these vehicles was built by Thomas Harrington of Hove, a concern traditionally associated with fleets in the south of England, and in particular Southdown, a fleet which had many parallels to Ribble yet with its own strong traditions. Twenty seated 32 for touring duties, the remainder, with 41 seat capacity, were for general coach duty though 1039-48 also became 32-seat in 1962 – in later years most became 41-seat, though three became 39-seat in 1968. Four were withdrawn in 1969 but most ran until 1971-2.

1019-38	PCK 601-620	Leyland L2T	Harrington	C32F	1961
1039-53	PCK 621-635	Leyland L2T	Harrington	C41F	1961

Ribble's introduction to the Leyland Leopard involved the early version whose roots in the Tiger Cub chassis were self-evident from such details as the front wheels. The first 20, delivered in the spring and summer of 1961, were touring coaches, to which the relaxed output of the O.600 engine in a vehicle weighing 7tons 3cwt was well suited. These also introduced Harrington bodywork to the fleet at a time when that concern's Cavalier design was widely admired. At the time, Southdown was also taking delivery of a very similar fleet of touring coaches – the two operating companies, often having parallels, rarely found themselves so completely in step. Here 1038 is seen passing the Ribble and Standerwick booking office in St Annes when new.

Leyland Leopard PSU3/3RT coaches, 1962-65

The increase in maximum permitted length to 36ft (11 metres) in 1961 led to the introduction of the PSU3 series of Leopard models, longer and uprated in specification to allow for the extra weight. Ribble's first batch were six coaches on the PSU3/3RT chassis, which was a coach version with the four-speed synchromesh gearbox and two-speed axle. They had been ordered by Scout for its London service, but following the acquisition of that business were transferred to Ribble before entering service, being given numbers 701 upwards at the beginning of the series reserved for coaches, by then blank with the withdrawal of the PS1 coaches, and thus starting a new generation. They had bodywork by Duple (Northern), which was the name given for a time to the ex-Burlingham factory in Blackpool, to a design known as the Continental, one of a succession of styles from that works that came and went after the strong succes of the Seagull. They were equipped to quite high standards, having toilet compartments and seats for 40.

In April/June 1963, Harrington was again the favoured bodybuilder, with an extended version of the Cavalier design, seating 49 for general coach duties. In the period from October 1963 to March 1964, it was Plaxton's turn, this Scarborough-based concern having joined the ranks of approved suppliers to BET companies by virtue of its Panorama design with long and relatively deep side windows. A total of 25 examples were supplied in that period, though the first ten were allocated to Standerwick, having numbers with an S suffix, while four more were for Scout, with S-prefix numbers in the way used for a time. A final batch of coaches, 20 for Ribble, nine for Standerwick and four for Scout, on this version of the chassis appeared in April-June 1965, again with Plaxton bodies but to a revised Panorama design. These vehicles were withdrawn between 1970 and 1976.

701-706	SCK 866-871	Leyland PSU3/3RT	Duple (N.)	C40FT	1962
707-728	TCK 707-728	Leyland PSU3/3RT	Harrington	C49F	1963
729-738S	TRN 729-738	Leyland PSU3/3RT	Plaxton	C49F	1963
S739-742	TRN 739-742	Leyland PSU3/3RT	Plaxton	C49F	1963
743-763	TRN 743-763	Leyland PSU3/3RT	Plaxton	C49F	various
775-794	ARN 775-794C	Leyland PSU3/3RT	Plaxton	C49F	4/65
795-803S	ARN 795-803C	Leyland PSU3/3RT	Plaxton	C49F	4/65
S804-807	ARN 804-807C	Leyland PSU3/3RT	Plaxton	C49F	4/65

Ribble's first 36ft vehicles, placed in service in November 1962, were 'inherited', the six Leopards having been ordered by Scout. The body order went to Duple (Northern) for the Continental style which attracted only limited buyers, though these examples were equipped to a high standard, no doubt influenced by the competition on the London services from the Gay Hostess double-deckers. Here 705 (SCK 870) is seen in Bolton, with a Corporation PD3/East Lancs in the background.

The Harrington Cavalier was favoured in 36ft form for the 1963 batch of 22 coaches, the design being very similar to the shorter version, save for an extra bay. By this date, the idea of fixing the side windows and providing air-liner style forced-air ventilation had become generally accepted. Seen here when new in April 1963 are 707 and 708, with a pair of similar coaches for Standerwick.

The Plaxton Panorama body was chosen for Ribble's coach deliveries on Leopard chassis in 1963/4 and 1965, but the two batches differed quite considerably, the bold emphasis of length of the earlier style, represented (left) by 757, being abandoned in favour of a rather odd design with a deliberate break in the trim at about one-third of the length for the later version, restyled by Ogle, of which 777 is seen in a motorway view.

Leyland Leopard PSU3/1R buses, 1963-66

Leopard 36ft models in 53-seat bus form began to appear in the fleet in 1963, using the appropriate version of synchromesh chassis, these being the first new single-deck buses since the Tiger Cubs of 1954, the capacity enabling them to directly replace lowbridge Titans on appropriate duties. The BET group had operated a central purchasing system from its tramway days, going on to producing standardised designs for bus bodywork used by many associated companies. Apart from some of the early Daimler Y-types, Ribble had favoured manufacturers' or its own designs, but the standard BET Federation single-decker design was adopted for these vehicles concurrently with the arrival of a new General Manager, George Brook, who sought to stamp his own authority on the Company image.

Marshall was a concern with aircraft connections which had begun bus bodybuilding in the post-war period, but mainly for export until it began tendering successfully for BET orders in the early 'sixties. The first 40, delivered between June and October 1963, were to the then new Federation design, with the style of curved-glass windscreen that was later to be adopted for several other types, and 50 more delivered in March-May 1964 were almost identical, though one vehicle, 498, was used for development work on suspension by Leyland and not placed in service until November. The 1965 batches were split, with 70 by Weymann and 20 by Marshall, though the deliveries were divided in the more complex way shown, and spread from three early Weymann examples in December 1964, most of the rest through 1965 but the final vehicle, 627, in May 1966. Weymann's factory closed in 1965 and some of the last examples were completed by Metro-Cammell.

When new, these buses ran with conductors, but conversions to one-man operation were carried out from 1966, many of the earlier conversions being reduced to 45-seat capacity at the same time because of the restrictions imposed by the agreement with trade unions at the time, though this was not needed when the agreement was revised and earlier conversions later reverted to 53-seat. Renumbering of 458-61 to 683-6 took place in 1973 to avoid a clash with new Leyland Nationals. General withdrawal began in 1976, but quite a number survived to 1982.

458-497	TCK 458-497	Leyland PSU3/1R	Marshall	B53F	1963
498-547	UCK 498-547	Leyland PSU3/1R	Marshall	B53F	1964
548-567	ARN 548-567C	Leyland PSU3/1R	Weymann	B53F	various
568-587	ARN 568-587C	Leyland PSU3/1R	Marshall	B53F	1965
588-607	ARN 588-607C	Leyland PSU3/1R	Weymann	B53F	1965
608-627	CCK 608-627C	Leyland PSU3/1R	Weymann	B53F	various

A fleet of 170 almost identical buses with bodywork to the latest BET Federation design on Leopard PSU3 bus chassis was built up between 1963 and 1966. Hitherto, the lack of cream relief on Ribble's post-1951 single-deck bus livery had been offset by the use of polished aluminium trim, but here the effect was rather gloomy once the initial gloss wore off, despite the attractive lines. Marshall built the bodywork on a total of 110, including the first 40, of which the vehicle shown, 489, was one, arriving in Blackpool on an X4 working soon after delivery in August 1963. Alongside, a Lancashire United Guy Arab can be seen on similar duty on the X60.

Vehicles acquired from Standerwick, 1963-65

During this period, the following Royal Tiger coaches were transferred to Ribble, 1054-9 in March 1963, 1062 in January 1964 and 1077-8 in April 1965.

1054-59	EFV 145-150	Leyland PSU1/15	Duple	C41F	1951
1062	FFR 690	Leyland PSU1/15	Leyland	C41C	1952
1077-8	FFR 360,691	Leyland PSU1/15	Leyland	C41C	1952

Vehicles acquired from Michelin Tyres Ltd, Stoke-on-Trent, November 1963

The following pair of Leyland Leopard coaches had been used to demonstrate Michelin X radial tyres, then new in coach sizes.

1060-1	821-822 YEH	Leyland L2T	Plaxton	C41F	1/63

Vehicles acquired from Scout, 1964-65

Various transfers to and from Scout took place whilst it was run as a subsidiary, including two PD2 buses that had been Ribble 2642/51 but returned from Scout in February 1964 as 2778/9. The following Tiger Cubs, acquired by Ribble in April 1965, had been new to Scout:-

1079-80	JCK 688, 691	Leyland PSUC1/2	Duple	C41C	3/56

Leyland Leopard PSU3 dual-purpose vehicles, 1964-65

The 'layer-cake' cream and crimson livery gave a suitably glamorous look to the BET Federation single-decker – this view of 765, 767 and 772 shows the curved glass rear window which was also a feature of the design.

The BET Federation body was also produced in dual-purpose form, with coach seats and livery but based on the bus shell, and capable of use on either coach or bus duties – most vehicles in these batches were equipped for one-man working in 1966-8. The first ten were produced by Marshall in 1964, but a further ten of generally similar design by Weymann in April-June 1965, were on 'coach'-type chassis, all of the foregoing having synchromesh gearboxes, though 767 was fitted with a Pneumo-cyclic gearbox in 1967 and ran until 1980, being renumbered to 889 in 1977. The rest were withdrawn in 1976-7.

764-773	TRN 764-773	Leyland PSU3/1RT	Marshall	DP49F	3/64
808-817	ARN 808-817C	Leyland PSU3/3RT	Weymann	DP49F	1965

Albion Lowlander LR1 double-deckers. 1964-65

The Ribble version of the Lowlander had a full-fronted cab but differed from the designs used on the PD3 in having a projecting front cowl and, with the variations in window levels of the Alexander body, lacked their cleanness of line. Seen here is 1855 (UCK 855), in company with 1955 (ECK 955E), one of the Atlantean PDR1/2 buses with Northern Counties bodywork, a later essay at the low-height double-decker concept.

A front-engined low-floor double-deck model called the Lowlander was introduced as a joint exercise by Leyland and Albion (which had been a Leyland subsidiary since 1951) in 1961, primarily to suit the needs of the Scottish Bus Group. It was based on the front end of the PD3 chassis, complete with O.600 engine, but with a low frame and a drop-centre rear axle which allowed the lower-deck floor line to be low enough to permit centre gangways in both decks while maintaining overall height at the 'lowbridge' level, much in the manner first introduced on the Bristol Lodekka in the 'fifties. Ribble considered this a preferable design to the lowbridge version of the early Atlantean, and ten examples of the Lowlander LR1, with Pneumo-cyclic gearbox, were added to the fleet in February-March 1964, followed by six more in April-May 1965. Alexander had bodied most of the Scottish examples, and was given the Ribble order, based on its existing design, but with full-fronted cab to suit Ribble's preference. The result was rather oddly proportioned, but quite practical, and they remained in service until 1976-7. Although built by Albion, Leyland practice at the time was to market those sold in England as Leyland products but Ribble always regarded them as Albions.

1851-60	UCK 851-860	Albion LR1	Alexander	H41/31F	1964
1861-66	ARN 861-866C	Albion LR1	Alexander	H41/31F	1965

Leyland Panther PSUR1/2RT dual-purpose vehicle, 1964

Leyland introduced a new single-decker model in 1964, using many of the components of the Leopard, but with the O.600 engine mounted horizonatlly behind the rear-axle instead of amidships. The Pneumo-cyclic gearbox was standard. It was offered mainly in low-frame form for bus work, but the example built for Ribble was the first, and one of only a few, of the straight-framed type, intended as a coach chassis, though in this case with Marshall dual-purpose body, very like the 764-773 batch which immediately preceded it numerically. It was displayed in the demonstration park at the Commercial Motor Show that year, though initially placed in service a few months earlier. It proved to be less reliable than the Leopard, being prone to the overheating problems that plagued many early rear-engined types, and Ribble did not order any further examples. It was withdrawn in 1975. It introduced the suffix registration system into the fleet, this having begun with A in 1963.

774	ACK 774B	Leyland PSUR1/2RT	Marshall	DP49F	7/64

Leyland Panther 774 remained unique, proving to lack the Leopard's good reliability record. Here it is seen on private hire duty.

A return to 44-seat single-deckers only slightly longer than those of the 'fifties was made with the Leopard PSU4 models added to the fleet in 1966-7

Leyland Leopard PSU3 and PSU4 buses, 1966-67

In 1965, a new generation of short-wheelbase Leopard, the PSU4, appeared, replacing the L1 and L2 and having more in common with the longer PSU3. In 1966-67, Ribble took batches of PSU4 before reverting to PSU3, standardising on the Pneumo-cyclic transmission instead of the synchromesh gearbox from this period. There were 30 PSU4/2R in April-July 1966, and 25 PSU4/4R (this being nominally a 'coach' chassis, but it was not uncommon for such apparent mismatches to be made because of the layout of auxiliaries) in November 1966-February 1967, all with Marshall 44-seat bodywork. In March-July 1967, 20 PSU3/4R with similar but longer bodywork were delivered, and as built these seated only one more, but this was a temporary expedient to suit the union agreement, and they were reseated to 53 in later years. General withdrawal began in 1977 though some vehicles remained in service to 1982.

628-657	CRN 628-657D	Leyland PSU4/2R	Marshall	B44F	1966
658-682	DRN 658-682D	Leyland PSU4/4R	Marshall	B44F	various
201-220	ECK 201-220D	Leyland PSU3/4R	Marshall	B45F	1967

Leyland Leopard PSU3 dual-purpose vehicles, 1966-68

This was a growing vehicle category, well matched to Ribble's need for vehicles suited to medium-distance express services. They followed a similar pattern to the buses in terms of specification, with fourteen PSU3/4R bodied by Marshall in April 1966 and again in June 1967, and 30 of the 'bus-type' PSU3/2R with Willowbrook bodywork in April-May 1968, the latter, built in Loughbrough, being an unfamiliar body maker for Ribble, though a supplier to other BET companies for many years. Conversion of the first batch for one-man operation took place in 1967, the second was so equipped from new and the rest altered in 1972-6. Withdrawals took place in 1977-81.

818-831	CRN 818-831D	Leyland PSU3/4R	Marshall	DP49F	4/66
890-903	ECK 890-903E	Leyland PSU3/4R	Marshall	DP49F	6/67
904-933	FCK 904-933F	Leyland PSU3/2R	Willowbrook	DP49F	1968

Leyland Leopard PSU3/4R coaches, 1966-68

The switch to Pneumo-cyclic transmission extended to coaches and indeed from 1966 onwards, gearboxes of this type or their equivalents of other makes were usual on new additions of most types to Ribble's fleet. The Plaxton Panorama had become Ribble's standard coach body, with batches of 22, fourteen and twelve in the three years, sub-divided by variations in specification to suit use, including allocations to Standerwick or Scout, with the 44-seat version with toilet for London services. Withdrawals began in 1976.

832-841	CRN 832-841D	Leyland PSU3/4R	Plaxton	C49F	1966
842-849S	CRN 842-849D	Leyland PSU3/4R	Plaxton	C44FT	1966
S850-853	CRN 850-853D	Leyland PSU3/4R	Plaxton	C44FT	1966
864-875	ECK 864-875E	Leyland PSU3/4R	Plaxton	C49F	4/67
876-880S	ECK 876-880E	Leyland PSU3/4R	Plaxton	C49F	5/67
881-885S	ECK 881-885E	Leyland PSU3/4R	Plaxton	C44FT	5/67
S886-887	ECK 886-887E	Leyland PSU3/4R	Plaxton	C49F	5/67
S888-889	ECK 888-889E	Leyland PSU3/4R	Plaxton	C44FT	5/67
934-941S	FCK 934-941F	Leyland PSU3/4R	Plaxton	C49F	4/68
S942-945	FCK 942-945F	Leyland PSU3/4R	Plaxton	C49F	4/68

Bedford VAM5 coaches, 1966

A surprising purchase was that of ten Bedford VAM5 coaches in April-May 1966. These were Ribble's first examples of the make, the VAM introduced in 1965 being a front-engined model, though with set-back front axle. It thus allowed the use of bodywork, in this case Plaxton Panorama, looking outwardly like that of underfloor-engined models, though of shorter 9.5-metre length. It used many components in common with Bedford's mass-produced goods range, including the vertical Bedford 330cu in (5.4-litre) diesel engine and a synchromesh gearbox. They received the seats from the 1961 Leopard L2T Harrington coaches 1019-28, being intended for Kingfisher tours, but, perhaps not surprisingly, were found to be less satisfactory, especially in terms of noise level, and were sold in 1969.

854-863	CRN 854-863D	Bedford VAM5	Plaxton	C32F	1966

For the first and only time, Bedford was included among the makes of new vehicle added to the fleet in 1966, when ten of the VAM5 type with Plaxton Panorama bodywork were purchased. They looked very like contemporary underfloor-engined models, as can be seen in this view, showing Bedford 855 at the right of a line otherwise comprised of Leopards 644 (Marshall bus), 840 (Plaxton coach) and 818 (Marshall dual-pupose). The vertical engine of the Bedford was mounted ahead of the front axle and covered by a cowl between the driver and entrance step.

Leyland Atlantean PDR1/2 double-deckers, 1966-67

The PDR1/2 was a means of producing the Atlantean in low-height form without the need for using the 'lowbridge' sunken side gangway layout at all. The Daimler Fleetline had solved this problem and its Daimatic gearbox, similar to the Pneumo-cyclic in principle, but with an ingenious concentric drive allowing a simple transmission layout, was used in conjunction with an Albion Lowlander rear axle to produce an equivalent version of the Atlantean – it is noteworthy that at that date Daimler was a very successful competitor to Leyland with the Fleetline. Alexander got the body order for Ribble's first ten, supplied in June-July 1966, and having the well-rounded look then becoming well-established as the D-type on Fleetline chassis, though these particular bodies were designated H-type in Alexander's alphabetical system. In 1967, Northern Counties was successful, bodying fifteen delivered in May-June, making Ribble a customer for the first time since 1944, its body design being noteworthy in using BET-type windscreens. Examples of both types ran until 1979-82.

1867-76	CRN 867-876D	Leyland PDR1/2	Alexander	H44/31F	1966
1951-65	ECK 951-965E	Leyland PDR1/2	N.Counties	H41/31F	1967

The PDR1/2 version of the Atlantean was a surprising co-operative effort between Leyland and Daimler at a time when they were direct, and fierce, competitors for double-deck bus market leadership, Leyland conceding, in effect, that the lowbridge version of the PDR1/1 was unsatisfactory, and Daimler willing to sell the gearbox which was the key exclusive feature of the Fleetline – perhaps the moral victory appealed to them. Ribble had two batches, both notable for use of curved windscreen glass designed for single-deckers, the front transferring directly and the rear going to the upper-deck front. The first batch, with Alexander bodywork, is illustrated on page 127 of Volume 1. The second, comprising fifteen buses with Northern Counties bodywork, is represented by 1952 (ECK 952E) seen on the Lancaster-Keswick route which was regularly operated by these vehicles.

Only one of the vehicles added to Ribble's fleet from the BBMS business had been new to that operator, this being Atlantean 2295 TE, with lowbridge body, built by Weymann but virtually identical to the Metro-Cammell examples supplied direct to Ribble. It is seen in the smart condition so typical of this operator.

Vehicles acquired from Bamber Bridge Motor Services, April 1967

The business of J. and T. Prescott, of Bamber Bridge, using the abbreviated B.B.M.S. form of its title as fleetname, had operated quite a number of interesting vehicles but only three, two Leyland Atlantean and an Albion Lowlander, passed into Ribble's fleet on takeover, numbers 1966 and 1968 havng been demonstrators. They remained in Ribble service until 1972, 1979 and 1975 respectively.

1966	661 KTJ	Leyland PDR1/1	Weymann	L39/34F	9/59
1967	2295 TE	Leyland PDR1/1	Weymann	L39/33F	1/63
1968	747 EUS	Albion LR1	Alexander	H41/31F	2/62

Vehicles acquired from Standerwick, 1967-68

Further coaches transferred were Tiger Cubs 1062-8 in March 1967, and Leopards 729-730 in January 1968. The former ran until 1968-9, and the latter until 1974-5.

1062-68	NFR 956-962	Leyland PSUC1/2	Burlingham	C41F	6/58
729-730	TRN 729-730	Leyland PSU3/3RT	Plaxton	C49F	1963

Vehicles acquired from Scout Motor Services Ltd, 1968

Scout was absorbed by Ribble in October 1968, but the four Tiger Cub coaches with Duple (Midland) bodywork listed first had been transferred in March of that year. The final transfer was largely of vehicles that originated with Scout when independent, though Atlantean 1970 was originally a Leyland demonstrator. The PD3/3 buses had bodywork basically like Ribble's contemporary PD3/4, but had half cabs

Scout's PD3 buses were basically a half-cab version of the Ribble eqivalent, with similar Burlingham bodies, though on the PD3/3 chassis having the concealed radiator front-end then offered by Leyland. MCK 370 of the final batch is seen here when Scout was a Ribble subsidiary – it was to become Ribble 1977, running until 1975. Alongside is one of the 'White Lady' Atlanteans, 1282 (RRN 431).

Among the coaches taken into Ribble's fleet when Scout was absorbed was 1074, the Leyland Leopard L2 seen here, with Duple (Midland) bodywork to a rare straight-waisted design with relatively large windows and Brittania-style external trim – it was one of five dating from 1961. The batch did not remain in the fleet for long, being withdrawn in 1969 and sold to a dealer in February 1970. This vehicle was one of two rebodied by Plaxton in 1971, in this case going to Healey of Westport, Eire.

and the standard concealed radiator front-end of the time, the only examples in Ribble's fleet. The PD3/3 was a vacuum-brake model, but it is thought that they may have been converted to air-pressure by Ribble. In addition to the vehicles listed, Titan PD2 double-deckers 1396, 1446/7/56 had been transferred from Ribble to Scout in 1965, reverting to their original status and numbers on return, and Leopard PSU3/4R coaches S886-8 dating from 1967 joined the Ribble fleet as 886-8.

1069-72	NRN 166-169	Leyland PSUC1/2	Duple (M.)	C41F	1/60
1073-7	PRN 146-150	Leyland L2	Duple (M.)	C38FT	1961
1969	OCK 500	Leyland PDR1/1	Met.Camm.	H44/33F	5/60
1970	398 JTB	Leyland PDR1/1	Met.Camm.	H44/33F	6/59
1971-3	PRN 143-145	Leyland PDR1/1	Met.Camm.	H44/33F	1961
1974-5	LRN 62-63	Leyland PD3/3	Burlingham	H41/31F	5/58
1976-8	MCK 369-371	Leyland PD3/3	Burlingham	H41/31F	1/59

Bristol RE buses, 1968-72

A profound change began to occur in the bus operating and manufacturing industries in the late 'sixties, and additions to the Ribble fleet reflected this. In 1965, Leyland took a 25% shareholding in Bristol Commercial Vehicles Limited, which had been State-owned since 1948 and prevented by legislation from selling to operators in other sectors. This arrangement enabled BCV to sell on the open market, and Ribble was one of several operators interested. The RE model, first introduced in 1962, was widely agreed to be the most successful of the first generation of British rear-engined single-deckers. An initial order for ten was placed. Meanwhile, and unbeknown to the operating companies or indeed anyone outside those directly involved, negotiations were in hand for the purchase of BET's interests in bus operation in Britain by the State-owned Transport Holding Company, which already controlled the Tilling operating companies, Bristol and ECW. Agreement was announced in November 1967. By the time the first vehicles were arriving, the purchase was being completed, and it was widely accepted that vehicle policies of ex-BET and Tilling companies would tend to come into line, but Ribble's initiative had ben taken before this was so. The first ten, entering service between May and August 1968, were on RELL6L chassis, with Leyland O.680 engines, and had ECW bodywork generally very similar to that supplied to Tilling companies, though with Ribble-type destination blinds. They were of two-door layout and had the modest seating capacity for 11-metre vehicles of 41, being licensed to carry up to 31 standing passengers, there being widespread interest in such 'standee' buses at the time, but quite soon this latter figure was reduced to 25. They were used on urban routes in Liverpool and Chorley. A further 30 generally similar buses, but with Gardner 6HLX engines, entered service between March and July 1969 – Ribble had

The first Bristol RE buses arrived in Ribble's fleet in May 1968, just after the company became State owned. In fact, the agreement in principle to buy them, complete with ECW bodywork, had been made on 11th July 1967, when Ribble was still part of the strongly free-enterprise BET group. Even though Leyland was helping Bristol and ECW to compete in the open market, such success right on Leyland's doorstep was embarrassing. This vehicle is part of the second batch of 36ft RELL saloons, although by now Gardner 6HLX engines were fitted. The ECW body, although seating 41 like the earlier batch, was fitted with the tall flat windscreen later adopted (to assist tall drivers!) and normal centre doors. The plug type fitted to the 221-30 batch had not been successful.

The last batch of Bristol REs to be bought was one of forty RESL6L vehicles with ECW body, by now fitted with the BET windscreen. Number 347 (OCK 347K) is seen in standard National bus livery just before the split of the company.

become part of the National Bus Company group on its activation on 1st January 1969. Even so, the choice of Gardner engines for these vehicles was noteworthy, they being the first of this make for Ribble since the wartime Guys. After this 'Tilling-like' beginning, the deliveries made in the period from November 1970 to July 1971 of 49 RE models to Ribble reverted to a more BET-style choice of bodybuilder and appearance – work in hand and the need to set up a new integrated organisation meant that in early NBC days, existing patterns tended to continue to some degree. They were of the shorter RESL chasis, with Leyland engines, and had Marshall 47-seat bodywork, with single doorway. Finally, a return to ECW was made for 40 more RESL 47-seat buses entering service between April 1971 and July 1972. Withdrawals began in 1980 but some survived to be transferred to the new North Western Road Car Co Ltd in 1986.

221-230	FRN 221-230F	Bristol RELL6L	ECW	B41D	1968
231-260	HRN 231-260G	Bristol RELL6G	ECW	B41D	1969
282-330	LRN 282-330J	Bristol RESL6L	Marshall	B47F	1970
331-338	NCK 331-338J	Bristol RESL6L	ECW	B47F	1971
339-340	NCK 339-340K	Bristol RESL6L	ECW	B47F	8/71
341-370	OCK 341-370K	Bristol RESL6L	ECW	B47F	1971/2

Leyland Leopard coaches with Plaxton bodywork, 1969-71

Ribble continued to favour Plaxton coach bodywork in this period, but a marked change in appearance resulted from the adoption of the new Panorama Elite style introduced at the 1968 Show, with its curved-glass side windows, which set the styling pattern for most coaches placed in service by NBC fleets for its first decade or so. Leyland was using suffix letters to indicate design changes to an increasing degree, and the PSU3A and PSU4A signified the 'rationalised' Pneumo-cyclic gearbox, while new axle units were denoted by PSU3B and PSU4B. The 30 examples delivered in April-May 1969 were 49-seat 11-metre models but in March-April 1970 a switch was made to approximately 10-metre length with relatively spacious 36-seat capacity for 25 coaches intended largely for touring duty. The April-June 1971 batch of eleven were also to this length, but with 43 seats for express duty. General withdrawal occurred in 1975-77, though 1024 were transferred to Standerwick in 1972; many passed to National Travel and quite a number to other NBC fleets.

A landmark in coach design was Plaxton's Panorama Elite, with curved-glass side windows, setting the pattern for most of the coaches produced by British bodybuilders in the 'seventies. Ribble can claim to have been in at the beginning, since its first example, 946, was one of the first of the type to be revealed, having been displayed on the Plaxton stand at the Commercial Motor Show in October 1968, though not entering service until the following spring. The 1970/71 deliveries were of similar style, but on the shorter PSU4 chassis – 976, seen here being the first, dating from March 1970, with 36-seat capacity for touring duty.

946-975	HRN 946-975G	Leyland PSU3A/4R	Plaxton	C49F	1969
976-999	KCK 976-999H	Leyland PSU4A/4R	Plaxton	C36F	1970
1000	KCK382H	Leyland PSU4A/4R	Plaxton	C36F	1970
1001-11	NCK 101-111J	Leyland PSU4B/4R	Plaxton	C43F	1971

Vehicles acquired from United Automobile Services Ltd, January 1969.

The majority of the buses transferred from United along with its Carlisle services on 5th January 1969 were Bristol MW models with ECW 45-seat bodywork, the most recent five being of the MW6G type with Gardner 6HLW engines. Number 278 (8687 HN) dating from 1963, seen here, was among those that remained in service until 1974. After sale, it ran for S. M. Ementon, of Cranfield, for a couple of years. As with later generations of ECW body, the traditional Ribble colours suited the design well, introducing a touch of variety to the brighter red then so familiar with United and many other former Tilling fleets.

The merger of the BET and Tilling operating groups allowed some rationalisation of services, and four days after the commencement of NBC the transfer of United's share of the Carlisle local services was effected, together with 21 vehicles. United had run some double-deckers in Carlisle and at first it was planned that three Bristol KSW6B were to be included. However such vehicles, with Bristol engines as well as being quite old, though intriguing from an enthusiast's viewpoint, would have been inappropriate for the Ribble fleet, and three delicensed PD2 buses were reinstated instead.
The fleet transferred comprised five of the Bristol-ECW LS5G integral model and sixteen of the mechanically similar but conventional MW chassis with separate ECW body. Most were withdrawn in 1970-72, but the newest six ran with Ribble until 1974.

261	689 BHN	Bristol LS5G	ECW	B45F	2/56
262/7	632/59 CHN	Bristol LS5G	ECW	B45F	1957
263-264	271/5 EHN	Bristol LS5G	ECW	B45F	1957
265	514 FHN	Bristol MW5G	ECW	B45F	1958
266/8-9	543/72/9 LHN	Bristol MW5G	ECW	B45F	various
270	2590 HN	Bristol MW5G	ECW	DP45F	1961
271	2619 HN	Bristol MW5G	ECW	B45F	1961
272-276	5040-3/51	Bristol MW5G	ECW	B45F	1962
277-279	8685/7/96 HN	Bristol MW6G	ECW	B45F	1963
280-281	KHN 729-730D	Bristol MW6G	ECW	B45F	1966

Vehicles acquired from Standerwick, 1970

Four Gay Hostess Atlantean double-deck coaches were transferred to Ribble in March 1970, 1286-7 having begun life as Ribble 1263-4, having passed to Scout in 1963 and Standerwick in 1968, while 1288-9 had been new to Standerwick. They were withdrawn in 1971.

1286-7	NRN 612-613	Leyland PDR1/1	Weymann	H34/16FT	8/60
1288-9	SFV 413/20	Leyland PDR1/1	Weymann	H34/16FT	6/60

Bristol VRT double-deckers, 1971-72

Bristol's original intention to use the longitudinal rear-engine layout for its production VR double-deckers was abandoned in favour of a transverse engine position. Thus the VRT model went into production at the end of 1968, with ECW 70-seat bodywork as standard, almost instantly becoming the main double-decker for NBC fleets. Ribble had not added any new double-deckers to its fleet since 1967, and its first VRT appeared in May 1971, delivery continuing intermittently until July 1972, by which date the batch of 23 had been completed. Like almost all NBC orders at that stage, they were of the low-height type, the VRT/SL chassis permitting this with centre gangways. They had Gardner 6LX engines and were of the early body style with flat-glass windscreens, entering service equipped for one-man operation, as was to be standard henceforth, though 1979-84 were converted after delivery. The earlier vehicles of this batch were delivered in traditional Ribble cherry red but the corporte NBC poppy red appeared on the last examples. Five went to the Crosville fleet in 1983 – by that date inter-company transfers were quite commonplace within NBC.

The Bristol VRT with ECW body of the early standard type, built to 13ft 8in overall height, was another instance of a standard Tilling design looking well in Ribble cherry red (sometimes described as crimson), and cream, but it was a combination only seen on a limited number of vehicles, this example, 1987 (OCK 987K), being among those dating from February 1972 whereas the last few of the batch, appearing in July, were in NBC poppy red and white. Carlisle depot was the recipient, gaining another strand of Tilling flavour in its rolling stock. The condensed destination blind lettering hardly made for legibility.

1979-80	NCK 979-980J	Bristol VRT/SL6LX	ECW	H39/31F	1971
1981-84	NCK 981-984K	Bristol VRT/SL6LX	ECW	H39/31F	9/71
1985-99	OCK 985-999K	Bristol VRT/SL6LX	ECW	H39/31F	1972
2000-01	OCK 100-101K	Bristol VRT/SL6LX	ECW	H39/31F	7/72

Bristol RELH coaches, 1972

The ECW coach body produced for the Bristol RE in 1972 was an ingenious design with overall appearance quite similar to the styles being offered by the major coach specialist bodybuilders, yet using flat glass for the side windows. Ribble had ten, though the main intake of coaches continued to be based on the Leyland Leopard, and thus these were rather regarded as odd men out in the fleet. The former Ribble 1021 is seen here in 1983, after sale to Crosville, in which fleet it had become ERL528. The switch to TF registration marks, breaking Ribble's previous virtually exclusive use of CK or RN for new vehicles, was a reflection of Preston becoming merged with Lancashire so far as motor vehicle licensing was concerned from the spring of 1972.

The Bristol RE had been produced in coach form since first going into production, but Ribble's first examples were ten delivered in August to October 1972. They had ECW coach bodywork to a style then newly put into production which had the same windscreens as the Plaxton Panorama Elite, but used flat glass for the side windows yet had an overall appearance which was in line with the generally accepted taste of the period. They had Leyland O.680 engines. These vehicles were not popular with Ribble as full coaches and were soon downgraded to dual-purpose status. This entailed the fitment of internal luggage bins and ticket-issuing equipment. They were repainted into 'local coach' livery (poppy red/white) with extra external trim under the windows being added at the same time. They were withdrawn in 1982-4, many going to Crosville.

1012-21	PTF 707-716L	Bristol RELH6L	ECW	C49F	1972

Leyland National buses, 1972-74

The Leyland National, developed from what at first had been primarily a Leyland project for a single-decker intended for city service, went into production in 1972 as a joint enterprise between Leyland and NBC, built in a factory expressly designed for its volume production. Its main features were the integral structure built up from pressed steel components, with the horizontal Leyland 510 turbocharged engine of 8.2-litre capacity mounted under the rear floor, and air suspension. Ribble chose the longer 11.3-metre length and two-door layout for its first 50 examples. The first few were supplied with 44-seat capacity to allow for a fairly large number of standing passengers, and painted in Ribble cherry red, though altered to 48 and resprayed NBC poppy red before entering service, beginning in November 1972. Delivery continued to July 1973, the next 40, of single-door type, began arriving in August, delivery continuing to April 1974. Most of the first batch were rebuilt to B49F between 1979 and 1983, those remaining as B48D being 372/81-3/5/96/7,400/15.

371-385	PTF 717-731L	Leyland National 1151/2R	B48D	1972
386-420	PTF 732-766L	Leyland National 1151/2R	B48D	1973
421-460	NTC 601-640M	Leyland National 1151/1R	B49F	various

The first Leyland Nationals in Ribble's fleet marked a change from previous practice in several respects, quite apart from the new thinking in terms of vehicle design. The first vehicle, 371 (PTF 717L), is seen in NBC's newly adopted unrelieved corporate poppy red livery and rather bland fleetname lettering with the double N logo. Grey wheels were now standard throughout the group so as to permit freedom of interchange if a wheel was changed in another company's garage. The bus was one of the initial fifteen examples that entered service in November 1972, they and the remainder of the first 50 having the two-door layout as built, though single-door was to be standard for subsequent Nationals delivered to the fleet and most of the early ones were rebuilt thus in later years.

Leyland Leopard PSU5 12-metre coach, 1972

There was speculation that 701, as well as being the third holder of the initial number in the 'coach' series, suggesting the beginning of a new Ribble coach generation, might be the precursor of a new nationwide fleet of similar coaches run by NBC when it was exhibited at the 1972 Commercial Motor Show. As it turned out, no more of the type were built, yet a decade or so later somewhat similar ideas were widely adopted.

This vehicle was exhibited at the Commercial Motor Show in 1972, joining the Ribble fleet in November of that year. Its bodywork was of Alexander's M type, largely as introduced in 1968 by the Scottish Bus Group for its overnight London services, though 701 used the 12-metre PSU5 version of the Leopard chassis rahter than the Bristol RE. It was intended to explore the views of the then recently-appointed NBC Chairman, Fred Wood, who was much impressed with the American Greyhound system and was seeking to emulate some of its ideas with the formation of National Travel and the white coach livery of which this vehicle was the first example in Ribble's fleet. It was lent to National Travel (South East) in 1974, but remained unique within NBC. It was renumbered 1200 in 1976, retaining that number with National Travel (North West) to whom it had passed in May of that year.

701	RTF 561L	Leyland PSU5/4R	Alexander	C46FT	1972

Vehicles acquired from Standerwick, 1972 & 1974

Five Leopards dating from 1965 and 1967 were transferred from Standerwick to Ribble in 1972 (the vehicles in question, originally 795-6S, taken into the latter's stock in January, and the former 876-8S, in December, simply losing the S suffix to their fleet numbers). Standerwick was in the process of vanishing as a result of the setting up of National Travel and the March 1974 transfer of eight more Leopards, dating from 1963, was the final such transfer. These had been 731/3/5/7S and S739-42 when new, the latter four having begun life allocated to Scout, and again regained their original numbers but without suffixes.

Leyland Leopard coaches with Duple bodywork, 1973-80

Duple introduced its Dominant range of coach bodywork in 1972, using a new steel-framed structure and having curved side windows of similar contour, though not quite as much length, as the Plaxton Elite and thus having quite similar overall appearance. Ribble standardised on the Dominant for the rest of the 'eighties. A total of 112 were supplied, beginning with nineteen in July 1973. Another nineteen followed in May-August 1974, twelve in June-July 1976, fourteen in January-August 1977, 23 in August-1978-May 1979 and 25 in October 1979-June 1980. The Leopard type designation successively changed, with PSU3C having uprated brakes, D signifying the standardisation of the close-

Ribble switched to Duple's then new Dominant as its standard coach on the Leopard chassis from 1973, thereby reverting to Blackpool as the source of its coach bodywork – the formerly Hendon-based concern had moved its entire operation to that town by 1970, concentrating its activities on what had been the Duple (Northern) and, before that, Burlingham premises. The general resemblance in style to that of the Plaxton Panorama Elite was related to the recruitment by Duple from the Scarborough concern of John Ruddy, though under the skin it was of quite different construction. The ribbed stainless-steel strip below the side windows was perhaps the most obvious recognition point, as shown here by 1048 (UTF 728M), when new in June 1974. This example is in the second version of the National Coach livery.

ratio Pneumo-cyclic gearbox and E altered reservoir positions. Withdrawals of the earlier vehicles began in 1980, many going to other NBC fleets. The Duple body style also evolved; the original design had two distinct phases at this time, becoming known as the Dominant I. Subsequent examples for the Ribble group were of the Dominant 2 which had been restyled by Michelotti. These had deep front windscreens, a shallow single-piece rear screen, and new light clusters both front and rear. Ribble's examples were of the National Bus variant of the Dominant 2, having simplified side mouldings to accomodate the 'National' fleetname on appropriate examples and, over the windscreen, destination indicators in the so-called 'Bristol dome '. Many vehicles were of 'Express' pattern, having two-piece doors in laminated glass to facilitate one-man-operation. These would have qualified for Standard New Bus Grant, then 50% of original cost, providing they spent at least half their time on Stage Carriage Work. All vehicles of the Express pattern were delivered and operated in red/white Local Coach (Dual-Purpose) livery. Earlier full-coach examples staying with Ribble were painted in this livery when downgraded for one-man-operation later.

1022-26	WTF 568-572L	Leyland PSU3B/4R	Duple	C49F	7/73
1027-40	XTF 801-814L	Leyland PSU3B/4R	Duple	C49F	7/73
1041-59	UTF 721-739M	Leyland PSU3B/4R	Duple	C49F	1974
1072-83	PCW 672-683P	Leyland PSU3C/4R	Duple	C49F	1976
1084-86	VRN 84-86R	Leyland PSU3D/4R	Duple	C49F	1977
1087-97	YFR 487-497R	Leyland PSU3E/4R	Duple	C47F	1977
1098-1120	KRN 98-120T	Leyland PSU3E/4R	Duple	C47F	various
1121-45	WCK 121-145V	Leyland PSU3E/4R	Duple	C49F	various

Leyland National 10.3 metre bus, 1973, battery-electric conversion, 1974

A single Leyland National of the shorter 10.3-metre length was delivered in October 1973 and its conversion to battery electric conversion undertaken by Ribble, on behalf of NBC, at Government request. The shorter model was favoured to keep down the overall length, as a two-axle Dyson trailer was used to house the 7 tons of batteries required, the complete outfit being 44ft 8in (13.7 metres) long overall. A Bosch 120hp motor replaced the diesel engine. It was capable of 39mph but the range on an 8-hour charge was only 60-80 miles, and it was decided to lend it to Crosville for operation on the Runcorn busway, where operating conditions were more favourable than in normal road traffic, from November 1975. It was sold to Crosville in February 1978, although broken up for body spares by that company in September 1981. It is illustrated on page 131 of Volume 1.

461	OTF 354M	Leyland National 1051/1R		B41F	1973

Leyland Atlantean AN68 Park Royal double-deckers, 1973-76

An unexpected departure from the initial NBC standardisation on Bristol-ECW double-deckers led to the supply of batches of the much-improved AN68 version of the Atlantean. Park Royal bodywork to a style based on that builder's standard of the time, derived from a version first produced for London Country using the Alexander design of windscreen was fitted. The distinctive overall appearance belied this rather complex ancestry, as conveyed by this view of two at Crosby in May 1974 – 1339, nearer the camera, had entered service the previous month and 1320 in January of that year. Note the grey glazing gasket favoured by NBC for a short period in the mid 'seventies.

Leyland introduced the AN68 series of Atlantean in 1972, not greatly altered in basic design from the PDR1/1 but with much detail revision designed to improve reliability. NBC placed orders for such vehicles with Park Royal bodywork for some of its subsidiaries, mainly of BET origin, including Ribble, which built up a fleet of 104. The first 42 entered service between December 1973 and April 1974, a further 48 following from September 1974 to January 1975 and the final 34 between December 1975 and March 1976. These distinctive vehicles proved very successful, the class remaining intact until the splitting of the fleet to form the new North Western company in 1986.

1301-42	RTF 612-653M	Leyland AN68/1R	Park Royal	H43/30F	various
1343-70	GBV 121-148N	Leyland AN68/1R	Park Royal	H43/30F	various
1371-1404	NRN 371-404P	Leyland AN68/1R	Park Royal	H43/31F	various

Vehicles acquired from North Western Road Car Co Ltd, Stockport, 1973-74

The old North Western company had lost its bus operations as the result of the take-over of most of them by SELNEC PTE (later Greater Manchester Transport), becoming effectively a coach company and indeed used as the basis of National Travel (North West). Hence the process of 'cascading' older Leopard coaches not considered suitable for the latter's needs resulted in them being transferred to Ribble. 1067-71 were acquired in October 1973 and 1062-6 in March 1974. The Harrington bodies were of the Grenadier type, a mildly updated version of the Cavalier, while the Alexander bodies were of the well-known Y type, not hitherto seen in Ribble's fleet.

1062-63	AJA 150-151B	Leyland L2T	Harrington	C41F	1964
1064-66	DDB 152-154C	Leyland L2T	Harrington	C41F	1965
1067-71	NJA 310-314G	Leyland PSU3A/4R	Alexander	C49F	1969

Leyland Atlantean AN68 ECW double-deckers, 1976-81

The combination of AN68 chassis with ECW body was chosen for much of Ribble's double-deck needs in the late 'seventies, the combination being of full height. The first 32 entered service in April-September 1976, 20 more following in August 1979-February 1980 and a final 30 in December 1980-February 1981. The AN68A had a modified gearbox with G2 automatic control and the AN68B incorporated further minor changes.

The ECW body for Atlantean chassis was of full 14ft 6in height, unlike the more usual version for the Bristol VRT chassis. The main body structure was higher-built, but the windscreen, by then of BET type on ECW bus bodies, remained in much the same relationship to the driving position, resulting in a deeper between-decks white band across the front of the vehicle. In addition, the familiar Atlantean 'bustle' remained at the rear. Seen here is 1435 (SFV 435P) bound for Blackpool – by coincidence, in an earlier era its registration letters would have implied origination in that town, but the FV combinations were among those transferred to the Preston LVLO under the post-1974 redistribution. These were sound vehicles, even if they did not have quite the eye-catching 'presence' of the Park Royal type and, with 82 examples, were not far short in numbers.

1405-24	RFR 405-436P	Leyland AN68/1R	ECW	H43/31F	1976
1425-36	SFV 425-436P	Leyland AN68/1R	ECW	H43/31F	1976
1466-85	TRN 466-485V	Leyland AN68A/1R	ECW	H43/31F	various
1486-1515	FBV 486-515W	Leyland AN68B/1R	ECW	H43/31F	various

Leyland National buses, 1976-79

A revised specification for the National was adopted from the spring of 1976, called Phase II at the time, but not to be confused with the National 2 of 1980. The most important change was the repositioning of the batteries under the cab to aid weight distribution and balance brake operation. Ribble took delivery of 74 of the 11.3-metre version in July 1976-April 1977, except that one, 755, which entered service in July, acted as a precursor of the National 2 in having a Leyland O.680 engine. A further batch of five also arrived in July 1977, followed by 33 in August 1977-July 1978. A pre-production example of the 'B' type National, with under-seat heating system and other features to simplify the specification, was operated from February 1978, at first on loan from Leyland Vehicles, using the fleet number 461 vacated by the battery-electric National. It was acquired in April 1979. The model was offered only in 10.3-metre form and eleven more were added in August-September 1979.

687-715	SCK 687-715P	Leyland National 11351A/1R	B49F	1976
716-760	UHG 716-760R	Leyland National 11351A/1R	B49F	various

The Classic Leyland National. An 'A' series Mark I, 761 (ACW 761R) of 1977 shows the clean line of the model and NBC bus livery when brand new. Ribble, however, always managed to retain its own typeface for route numbers – from the war right on to privatisation. No other company used this version. The white waistband had been introduced as a concession from the unrelieved red of earlier examples.

The type B version of the National was readily identifiable by the lack of roof pod, as well as the rows of louvres in the front panel, both features giving clues to the simplified heating and ventilating system. It was available only in the 10.3-metre length. When a pre-production vehicle was taken into the fleet in February 1978, at first on loan, it was given the number 461 vacated by the previous Leyland National of this length in the fleet, the battery bus, by then sold to Crosville. It is seen here two months later in Preston bus station, long a favourite location for photography, though the modern structure with multi-storey car park produced a very different background from the old Tithebarn Street premises.

761-765	ACW 761-765R	Leyland National 11351A/1R	B49F	7/77
766-798	CBV 766-798S	Leyland National 11351A/1R	B49F	various
461	GCW 461S	Leyland National 10351B/1R	B44F	2/78
802-812	TRN 802-812V	Leyland National 10351B/1R	B44F	1979

Ribble took delivery of one batch of eleven type-B Nationals in 1979, of which 802 (TRN 802V), seen in company with an MG Midget in Kendal five years later, was the first – the numbers 799-800 were allocated to National 2 prototypes and 801 left blank, its registration number being used for Ribble's first minibus.

Bristol VRT double-deckers, 1977-80

Further Bristol VRT buses with ECW bodywork entered the fleet after a five-year gap since the arrival of the previous 23, sixty being added in 1977-80, though this time split between lowheight and full-height versions, and all of the Series 3 type by then current. The first to arrive were 20 lowheight buses taking numbers which followed on from their predecessors of 1972, the example seen here being 2010 (CBV 10S), which had a Leyland 501 engine when new but had received a Gardner 6LXB by the time it was photographed in August 1985. Most of the type were similarly treated.

The full-height version of the ECW-bodied VRT had proportions much the same as the Atlantean-based vehicles, though readily distinguished from them by the grille needed with the front-mounted radiator of this model, and the rear-end, with engine housing incorporated within the body outline in usual VRT style. This scene in Carlisle in May 1984 shows the 'Autofare Bus' lettering, applied to quite a number of buses with this form of fare-collection equipment operating in that city, conveniently fitting within the deep white band over the windscreen on this body type. These vehicles were numbered in the same series as the AN68 buses of similar overall height, this being 1461 (TRN 461T), one of the last of the type, having entered service in November 1979. This version had the lower deck floor built ***on top*** *of the upsweep of the chassis at the front, giving an extra step into the saloon. Stability was not one of their strengths. The Marks & Spencers store on the left displayed plaques recording the use of earlier premises on the site by Bonnie Prince Charlie on his southward march in 1745 and by the Duke of Cumberland in 1746.*

Further deliveries of the Bristol VRT began in August-December 1977, when 20 on chassis with Leyland 501 engines were added to the fleet. They had 13ft 8in ECW bodywork and took fleet numbers 2002-21, which followed on from the previous batch of this height. A further 29 dating from November 1978 to a year later were of full height and were numbered 1437-65 to follow the Atlantean buses of similar height. Finally, eleven more buses, but built with Gardner 6LXB engines, became 2022-32 in August-October 1980. The Leyland 501 engine, a vertical version of the unit used in the Leyland National, was found to be unsatisfactory and all those so powered but 2003-5/712-4/8 were fitted with Gardner 6LXB units in 1982-3.

2002-21	CBV 2-21S	Bristol VRT/SL3/501	ECW	H43/31F	1977
1437-59	LHG 437-459T	Bristol VRT/SL3/501	ECW	H43/31F	various
1460-65	TRN 460-465V	Bristol VRT/SL3/501	ECW	H43/31F	1979
2022-32	DBV 22-32W	Bristol VRT/SL3/6LXB	ECW	H43/31F	1980

Ford Transit minibus

Ribble's first minibus was purchased for the Fell Runner service in the Penrith area. It was withdrawn in 1981, becoming a Ribble service vehicle.

1001	TRN 801V	Ford Transit	Dormobile	B16F	1979

Leyland National 2 buses, 1979-82

The casual observer, coming across 800 (NCW 880T) might well have deduced it was a series-B version of the National, built to 11.3metre length – a variant that was never offered. It was of that length but was the prototype National 2, which had the O.680 engine associated with that model but retained the early type of front-end because the radiator remained at the rear. It is seen here at Burnley in April 1985.

All but the last ten of Ribble's 75 production National 2 buses with L11 engines were of the shorter 10.6-metre length, which seemed to emphasise the different proportions given by the modified front-mounted radiator and the more deeply curved windscreen. Seen here is 848, (JCK848W), in the intermediate livery following Deregulation. This was poppy red and white, but with yellow fleetnames on the roof and 'Info-line' posters for its home area.

Ribble had carried out a test installation of a Leyland O.680 engine in a 1977 National, number 755, and it was logical that the prototype Leyland National 2, exhibited at the Motor Show in 1978 was for Ribble, numbered 800 and joining the fleet in January 1979. It had a Leyland 690 engine, another stage in the development of the 680, but was outwardly like previous Nationals, as it retained the rear-mounted radiator. It began running from Chorley depot the following month. By mid-1980, this vehicle had progressed to an L11 engine, the name given to a new-generation unit which was of the same 11.1-litre size and was to replace the 680. The number 799 and registration NCW 799T had been reserved for a second development vehicle, which had started life in 1978 as a pre-production prototype of the series B version of the National but in the event that was retained by Leyland for further modification and development into National 2 specification, eventually being registered as GFR 799W and not entering Ribble's fleet until 1981.

In January 1980 the first production National 2 models began to be delivered to operators, these having a front-mounted radiator and a more rounded windscreen of DAB origin, the length being increased by 300mm as compared to the earlier versions. Ribble's first examples, of the shorter type, now of 10.6-metre length, arrived in May. taking numbers 813 upwards, following those of the B-series buses. Thirty, with L11 engines, were delivered by the end of 1980, followed by 35 (in addition to the delayed 799, of 11,6-metre length) spread through 1981 and January to September 1982. Deliveries switched to 11.6-metre buses, with ten in August-December 1982.

800	NCW 800T	Leyland National 2	113690/1R	B52F	1/79
813-822	YRN 813-822V	Leyland National 2	NL106L11/1R	B44F	1980
823-827	BCW 823-827V	Leyland National 2	NL106L11/1R	B44F	7/80
828-842	DBV 828-842W	Leyland National 2	NL106L11/1R	B44F	1980
843-846	DBV 843-846W	Leyland National 2	NL106L11/1R	B44F	1981
799	GFV 799W	Leyland National 2	NL116690/1R	B49F	2/81
847-853	JCK 847-853W	Leyland National 2	NL106AL11/1R	B44F	1981
854-877	LFR 854-877X	Leyland National 2	NL106AL11/1R	B44F	various
878-887	RHG 878-887X	Leyland National 2	NL116AL11/1R	B52F	1982

Leyland Olympian double-deckers, 1980-83

Leyland developed a new double-deck chassis, initially given the project number B45, to replace the Atlantean, Fleetline and the Bristol VRT. Ability to accept low-height bodywork was one of its key features with a particular view to acting as a replacement for the VRT as hitherto supplied in this form to most NBC fleets. It was decided that it would be assembled by Bristol, though many features of its mechanical design were derived from that of the integral-construction rear-engined Leyland Titan then in production for London Transport. The most obvious differences were the use of air-pressure brakes and a rigid front axle. The second prototype chassis, B45-02, with Gardner 6LXB engine, was fitted with a new type of ECW 76-seat body to meet this requirement, and the completed vehicle supplied to Ribble in August 1980. Production of the model, by then called the Olympian, to generally similar design began in 1981 together with ECW lowheight bodywork,

The Leyland Olympian with ECW body was the direct successor to the VRT as the NBC group's standard double-decker, the earlier examples carrying this follow-on effect further by having chassis built in the Bristol works. There were strong elements of the Titan in the design, but the equal-height windows on both decks and the continuity of windscreen style gave the type its own distinctive appearance, as conveyed by 2113 (JFR 13W) of Ribble's first production batch, dating from October 1981.

The ECW body design of later Olympians did not alter significntly in general appearance but a coach-seated version was produced in response to the growing interest in such vehicles. Ribble's first three examples in the blue Timesaver livery are seen posed for a publicity photograph at Burnley garage soon after delivery in May 1984, carrying blinds set for the X43 route to Manchester, where in earlier times the White Lady double-deck coaches had operated.

now seating 77, and in August Ribble also received the first example, with chassis number ON-1, this becoming Ribble 2101. A further twelve followed in the period up to October, and in 1982 there were deliveries of ten in January and seven between June and October. The 1983 batch comprised a further seven which arrived in June-July. Production of Olympian chassis switched to Workington that year with only minor changes in design, Ribble's first examples being the batch numbered 2138 upwards delivered in 1984, of which there were eighteen buses plus four of a version with 70 coach seats. In 1985, the split was ten each of the bus and coach-seated versions the latter now accomodating 72. All of the foregoing had Gardner engines, generally of the 6LXB type, but 2124/7-30 received units of a turbocharged variant not generally marketed, 6LXBT.

2100	DBV 100W	Leyland B45-6LXB	ECW	H45/31F	8/80
2101	GFR 101W	Leyland ONLXB/1R	ECW	H45/32F	8/81
2102-13	JFR 2-13W	Leyland ONLXB/1R	ECW	H45/32F	1981
2114-23	OFV 14-23X	Leyland ONLXB/1R	ECW	H45/32F	1/82
2124-26	SCK 224-226X	Leyland ONLXB/1R	ECW	H45/32F	1982
2127-30	VRN 827-830Y	Leyland ONLXB/1R	ECW	H45/32F	1982
2131-37	DBV 131-137Y	Leyland ONLXB/1R	ECW	H45/32F	1983
2138-43	A138-143 MRN	Leyland ONLXB/1R	ECW	H45/32F	1984
2144-47	A144-147 OFR	Leyland ONLXB/1R	ECW	H45/32F	3/84
2148-55	B148-155 TRN	Leyland ONLXB/1R	ECW	H45/32F	1984
2156-59	A156-159 OFR	Leyland ONLXB/1R	ECW	CH42/28F	5/84
2160-69	B960-969 WRN	Leyland ONLXB/1R	ECW	H45/32F	1985
2170-79	C170-179 ECK	Leyland ONLXB/1R	ECW	CH42/30F	various

Bristol LHS6L buses, 1980

A curious throwback to the past was the purchase of two of the Bristol LHS buses in 1980, not only because this model, not previously seen in the Ribble fleet, was in its twilight years, its ECW bodywork reviving the architecture of the RE model, but its Leyland O.400 engine was derived from that of the Tiger Cub and thus recalling the 'fifties. Seen here in Blackburn on a private hire duty in May 1982 is 271 (FBV 271W) – it carried the slogan 'Betty's bus' in tribute to the popular driver of the community bus service based on Clitheroe for which these vehicles were acquired. Despite the success of 'Betty's Bus' Ribble lost the tender to operate the service upon Deregulation in 1986. There was a reversion to the all-red livery in response to an NBC economy drive – some companies, however, did not seem to be seized of NBC's directive in this regard . . .

Two Seddon Pennine IV midibuses had been borrowed from Greater Manchester Transport in 1978 to operate a community bus service from Clitheroe garage and, to replace these, two Bristol LHS6L models were added to the fleet in October 1980. The Bristol LH had been introduced as a lightweight mid-underfloor-engined model in 1968, generally having the Leyland O.400 engine, used in much the same form as in the Tiger Cub. By 1980, it was being produced only in the short LHS form, although the LH, with standard ECW bodywork, had been used extensively by some NBC fleets. Its appearance in Ribble's fleet thus reintroduced a type of engine reminiscent of the 'fifties, though well on top of the job in a light 35-seat midibus.

271-272	FBV 271-272W	Bristol LH6L	ECW	B35F	1980

Vehicles acquired from Potteries Motor Traction Co Ltd, March 1983

Under an exchange arrangement, two pairs of Bristol VRT buses with Leyland 501 engines and almost identical specification and age were swapped between PMT and Ribble in March 1983, the outgoing Ribble buses being 2003 and 2004. In November 1983, 2034, in common with many other 501-powered VRTs, received a Gardner 6LXB engine. The reason was to give Ribble two ultra low-height (13ft 5in) examples.

2033-4	URF 661-662S	Bristol VRT/SL3/501	ECW	H43/31F	1977

Vehicle acquired from Leyland Vehicles, January 1983

One further Leyland National of the type B specification that had been operated on loan since November 1979 was acquired in January 1983. When first operated, it had been given the fleet number 880, but in May 1982 it was renumbered 686 to make way for National 2 vehicles tnen on order.

686	WFR 392V	Leyland National	10351B/1R	B44F	1979

Leyland National 2 buses with Gardner engines, 1983-84

Leyland introduced a Gardner engine option for the Leyland National at the beginning of 1983. Ribble, although traditionally wedded to Leyland products, had built up enough experience of Gardner units by that date to respect their efficiency and durability, and they were specified for the last new Nationals to be added to the fleet. Ten, delivered between March and July of that year, had the 6HLXB and one, not added to the fleet until January 1984, the turbocharged 6HLXCT. These were to be the last new Leyland National buses for Ribble.

888-893	ARN 888-893Y	Leyland National 2	NL116HLXB/1R	B52F	1983
894	ARN 894Y	Leyland National 2	NL116HLXCT/1R	B52F	1/84
895-898	ARN 895-898Y	Leyland National 2	NL116HLXB/1R	B52F	1983

Leyland Tiger TRCTL11 coaches, 1983-84

A replacement for the Leopard coach chassis was developed by Leyland, largely on the basis of consultation with NBC, and first shown to the public at the 1980 Motor Show as the B43, the name Tiger being applied at its official launch early in 1981. It could be described as an extensively updated successor to the Leopard, with the turbocharged TL11 engine as the initial power unit, and air suspension as standard. The TRCTL11/3R was a 12-metre coach model, equvalent to the Leopard PSU5, this length having become much more widely accepted by that time. Ribble's reduced need for coaches because of the creation of National Travel meant that its first examples did not join the fleet until April 1983, and even then the five vehicles in question, with Plaxton Paramount 3500 high-floor bodywork, were operated by National Travel (East) for their first six months. One further Tiger was added to the fleet in December of that year, numbered 1150, but that was a replacement for a 1978 Leopard, 1098, that had been burnt out and was an 11-metre TRTC11/2R with Duple Dominant IV Express body, believed to be the last Dominant coach shell body built – it is illustrated on page 136 of Volume 1.

1001-5	BRN 1-5Y	Leyland TRCTL11/3R	Plaxton	C50F	4/83
1150	A150 LFR	Leyland TRCTL11/2R	Duple	C51F	1983

Vehicles owned by Ribble and leased to other NBC Subsidiaries

One of the financial endeavours of the National Bus Company in its later years was to have the richer bus operating subsidiaries fund the purchase of high specification coaches for use by certain National Travel coach-oriented companies. Amongst these 'lessors', frequently operating in PTE areas under Agency Arrangements, were United Automobile, West Riding, Northern General Transport and Ribble. The full extent of these arrangements is difficult to unravel but it is known that the vehicles below were amongst the Ribble contribution. They were always **owned** by Ribble but exclusively **used** by National Travel (East) Ltd whose name would appear on the lower bodyside and on the Vehicle Registration Document in the status as 'Registered Keeper' as distinct from beneficial owner. Upon Privatisation some vehicles were returned to their actual owner for disposal, or, occasionally, re-use. The vehicles below passed to the buyers of National Travel (East) – NTE Coaches Ltd.

	THL 293-8Y	Leyland TRCT11/3R	Plaxton	C50F (293)	1983
				C51f (rest)	1983

Vehicles acquired from National Travel (West) Ltd, Manchester, November 1983 and March 1984

Among coaches added to the fleet by transfer from National Travel (West) in November 1983 was 1066 (TTF 222M), this Leyland Leopard with Duple Dominant body dating from 1973, very similar to those supplied to Ribble at the time. It is seen when visiting Clitheroe garage in May 1964 and illustrates the 'stripey' type of livery used in various forms by NBC fleets at that time.

These were transfers of older coaches in the manner that had occurrred from time to time though soon to be followed by the take-over detailed below. 1060-63 were acquired in November 1983 and 1064-5 in March 1984.

1060-63	XTF 818/22-4L	Leyland PSU3B/4R	Duple	C49F	1973
1064-65	XTF 827/8L	Leyland PSU3B/4R	Duple	C49F	1973
1066	TTF 222M	Leyland PSU3B/4R	Duple	C49F	1974

Vehicles acquired from National Travel (West) Ltd, Manchester, May 1984

The concentration of much express coach operation and ownership under National Travel in 1974 was reversed to a substantial degree so far as Ribble was concerned almost exactly a decade later, when it took over the 147 vehicles of National Travel (West) in May 1984. They had fleet numbers below 200 which did not clash with Ribble's existing stock, and thus were retained. The fleet reflected general NBC coach policy, being largely made up of Leyland Leopards, with standardisation on the 12-metre PSU5 version from 1976, mostly with Duple or Plaxton bodywork, though there were also examples from Willowbrook and ECW. Many of these earlier vehicles were soon transferred to other NBC fleets or sold off, but some were converted to allow fare-collection by the driver, being renumbereed in the 12xx series. From 1982/3, the Tiger had become NT(W)'s standard choice of chassis, the initial vehicle (95) having a Duple Dominant IV body, followed by 105 with Plaxton Paramount 3200 and then 106-110 and 122-134 with the taller 3500 type. In 1984, four examples of the MCW Metroliner six-wheel double-deck coach with rear-mounted Cummins engine had just come into the fleet at the time of transfer, as had one example (121) of the Plaxton 4000, in a similar category but based on an Auwaerter Neoplan underframe, this latter being used for contract holiday travel to Spain, for which its lower overall height was suited. The MCW coaches (113/6-8) had been lent from new to United and were sold to that operator in July 1984. Two further Metroliners (119-120) and two Tigers (124-5) were on order at the time of transfer but delivered direct to Ribble the same month. 119-120 were transferred to Shamrock & Rambler in 1985. At least one operated in Lakeland Experience colours in its first summer, prior to use on National Express duties.

The 12-metre Leopard PSU5, with its capability to provide coach seating for 50 passengers or more, had been favoured by National Travel (West) from 1976 and 94 of the type formed nearly two-thirds of the fleet transferred to Ribble. Having been based in Manchester, NT(W) had many vehicles with registrations issued by the local LVLO, among them this example, BNB 234T, numbered 34 at the time of take-over, but which had become 1234 on conversion to one-man-operation. It was new in 1978 with Duple Dominant 2 coach body. By this time (1986) the NBC Corporate Image Manual permitted more local choice of colour, albeit to a (new) standard layout. This vehicle is painted in White/Red/Grey. Note the disappearance of the NBC symbol by this time – a sign of the break up of the Group.

Towards the end of the NBC era there was a growing trend towards coach liveries related to the business on which the vehicles were intended to be used rather than the identity of their owning company. Thus 75 (MRJ 275W) was one of eight ex-National Travel (West) Leopard PSU5 coaches repainted in Kingfisher livery during 1985. The Plaxton Panorama Supreme IV bodywork on this 1980 vehicle had a clear line of descent from the Elite style of 1968.

The Rapide services of National Express called for coaches of appropriate specification. Number 109 (ANA 109Y), seen here at Victoria Coach Station in May 1985, was one of five with Plaxton Paramount 3500 bodywork in 46-seat form with toilet facility which had been placed in service by NT(W) in 1983.

Operated on contract tour duty to Spain was 121 (A121 MBA), a Plaxton 4000 double-deck coach painted in the livery of Anglo Continental Travel when placed in service by National Travel (West) in 1984, shortly before the fleet was transferred to Ribble – NT(W) lettering was still evident when photograped in July 1985. The model used the underframe and mechanical units of the Neoplan Skyliner model which had popularised the idea of the six-wheeled double-deck coach with operators in several European countries from its introduction in 1968.

1-7	SFV 201-207P	Leyland PSU5A/4R	Plaxton	CvarF	1976
8-18	URN 208-218R	Leyland PSU5/4R	Duple	C51F	1976
19-21	XCK 219-221R	Leyland PSU5B/4R	Willowbrook	C51F	1977
22-23	SEA 311-312R	Leyland PSU5B/4R	Willowbrook	C51F	1977
24-26	WUE 611-612S	Leyland PSU5B/4R	Willowbrook	C51F	1977
27-33	VVU 227-233S	Leyland PSU5C/4R	Duple	CvarF	1978
34-48	BNB 234-248T	Leyland PSU5C/4R	Duple	C50F	various
49-55	HNE 249-255V	Leyland PSU5C/4R	Duple	C53F	1980
56-64	JND 256-264V	Leyland PSU5C/4R	Duple	C53F	1980
65-80	MRJ 265-280W	Leyland PSU5C/4R	Plaxton	CvarF	various
81-90	SND 281-290X	Leyland PSU5D/4R	Duple	CvarF	1981
92-94	ANA 92-94Y	Leyland PSU5E/4R	ECW	C53F	1982
95	WVR 60X	Leyland TRCTL11/3R	Duple	C53F	1982
99	FDV 799V	Leyland PSU3E/4R	Plaxton	C49F	1979
105	A105 HNC	Leyland TRCTL11/3R	Plaxton	C46Ft	1983

106-110	ANA 106-110Y	Leyland TRCTL11/3R	Plaxton	C48FT	1983
113/6-8	A113/6-8 KBA	MCW Metroliner	MCW	CH53/18DT	1984
119-120	A119-120 KBA	MCW Metroliner	MCW	CH59/27F	1984
121	A121 MBA	Auwaerter N722/3	Plaxton	CH53/20DT	1984
122-134	A122-134 MBA	Leyland TRCTL11/4R	Plaxton	C48FT	1984
135-139	TTF 235-239M	Leyland PSU3B/4R	Duple	C49F	1974
145-149	PCK 145-149P	Leyland PSU3C/4R	Duple	C47F	1976
153-157	BWE 203-207T	Leyland PSU3E/4R	Duple	C46F	1979
158	PWD 841R	Leyland PSU3D/4R	Willowbrook	C47F	1977
159-160	VDH 243-244S	Leyland PSU3E/4R	Willowbrook	C28FT	1977
161-165	YTU 321-325S	Leyland PSU3E/4R	Duple	C49F	1977
172-176	PCW 672-676P	Leyland PSU3C/4R	Duple	C49F	1976

In 1985, 34-9,41/3-8 were renumbered 1234-9/41/3-8. 95 received the registration HCK 466 from a withdrawn PD2 trainer in late 1986, Ribble's first instance of application of a 'non-dating' registration.

Leyland Atlantean open-top double-decker, acquired 1984, and other open-top conversions

A Sea Dog inland – 927 GTA had begun life as 'Sir Martin Frobisher', one of Devon General's Atlantean convertible open-top buses used in the Torbay area. It is seen, left, in Clitheroe garge in July 1986, wearing NBC-style 'stripey' livery. The idea of converting double-deckers to open-top had caught on within Ribble, and a Park Royal roof is seen above perched in a corner of Southport depot in August 1985.

The idea of open-top double-deckers as a tourist attraction had tended to be associated with the south of England and its generally warmer climate, but gradually the possibilities were pursued in other areas, though not hitherto by Ribble. This vehicle began life as one of nine placed in service in 1961 by Devon General, basically to the standard Atlantean design with Metro-Cammell bodywork, much the same as Ribble's examples of the period but with detachable roof. They were used in Torquay on sea-front service, in this case until 1982, when it passed to Amalgamated Passenger Transport, which was the name taken up by NBC's central bus disposal and unit reclamation centre based at the Lincolnshire company's former overhaul works. It was lent to Lincolnshire for two summers and acquired by Ribble in November 1984, entering service in May 1985. During that time, Ribble had converted one of its own AN68 Park Royal buses (1377), so it seems that 1927 may have been purchased partly as a form of prototype for such conversions – two second-hand double-deckers were also converted to open-top in 1987 – Atlantean 1622 (ex-Blackburn) and Fleetline 1733 (ex-Midland Red).

1927	927 GTA	Leyland PDR1/1	Met.Camm	CO44/31F	1961

Leyland Tiger coaches, 1985

The Duple Laser body was immediately recognisable by its sharply raked windscreen. Seen here in April 1985, soon after entering service, is 1154 (B154 ERN) in Timesaver livery of red, silvergrey, white and black. The photograph is taken at Chorlton Street Coach Station in Manchester.

The Caribbean body, by contrast to the Laser, was quite square-cut and only such details as the grille gave the clue that it was also a Duple product. Here 146 (B146 ACK) demonstrates its higher build alongside 1234, representing a Leyland/ Duple Dominant 2 combination of seven years earlier.

Additions to the coach fleet made in 1985 were divided into various categories for different types of duty, with the 245bhp version of the engine specified in place of the standard 218bhp unit for 155-168. The bodies on 1151-4 and 155-168 were Duple Laser II, 1006 was Plaxton Paramount 3500 II, and 135-150 were Duple Caribbean II, to Rapide specification.

1151-4	B151-154 WRN	Leyland TRCTL11/2RH	Duple	C49F	1985
155-168	B155-168 WRN	Leyland TRCTL11/3RH	Duple	C53F	1985
1006	B66 YFV	Leyland TRCTL11/3RZ	Plaxton	C49F	5/85
135-150	B135-150 ACK	Leyland TRCTL11/3RZ	Duple	C48FT	5/85

Leyland Tiger bus, 1985

The solitary Duple Dominant bus body, on Leyland Tiger chassis, seen in Lancaster bus station in September 1993, wearing Stagecoach livery.

One Tiger chassis with Duple Dominant bus body was added to the fleet, having been built with a batch supplied to Midland Red (North) but not required by that company. It thus revived the concept of the mid-underfloor engined single-deck bus in the fleet almost 20 years after the big deliveries of Leopard buses ended, but it was to remain unique despite the allocation of a fleet number suggesting a possible new series. It was allocated to Blackpool depot and is also illustrated on page 95 of Volume 1.

900	B900 WRN	Leyland TRCTL11/2RH	Duple	B49F	1985

Transfer of stock to Cumberland Motor Services Ltd, 22nd February 1986

In response to Government directive, NBC orders resulted in the transfer of 71 vehicles, along with the Carlisle and Penrith depots, to Cumberland. The double-deck vehicles involved Bristol VR with full-height ECW bodies 1449-65, Atlantean-ECW 1467-85 and low-height VR-ECW 2002/17/24/32. Single-deck buses transferred were Nationals 748/52/6, 801/2/9-12; National 2s 882/3/5/7/95-8. Coaches were Leopard-Duple 1082/6, 1108-10/5/6/8/9/26-9/33/6/40.

Vehicles acquired from United Automobile Services , April 1986

These three almost new coaches had Plaxton Paramount 3500 Mark II bodies to Rapide specification. United had acquired them in lieu of Royal Tiger Doyen vehicles, but replaced them with Bova Europa coaches.

111-113	B107-109 NPY	Leyland TRCTL11/3R	Plaxton	C48FT	1985

Vehicles acquired from Crosville Motor Services Ltd, June 1986

Five MCW Metroliner double-deck coaches had barely had time to settle down in service with Crosville before being transferred to Ribble. They had Cummins 290bhp engines and Voith automatic transmission. The transfer resulted from industrial action taken at Crosville Motor Service's Love Lane Liverpool depot.

213-217	C213-217 KMA	MCW Metroliner	MCW	CH57/22F	1986

The MCW Metroliner had been developed as a response to the demand for high-capacity double-deck coaches, itself reflecting an upsurge of interest in travel by express coach in the early 'eighties. The six-wheel chassis was derived from a version of the maker's Metrobus for Hong Kong, but developed to suit high-speed motorway running, with 290bhp Cummins engine and Voith automatic gearbox. Not being as low-built as their counterparts enabled them to have more generous internal headroom. NBC's very fluid organisation at the time caused some confusing transfers of ownership. In much the same way as four of these vehicles allocated to National Travel (West) in 1984 had been sold to United almost immediately after Ribble had become their owners, so, in 1986, Ribble received these five run briefly by Crosville. In both cases industrial disputes were the cause. Seen here is 216 as running in August 1986, with National Express and Kingfisher lettering.

Auwaerter/Plaxton Paramount 4000 double-deck coaches, 1986

The Auwaerter/Plaxton 4000 became the main double-deck coach type in the fleet with the delivery of ten in 1986. This view, taken in July of that year, of the almost new 174 in Rapide livery and with electronic destination set for the London service makes an interesting comparison with earlier generations of Ribble double-deck coach. All the double-deck coaches and many of the more modern Tigers were destined to pass with the National Express activities to Amberline in 1988.

Ten more of the Plaxton Paramount 4000 double-deck coaches based on Auwaerter (Neoplan) N722 underframes were delivered for the summer of 1986. Of these, 171-8 had Mercedes-Benz V10 engines and 179-180 had the then recently introduced Gardner 6LYT 15.5-litre in-line six-cylinder. Sadly, 173 was destroyed by fire within a week of entering service in June 1986 as a result of an electrical fault in the body.

171-180	C171-180 KHG	Auwaerter N722	Plaxton	CH53/18CT	1986

Leyland Lynx bus, 1986

Another 'false dawn' in terms of a possible new major single-deck class was given by the delivery of a pre-production example of the Leyland Lynx underfloor-engine single-decker. Envisaged as a successor to the Leyland National it was built, like that model, at Workington, accounting for the registration issued via the Carlisle LVLO. It differed from the latter in being built in more traditional style, with underframe almost equivalent to a separate chassis, though dependent on the body structure for rigidity. The TL11 was the initial standard power unit.

901	C544 RAO	Leyland Lynx	Leyland	B51F	5/86

Another new single-deck type, again with apparent grounds for high hopes, was the Lynx, of which C544 RAO became Ribble 901 in May 1986. The future of Ribble was already uncertain, as conveyed by the omission of the NBC logo from the fleetname, but in what, up to then, had been 'normal' circumstances, it could have been expected that within a few years there would be a hundred or more similar buses in the fleet. The Lynx sold quite strongly in a depressed market for several years, but this was to remain Ribble's only example.

Mercedes-Benz L608D minibuses, 1986

After several years when very few new buses, as opposed to coaches, had been added to the fleet, the sudden arrival of some 64 single-deckers in September-October 1986 was quite an event, even if they seated only 19 or 20 passengers apiece. The complete reversal of previous reasoning is underlined by the fact that Ribble had purchased only fifteen new buses of capacity as small as this in the 57 previous years since the company was founded – seven Vulcan of 1922/3, seven Dennis Ace of 1934/6 and the single Ford Transit of 1979. The Mercedes-Benz L608D was a popular choice, partly because the production panel van body lent itself to minibus conversion. Seen here in the Minilink livery in April 1987 is 554, one of those with bus seats for 20 passengers the vehicles numbered 501-521 were similar except for the coach seats which reduced the capacity by one.

The advent of deregulation and privatisation was making profound changes in vehicle policy. NBC, in one of its final decisions, determined to pre-empt anticipated competition from independent operators of minibuses by buying large fleets of its own. Initial experience elsewhere had led to the conclusion that slightly heavier-duty vehicles than the minimal 16-seat types were likely to be a better proposition, the main choice falling on the Mercedes-Benz, with its simple but relatively smooth four-cylinder engine and well-chosen ratios in its five-speed synchromesh gearbox. An order for 90 was placed by Ribble, but in the event 26 of these were diverted to the new North Western company. The remainder had their Mercedes-Benz panel van bodywork converted to passenger form by Reeve Burgess, of Pilsley, near Chesterfield, a concern which had specialised in small buses, often for welfare purposes, but soon became a major concern in this field. Some had coach-style seating to suit use on private hire duty. They entered service in September-October 1986, often at smaller depots in more rural areas, though some were based in Preston and Chorley.

501-521	D501-521 RCK	Mercedes-Benz L608D	M-B/Reebur	DP19F	1986
522-564	D522-564 RCK	Mercedes-Benz L608D	M-B/Reebur	B20F	1986

Transfer of stock to North Western Road Car Co Ltd, Bootle, September 1986

A name with a long and honourable history was chosen for the hived-off south-western part of Ribble, created as a further response to Government order, though the new North Western was centred about 30 miles to the west of the old one's headquarters at Stockport. Double-deckers transferred comprised Atlantean/Park Royal 1301/3/5-16/8/20-38/40/1/3-60/2-7/9-76/9-82/7/9/91,1403; Atlantean/ECW 1466/86-1515; Olympian/ECW 2133/5/6/9-41/4/6/751/3/5/60-9. Single-deck buses involved were Leyland Nationals 374/5/7/9/80/7-9/91/2/5,401/9/20,687-93/8-701/4/6/10-2/29/31/5/46/50/1/8-67/9/73/4/86/7/91-6; National 2s 799,844/5/50-5/65/7/9/746 and Bristol RESL/ECW 344/5/56/8/61/3/9/70. Coaches included were Leopards 12/3, 66, 71/2,81-3/6/8,90,1122/4/5/32/5/7/42-5, 1238-40/6/55 and Tigers 95,105-10,127/8/35-9/46-8,1004.

Used double-deckers acquired 1986-8

Another reaction to deregultion was the decision to acquire substantial numbers of used double-deckers to allow rapid deployment on new or existing services. They were drawn from a variety of sources, though most were relatively normal sales of time-expired buses, and their condition varied considerably. They were numbered in series beginning at 1601 for Leyland Atlantean, 1700 for Daimler Fleetline (seen in Ribble service for the first time) and added to the existing 20xx series for low-height Bristol VRT, most being added to Ribble's fleet in the later months of 1986, the exceptions being noted below.

The Atlanteans numbered 1601-19/26-33 were ex-Southdown and were similar to Ribble's own AN68/Park Royal buses of the period. Blackburn Transport was the source of 1620-5, introducing the East Lancs body design of the 'seventies to the fleet. Twelve more Park Royal-bodied AN68 buses dating from 1972-73 came from the Greater Manchester Transport fleet in 1987, but these were to GMT's specification. The final Atlantean additions were 1646-52, acquired in the latter part of 1988 and coming from the Plymouth Corporation fleet – their Park Royal bodywork was quite similar to the Ribble and Southdown batches in appearance.

The main batch of Fleetline buses (1700-18) were from South Yorkshire PTE, dating from 1974-5 and had non-standard ECW bodies to that operators' specification. The remainder, all with Alexander bodywork, came from the Midland Red companies, though some had quite complex histories. Numbers 1719-23 had started life with Alexander (Fife) and had bodies to a style quite like those of Ribble's Atlantean buses of 1966 – they were acquired from Midland Red Coaches. The remainder came from Midland Red (North), two (1724/5) originating with Trent, but the rest (1726-33) with Midland Red before it had been split into area companies, and dating from 1969-71.

Of the Bristol VRT buses, 2035-9 came from North Devon, having begun life with Western National or in the case of 2039, Devon General; 2040/1 from South Midland, originally City of Oxford; 2042 also came from South Midland but had previously been with Western SMT; 2043-5 were from Southdown and 2046-9 were from Northumbria, originally United.

Some of these vehicles ran in Ribble service for only a few months, but others remained longer, several of those with centre-exit doors having them panelled over and a seat for an extra three passengers fitted within.

Repainting was enough to make the ex-Southdown AN68/Park Royal buses look quite at home with Ribble – PUF 718M is seen in the paintshop on 18th October 1986, about to become 1618. The ex-South Yorkshire Fleetlines with their non-standard ECW bodies were more obvious 'foreigners' – GWA 809N-SYPTE 809 about to become 1708 leads this pair prior to repainting.

1601-14	PUF 131-144M	Leyland AN68/1R	Park Royal	H43/30F	1974
1615-19	PUF 715-719M	Leyland AN68/1R	Park Royal	H43/30F	1974
1620	UBV 68L	Leyland AN68/1R	East Lancs	H45/31F	1972
1621-25	JFR 393-397N	Leyland AN68/1R	East lancs	H45/31F	1975
1626-27	PUF 720-721M	Leyland AN68/1R	Park Royal	H43/30F	1975
1628-33	LCD 42-47P	Leyland AN68/1R	PRV/Roe	H43/30F	1975
1634-38	VNB124/33/48/55/70L	Leyland AN68/1R	Park Royal	H43/32F	1973
1639	WBN 971L	Leyland AN68/1R	Park Royal	H43/32F	1973
1640-42	VNB140/66/7L	Leyland AN68/1R	Park Royal	H43/32F	1973
1643-45	XJA 519/25/31L	Leyland AN68/1R	Park Royal	H43/32F	1974
1646-52	GDR 201/3/4/7-10N	Leyland AN68/1R	Park Royal	H43/28D	1975
1700	CWE 784N	Daimler CGR6LXB	ECW	H43/27D	1974
1701-18	GWA 800/2-5/7-9/17-20 832/6/10/22/13/30N	Daimler CRG6LXB	ECW	H43/27D	1976
1719-23	RXA 50/3/5/8/9J	Daimler CRG6LXB	Alexander	H44/31F	1971
1724-25	DRC 541/3J	Daimler CRG6LX	Alexander	H44/33F	1971
1726-33	SHA 857/8/73G, UHA 191-3H, UHA 216H, YHA 274J	Daimler CRG6	Alexander	H45/30D	various
2035-38	OTA 284/5/92/3G	Bristol VRTSL-6LX	ECW	H39/31F	1970
2039	VOD 542K	Bristol VRTSL-6LX	ECW	H39/31F	1972
2040-41	NUD 101/8L	Bristol VRTSL2-6LX	ECW	H41/27F	1973
2042	SMS 45H	Bristol VRTSL-6LX	ECW	H39/31F	1970
2043	WCD 519K	Bristol VRTSL2-6LX	ECW	H39/31F	1972
2044-45	NCD 556M, GNJ 569N	Bristol VRTSL2-6LX	ECW	H43/32F	1974/5
2046	YHN 654M	Bristol VRTSL2-6LX	ECW	H43/31F	1974
2047-49	BHN 761-763M	Bristol VRTSL2-6LX	ECW	H43/31F	1974

Awaiting attention, also on 18th October 1986, were Fleetline/Alexander RXA 55J and 58J, which had been new to Alexander (Fife) but latterly had been run by Midland Red Coaches, whose name they still displayed – they were to become 1721 and 1722. Also with a Scottish background was VRT/ECW 2042, which had entered service in 1970 with Alexander (Midland), moving to Eastern National in 1973 and to South Midland in 1985 before purchase by Ribble – it is seen in Blackburn in March 1988. The SBG destination box on these buses echoes earlier Ribble practice.

Iveco 49-10 minibuses, 1987

The initial example of the Iveco 49-10 model to join the fleet was 565, seen here, but the following year 20 more were added. Note that the Ribble travel service sign in the background of this September 1987 view was still displaying the NBC doubleN emblem.

A further delivery of minibuses introduced more new names, the first numerically being an Iveco 49-10. This marque name was by then being applied to commercial vehicles of Fiat origin. The body was by Robin Hood, of Southampton, another concern propelled into prominence in the bus world by the growth in minibus popularity. Further examples followed in mid-1987, those numbered 620-629 being diverted from Alder Valley, though four others were retained, producing a gap at 630-633 in the fleet numbers.

565	D565 TFV	Iveco 49-10	Robin Hood	DP20F	1986
610-619	D610-619 BCK	Iveco 49-10	Robin Hood	B21F	1987
620-629	D620-629 BCK	Iveco 49-10	Robin Hood	B25F	1987

Freight Rover Sherpa minibuses, 1986-7

The 'converted parcel van' style of minibus arrived in the fleet in 1987, with the delivery of 40 Freight Rover Sherpa models with 16-seat conversion from the high-capacity van body shell carried out by Dormobile, one of those concerns which greatly expanded its activities in the minibus field during this period. It had begun life under the name Martin Walter, specialising in convertible cars before turning to more utilitarian vehicles and adopting the name of its most famous product. The example shown is 593, seen soon after entering service.

The Freight Rover name had arisen as a result of the amalgamation of the van-manufacturing plant of British Leyland, of Austin-Morris origins, with Range Rover. The Sherpa was a little narrower in original form than the Ford Transit, but capable of carrying a similar 16-seat body, in this case by Dormobile, of Folkestone. The name reveals its origins in an early form of camper van, though that organisation too had turned to personnel carriers and then minibuses as the demand for the latter rose. The vehicles were leased from finance companies and, proving to be too small for many duties, were not retained for very long.

566-605	D566-605	Freight Rover Sherpa Dormobile	B16F	1987

Dodge S56 minibuses, 1987

Yet another name brought into the fleet by the minibus era which would have surprised earlier generations was Dodge. This had become the Chrysler group's commercial vehicle marque which a complex series of mergers had linked with both the former Rootes group and Renault, and indeed the model became known as a Renault. However, the antecedents of the S56 range had more to do with the Rootes

The S56 model had quite a chequered ancestry, with elements of Commer and Dodge in its design, but 643 has a Renault badge in this view.

group make, Commer, equally unfamiliar in most major British operator's fleets though at one time quite well known as a builder of chassis for independent operators' coaches.

634-647	E634-647 DCK	Dodge S56	Dormobile	B25F	1987

Privatisation

The management buy-out by I. A. E. Chapman and his colleagues took effect on 2nd March 1988, as explained in Volume 1. Among almost immediate consequences was the decision to withdraw from National Express and the sale of 25 coaches involved on such duties to Amberline, a Liverpool operator about to become a subsidiary of Crosville Wales and subsequently to the privatised National Express organisation. The vehicles involved were Tiger/Plaxton coaches 111-113; Tiger/Duple coaches 140-5/9/50; Plaxton Paramount 4000s 171/2/4-80, and the ex-Crosville MCW Metroliners 213-217. Various other coaches were sold to a dealer.

Vehicles acquired from United Transport Buses, Preston, March 1988

Another early action after privatisation was the conclusion of a deal with United Transport (an organisation that had concentrated on bus operation in Africa for many years but had opened up activities in Britain in the Deregulation era), under which the United Transport minibus operation using the Zippy fleet name and based in Preston was taken over by Ribble. Most of the vehicles taken over were of types in Ribble's existing minibus fleet, but the Carlyle conversions are worthy of mention in being products of a business formed to run the former overhaul works of Midland Red. The Talbot Pullman, of which ten examples were acquired, was noteworthy as an ingenious six-wheel conversion of a front-wheel-drive van.

Nine examples of the Zippy fleet operated by United Transport in the Preston area parked in the bus station in August 1987. On the right of the line is 024 (D81 PUK), one of the Freight Rover Sherpa models with Carlyle bodywork. The registration marks of many of these vehicles are complicated by virtue of their being allocated by the chassis maker in some instances and the body maker or operator in others.

001-020	various	Iveco 49-10	Robin Hood	B19F	1987
021-042	various	Freight Rover Sherpa	Carlyle	B18F	1987
043-048	various	Iveco 49-10	Robin Hood	B19F	1987
051-059	various	Iveco 49-10	Robin Hood	B19F	1987
060-064	D368-372 SGP	Iveco 49-10	Elme	B22F	1987
065-067	D831-833 PUK	Freight Rover Sherpa	Carlyle	B18F	1987
070-079	various	Talbot Pullman	Talbot	B20F	1987

The Zippy livery was still evident, though in combination with smaller Ribble lettering, on 015 (D405 FRV), an Iveco 49-10 with Robin Hood body when photographed soon after the take-over, in April 1988. On the right, Talbot Express 070 (D78 RVM) is seen in Barrow en route to South Walney in June 1989 shortly before this batch of ten vehicles was transferred to Cumberland. This model was converted to six-wheel from chassis brought over from France in a part of the former Humber works in Coventry where they were also bodied.

Vehicles acquired from Manchester Minibuses Ltd, September 1988

A further and final stage in the United Transport saga was its pull-out from the above, which traded under the name Bee Line (curiously fascinating to budding participants in bus operation at the time, there being a quite unrelated concern running an ex-NBC operation in Berkshire with similar fleetname) whose activities were taken over by Ribble. Some 188 minibuses came into Ribble ownership, comprising 138 Sherpa out of the 175 listed below, and 50 Dodge S56. However only 179 were acquired as a direct result of the operations of Manchester Minibuses, a further nine being acquired in October 1988 as a result of success in tendering for some work for Greater Manchester PTE. They continued operating as a separate entity.

3060-69	D60-69 NOF	Freight Rover Sherpa	Carlyle	B18F	1987
3106-10	D106-110 NOJ	Freight Rover Sherpa	Carlyle	B18F	1987
3111-3210	D111-210 NON	Freight Rover Sherpa	Carlyle	B18F	1987
3211-70	D211-270 OOJ	Freight Rover Sherpa	Carlyle	B18F	1987
3401-50	D401-450 NNA	Dodge S56	N.Counties	B22F	1987

Stagecoach takeover

The purchase of the Ribble business by the Stagecoach group on 21st April 1989 brought the company back into the same group as Cumberland Motor Services once again, for Stagecoach had purchased the latter direct from NBC in July 1987. This was soon to lead to further reduction in size for the Ribble fleet, although very briefly it grew, as explained below.

The month after Stagecoach took over Ribble, the Barrow Borough Council fleet was acquired, as detailed overleaf, and some of the vehicles involved were amongst the earliest to appear in Stagecoach livery with Ribble fleetnames, Leyland National 2 CEO 722W having become 897 in this view in Barrow in June 1989. That same month, Ribble's remaining operations in Cumbria, including the Barrow area, were transferred to Cumberland, but this vehicle was among those retained by Ribble, which has tended to add to its fleet of National 2 models in succeeding years. There was considerable movement of vehicles to achieve a degree of rationalisation in the period just before the split, with some ex-Barrow buses and all the Park Royal-bodied Atlanteans in the area moving south into the reduced Ribble territory, while ECW-bodied Atlanteans moved north into Cumberland's extended area.

Vehicles acquired from Barrow Borough Transport, in administration, May 1989

Following a period of intense competition from Ribble, the Barrow municipally-owned undertaking ceased trading and the fleet was purchased by Ribble. Numbers were allocated as follows, though the Nationals were almost immediately passed to Cumberland, and the older double-deckers numbered 1600 and 1653-4, respectively ex-Delaine (though originally Graham of Paisley) and Plymouth, were sold off, not having been used by Ribble.

648/9-52	D456/7/60 BEO	Dodge S56	East Lancs	B22F	1986
650/51	D458/9 BEO	Dodge S56	East Lancs	DP22F	1986
653	E779 DEO	Dodge S56	Reebur	C25F	1987
756-760	NEO 829-833R	Leyland National 11351A/1R		B49F	1977
761-762	UEO 478-479T	Leyland National 11351A/1R		B49F	1978
895	CEO 720W	Leyland National 2 NL116L11/1R		DP48F	1980
896-898	CEO 721-723W	Leyland National 2 NL116L11/1R		B49F	1980
1449-51	LEO 734-736Y	Leyland AN68D/1R	N.Counties	H43/32F	1983
1452	A266 PEO	Leyland AN68D/1R	N.Counties	H43/32F	1984
1600	NXS 100L	Leyland AN68/1R	Alexander	H43/31F	1973
1653-54	GDR 205/6N	Leyland AN68/1R	Park Royal	H43/28D	1975

Vehicles transferred to Cumberland, June 1989

It was decided very soon after Stagecoach's purchase of Ribble that it would be more logical to transfer all the latter's operations within Cumbria to Cumberland Motor Services Ltd. With them went the following vehicles:- 70-79, the ex-Zippy Talbot Pullman minibuses; 99,169 and 175 Leopard coaches; 156, Tiger coach; 271/2 Bristol LHS; 378,426/34/40/6, Nationals; 503/4/17-20/2-34/57-62, Mercedes-Benz L608D; 716,744,756-62, 803/4/6-8, Nationals; 813/4/42/7/56/7/60-4/72/3/81/92/5-8, National 2s: 1044/5/52/5/6, 1088/91/4,1103-5/13/7,1237/47/53. Leopard/Duple: 1405-13/5/7-23/4-6, Atlantean/ECW: 2134/75-7 Olympians.

Used Leyland Atlantean double-deckers purchased 1989

A further 30 used double-deckers were added to the fleet via Ensign, the London-based dealer which took various discarded double-deckers in part-exchange. The 'new' additions had all begun life in the mid-'seventies with Greater Manchester Transport, being AN68A/1R models, this time with Northern Counties bodywork. They had been used latterly on London Regional Transport contracts by Frontrunner (South East).

Former Greater Manchester Transport double-deckers became a familiar sight in many parts of the country in the years after Deregulation as many sold off found new owners. However, some found their way back to what had been home territory as a result of purchases by Ribble of ex-GMT Atlantean AN68 models, both in 1987 and again in 1989, when a further 30 became available after use by Frontrunner (South East) on contracted services in London. Seen here in Bury in July 1990 is 1666 (KBU 911P) of the 1989 purchases, all of which had Northern Counties bodywork. In the background are, on the left, similar but later bus 8232 (ANA 232T) and on the right an unidentified Leyland Olympian, both still with GMT.

1655-62	JND 112-5/7/9/21/2N	Leyland AN68A/1R	N.Counties	H43/32F	1975
1663-64	JND 984/5N	Leyland AN68A/1R	N.Counties	H43/32F	1975
1665	JVM 989M	Leyland AN68A/1R	N.Counties	H43/32F	1975
1666-71	KBU 911-5/7P	Leyland AN68A/1R	N.Counties	H43/32F	1975
1672-75	KDB 681/4-6P	Leyland AN68A/1R	N.Counties	H43/32F	1975
1676-84	LJA 600/1/3/15/6/20/9/36/41P	Leyland AN68A/1R	N.Counties	H43/32F	1975/6

Vehicles transferred to The Bee Line Buzz Co, September 1989

Under the agreement with the Drawlane group described in Volume 1, Ribble handed over to the newly-formed Bee Line company 187 minibuses from the previous United Transport subsidiary, Manchester Minibuses Ltd, plus Leyland Nationals 393/4/9,408/102/4; Leopard coaches 1059/80/9; Atlantean/Park Royals 1304/6/68 and the remaining 37 of the 'second-hand' Atlanteans, 1601/37/13-5/7-9/28-32/4-42/4/5.

Leyland Olympian double-deckers, 1989-91

The first allocation of new double-deckers to Ribble under Stagecoach management came towards the end of 1989, when ten Leyland Olympians were delivered – in accordance with general Stagecoach policy, the body order went to Alexander, the design being the RL type. They had coach seating. When a further seven similar vehicles, but with bus seating, were delivered in 1990, the number 2190 was left blank as the appropriate registration number was not available.

2180-89	G180-189 JHG	Leyland ONLXB/2RZ	Alexander	CH51/31F	1989
2191-97	H191-197 WFR	Leyland ON2R56G13Z4	Alexander	H51/36F	1990
2198-99	J198-199 HFR	Leyland ON2R56G13Z4	Alexander	CH47/27F	1991
2201-06	J201-206 HFR	Leyland ON2R56G13Z4	Alexander	CH47/27F	1991
2207-10	J207-210 HFR	Leyland ON2R56G13Z4	Alexander	CH47/27F	1991

After a period when no new full-sized vehicles were added to the fleet, welcome reinforcements began to appear in modest numbers from 1989. The Leyland Olympian was chosen in the 5.64-metre (18ft 6in) wheelbase form, giving 10-metre nominal overall length, longer than any previous Ribble double-deck buses. Alexander bodywork was chosen, similar vehicles being added to other Stagecoach group fleets. At first, a vee-shaped driver's windscreen using flat glass, rather as favoured 20 years or so earlier by Midland Red, was chosen, 2187 of the initial batch of ten being seen here. At that stage the fleetname was in capital lettering, not unlike the corporate NBC style.

The general style of later deliveries was similar, but a noticeable difference was the change to the BET-type windscreen, whose qualities in eliminating most internal reflections and giving a good external airflow to aid in keeping the driver's mirror and side windows clean were widely recognised. Seen here in 1993 with lettering for the service linking north-east Lancashire with Manchester is 2206 of the 1991 batch. The Ribble fleetname has all but vanished, appearing in small lettering on the front panel.

Good use was made of the offside on the Alexander-bodied Olympian buses operated on the Mancunian service to display explanatory lettering without destroying the overall style of the vehicle and livery application. As mentioned opposite, the Ribble name has now virtually disappeared.

The style of seat used in the more recent Olympian vehicles has a coach-like outline, with built-in headrest, though not as high backed as most seats in full-sized coaches. This view of the upper deck shows how the high-set rear emergency window of the Alexander body gives good rearward vision, often helpful to passengers seeking to identify their location before leaving the vehicle.

This lower-deck view shows how the seats over the rear wheel arches are considerably higher-mounted than those in the main part of the saloon. All views on this page show 2199 of the 1991 delivery. Comparison with photographs on page 106, and also page 67 in Volume 1, shows how much more spartan these vehicles are by comparison with earlier Ribble coaches.

Vehicles acquired from East Midland Motor Services Ltd, 1990

East Midland was another Stagecoach acquisition from the NBC empire, and transfers between Stagecoach companies were becoming even more common than in the latter days of NBC. The VRTs 1690-94 were acquired in 1990.

1690-1	RCH 154-155R	Bristol VRTSL3/6LXB	ECW	H43/31F	1976
1692-4	SNN 157-159R	Bristol VRTSL3/6LXB	ECW	H43/31F	1977

Vehicles acquired from Cumberland, 1990-93

In addition to the ex-Cumberland vehicles listed below, other instances of transfers to Ribble included vehicles originally new to the company and listed as such in earlier pages. They include Nationals 801/2/6-9/12, National 2s 813/4/42/7/56/7/60/1/3/7/81/92/5-8, Atlantean/ECWs 1407/8/10/1/5/8/9/21/76-73/5-82/4/5, in all cases reverting to their old numbers. Of the following, Nos. 1159/60/3 were originally registered D205/6 LWX, F410 DUG, having originally been new to Wallace Arnold Coaches. Nos. 303/4/88/97 were originally owned by Central SMT and 358/71,424 by Alexander (Midland), all passing to Kelvin Scottish before purchase.

301	CHH 214T	Leyland National 10351B/1R		B44F	1979
302	NEO 833R	Leyland National 11351A/1R		B49F	1977
303-304	SNS 825/8W	Leyland National 2 NL116AL11/1R		B52F	1980
305	HHH 371V	Leyland National 2 NL116L11/1R		B52F	1980
306/7	AHH 204/1T	Leyland National 10351B/1R		B44F	1978
311	AHH 206T	Leyland National 10351B/1R		B44F	1979
312	CHH 210T	Leyland National 10351B/1R		B44F	1979
318	AHH 208	Leyland National 10351B/1R		B44F	1979
357	KHH 377W	Leyland National 2 NL116L11/1R		B52F	1980
358	OLS 809T	Leyland National 10351B/1R		B44F	1978
367-368	MAO 367-368P	Leyland National 11351A/1R		B52R	1976
370	HHH 370V	Leyland National 2 NL116L11/1R		B52F	1980
371	OLS 807T	Leyland National 10351B/1R		B44F	1978
372-373	HHH 372-373V	Leyland National 2 NL116L11/1R		B52F	1980
374/6/8	KHH 374/6/8W	Leyland National 2 NL116L11/1R		B52F	1980
375	AHH 209T	Leyland National 10351B/1R		B44F	1979
377	WAO 397Y	Leyland National 2 NL116HLXB/1R		B52F	1982
379-382	NHH 379-382W	Leyland National 2 NL116L11/1R		B52F	1981
383	RRM 383X	Leyland National 2 NL116AL11/1R		DP52F	1981
384	CHH 211T	Leyland National 10351B/1R		B44F	1979
385	RRM 384X	Leyland National 2 NL116AL11/1R		DP52F	1981
386	RRM 386X	Leyland National 2 NL116AL11/1R		B52F	1981
387	SHH 387X	Leyland National 2 NL116AL11/1R		B52F	1982
388	SNS 822W	Leyland National 2 NL116AL11/1R		B52F	1980
389-394	SHH 389-394X	Leyland National 2 NL116AL11/1R		B52F	1982
395	RRM 385X	Leyland National 2 NL116AL11/1R		B52F	1981
396/8	WAO 396/8Y	Leyland National 2 NL116H6LXB/1R		B52R	1982
397	SNS 831W	Leyland National 2 NL116AL11/1R		B52F	1980
399	SHH 388X	Leyland National 2 NL116AL11/1R		B52F	1982
424	OLS 806T	Leyland National 10351B/1R		B44F	1978
533	D33 UAO	Mercedes-Benz L608D	Reebur	B20F	1987
643/5/6	WAO 643/5/6Y	Leyland TRCTL11/2R	Alexander	C47F	1983
1159	LJY 145	Volvo B10M-61	Plaxton	C50F	1987
1160	YDG 616	Volvo B10M-61	Plaxton	C50F	1987
1163	IIL 3507	Volvo B10M-60	Plaxton	C50F	1988

A high proportion of the vehicles transferred from Cumberland in the period from 1990 were Leyland National 2 buses. Ribble had a larger fleet of this type that had been delivered new than most former NBC subsidiaries, and hence adding more examples was a logical course of action. Retention of Cumberland fleet numbers where they did not clash simplified the process and was a sign of growing inter-relationship between the two companies. Seen here in Burnley in 1993 is 370, displaying the Ribble Buses fleetname in the style of lettering adopted as a corporate standard by Stagecoach.

Mercedes-Benz L709D minibuses, 1990

A further intake of Mercedes-Benz minibuses was made in 1990, this time of the L709D model and having purpose-built Alexander bodywork rather than the van conversions of earlier deliveries. No name or number lettering beyond the legal ownership had been applied to 586 (G186 PAO) when seen in Bury in July 1990. Stagecoach new vehicle choice and specification was carried out on a group basis and some vehicles of the same batch were temporarily diverted to Magicbus before arriving with Ribble. If anything this was more restrictive than in NBC days.

The L709D was a heavier-duty successor to the L608D, broadly similar in specification but updated in minor details and available in chassis form. In addition to new Alexander-bodied examples as supplied elsewhere within the Stagecoach group, 530 was fitted with a body built by Ribble Engineering, the name given to the former Ribble works at Frenchwood Avenue, Preston. Note the use of Carlisle registration marks, reflecting a growing Cumberland influence on Ribble. 579-580 had operated briefly for Magicbus before arrival with Ribble.

530	D672 SHH	Mercedes-Benz L709D	Ribble	B25F	1990
565-566	G665,566 PRM	Mercedes-Benz L709D	Alexander	B23F	1990
567-572	G567-572 PRM	Mercedes-Benz L709D	Alexander	DP25F	1990
573-575	G573-575 PRM	Mercedes-Benz L709D	Alexander	B25F	1990
576-577	G576-577 PRM	Mercedes-Benz L709D	Alexander	B23F	1990
579-580	G179-180 PAO	Mercedes-Benz L709D	Alexander	B23F	1990
583-592	G183-192 PAO	Mercedes-Benz L709D	Alexander	B23F	1990

Bristol VRT double-deckers acquired from other members of the Stagecoach group, 1990

The Stagecoach concern had begun as a small independent business in Perth, still in existence as a separate entity, and from which 2040 and 2043 were obtained. Magicbus had been an early Stagecoach enterprise, operating in the Glasgow area and was the source of 2044/5; these vehicles, had begun life with Devon General. United Counties was another of the Stagecoach group's ex-NBC acquisitions, and was the source of 2041/2, though 2041 was another vehicle originally in the Devon General fleet.

2040	FDV 813V	Bristol VRTSL3/6LXB	ECW	H43/31F	1979
2041	LFJ 857W	Bristol VRTSL3/6LXB	ECW	H43/31F	1980

Transfers of existing vehicles between subsidiaries has also been carried out on quite a large scale within the Stagecoach combine. Number 2043 (FDV 817V) is one of a batch of Bristol VRT buses was to standard NBC specification and had begun life with Devon General, which adopted a policy of extensive use of minibuses under the management of Harry Blundred. It sold off many of its larger buses relatively early, these examples passing to Magicbus. This June 1993 picture in Burnley shows the application of the corporate style of fleet name, the underlining bearing the words 'Part of the Stagecoach Group' – there was heavier emphasis on the group name in the run up to its quotation on the stock exchange.

2042	RRP 858R	Bristol VRTSL3/6LXB	ECW	H43/31F	1977
2043	FDV 817V	Bristol VRTSL3/6LXB	ECW	H43/31F	1979
2044/5	FDV 833,784V	Bristol VRTSL3/6LXB	ECW	H43/31F	1979

Vehicles acquired from Highland Scottish, 1991

The following Olympians were acquired from Highland Scottish. In addition the numbers 1138-44 were allocated to seven 1982 Leyland Leopards with Alexander bus or dual-purpose bodywork from the same source, but they did not enter service with Ribble, remaining in store for the few months they were in the area.

2211-14	A975/7-9 OST	Leyland ONLXB/1R	Alexander	H45/32F	1983
2215-23	B891-899 UAS	Leyland ONLXB/1R	Alexander	H45/32F	1985

Vehicles acquired from Hampshire Bus, 1991

The following were acquired for the Morecambe-Blackpool service 142. They were numbered as shown at first, but were renumbered 135-7 in September 1993.

1135-37	F135-137 SPX	Dennis Javelin	Duple	B63F	198?

Mercedes-Benz 709D minibuses, 1993

The 1993 delivery of Mercedes-Benz 709D minibuses was broadly similar to the 1990 ones but slightly taller build allowed room for a deeper destination screen. Seen here in Preston are 603 (L123 DRN), 596 (K116 XHG0 and 630 (L630 BFV) – some vehicles of the batch entered service with K registrations but others switched to L, disrupting the initial allocation of numbers.

These vehicles were all delivered with K registrations but some were re-registered as L-prefix, as shown, before entering service.

593-596	K113-116 XHG	Mercedes-Benz 709D	Alexander	B25F	1993
597	L119 DRN	Mercedes-Benz 709D	Alexander	B25F	1993
598-601	K118-121 XHG	Mercedes-Benz 709D	Alexander	B25F	1993
602-603	L122-123 DRN	Mercedes-Benz 709D	Alexander	B25F	1993
604	K124 XHG	Mercedes-Benz 709D	Alexander	B25F	1993
605-608	L125-128 DRN	Mercedes-Benz 709D	Alexander	B25F	1993
610-628	K610-628 UFR	Mercedes-Benz 709D	Alexander	B25F	1993
629-636	L629-636 BFV	Mercedes-Benz 709D	Alexander	B25F	1993
637	K112 XHG	Mercedes-Benz 709D	Alexander	B25F	1993

Vehicles acquired from Rainworth Travel, 1993

These were added to the fleet to reintroduce private hire operations and appeared in the yellow and tan 'Coachline' livery used on Cumberland's private hire coaches. They were originally C104/5 DWR, the current registrations coming from Routemasters in Stagecoach group ownership.

1161	WLT 391	Volvo B10M-61	Plaxton	C53F	1986
1162	WLT 980	Volvo B10M-61	Plaxton	C53F	1986

Vehicles ex-Lancaster City Transport, 22nd August 1993

In the period since Volume 1 was published, the history of co-operation between Ribble and Lancaster City Transport was brought to an abrupt end. In December 1992, Lancaster City Council, responding to Government pressure, recommended the sale of the LCT company by open tender. Ribble was inhibited from buying the company as a going concern by the official attitude to what were regarded as monopoly situations, and the management and employees decided not to bid. In an effort to counter the seeming likelihood of a major competitor buying LCT,

Ribble registered services over all LCT's main routes. This prompted the City Council to accept an offer from Stagecoach for the depot and twelve vehicles from the fleet (which in July had amounted to 60 buses), with effect from the above date – the Lonsdale Coach business was not included.

The vehicles acquired were ten of the most recent Atlanteans, having numbers 200, 205/6 etc in the Lancaster fleet and included the last example of the model off Leyland's production line, A214 MCK, and two Optare Metrorider midibuses. These, registered K200 LCT and K300 LCT, were re-registered, it being preferred to remove this reference to the initials of the former owners. As we go to press, the Atlanteans,transferred to operate from Preston, are still in Lancaster livery though with Stagecoach fleetnames, the Metroriders being in advertising liveries.

449-450	K449-450 YCW	Optare Metrorider	Optare	B31F	1992
1200	TCK 200X	Leyland AN68D/2R	East Lancs	H50/36F	1982
1205-6	LFV 205-206X	Leyland AN68C/2R	East Lancs	H50/36F	1981
1212	TCK 212X	Leyland AN68D/2R	East Lancs	H50/36F	1982
1213/5	WCK 213/5Y	Leyland AN68D/2R	East Lancs	H50/36F	1982
1214	A214 MCK	Leyland AN68D/2R	East Lancs	H50/36F	1984
1221-22	BFV 221-222Y	Leyland AN68D/2R	East Lancs	CH45/32F	1983
1223	A223 MCK	Leyland AN68/2R	East Lancs	CH45/32F	1984

Vehicles acquired from United Counties, 1993

These were mainly to cover for Leyland Olympians transferred from Chorley to Morecambe in the aftermath of the Lancaster City Transport episode.

2051/2/5/8	LFJ 882/3/5/4	Bristol VRTSL3/6LXC	ECW	H43/31F	1981
2053/4/6/7	LFJ 858/9/6/01	Bristol VRTSL3/6LXB	ECW	H43/31F	1981

Vehicles acquired from PMT, 1993

The following were acquired for National Express contracts, operating in that concern's livery, the vehicles being 'Expressliners'.

1164-65	B117/6 XRE	Volvo B10M-60	Plaxton	C46FT	1989

Vehicles acquired from Skyliner (Schofield), Mossley, 1993

These were also Expressliners for National Express contracts.

1166-67	H150/49 CVU	Volvo B10M-60	Plaxton	C46FT	1990

Dennis Javelin coaches, 1993-94

These are of dual-purpose character for longer routes. Many carry route branding, such as 'Ribble Valley Mancunian' for the X25 between Manchester, Bolton, Blackburn and Clitheroe, and 'Lancashire Coastliner' for X42 between Morecambe, Lancaster, Garstang and Blackpool. 144 was at the 1993 Coach & Bus Show at the National Exhibition Centre, Birmingham. The fleet numbers omit 147.

138-146	L138-146 BFV	Dennis 11SD2129	Plaxton Interurban	C47F	1993
148-151	L148-151 BFV	Dennis 11SD2129	Plaxton Interurban	C47F	1993
152-158	L152-158 BFV	Dennis 11SD2129	Plaxton Interurban	C47F	1994
159-161	L159-161 CCW	Dennis 11SD2129	Plaxton Interurban	C47F	1993

Volvo B6 single-deckers, 1993-94

This model, with six-litre vertical engine mounted longitudinally at the rear, has been chosen to replace minibuses on the busier routes, the first instance being the 'Hyndburn circulars' in the Blackburn, Accrington, Great Harwood and Oswaldtwistle area. The bodywork is of the Alexander Dash type. The first six examples were re-allocated from United Counties, and 231-3 saw a few days use with that operator, but 234-6 entered service with Ribble.

231-236	L423-428 MVV	Volvo B6	Alexander	B40F	1993
237-240	L237-240 CCW	Volvo B6	Alexander	DP40F	1993
241-250	L241-250 CCK	Volvo B6	Alexander	DP40F	1993
251-266	L251-266 CCK	Volvo B6	Alexander	DP40F	1994
267-269	L267-269 CCK	Volvo B6	Alexander	B40F	1993

Vehicles on order, correct to 25th March 1994

The 1994 order is for: 18 Volvo B6/Alexander
28 Volvo B10M/Alexander PS buses.

SUMMARY FLEET STRENGTH MARCH 1994

The current fleet strength of Ribble is roughly equivalent to what it was in 1929 though with a quite different spread of vehicle sizes. It is however more difficult to pinpoint the actual requirement as in these Deregulated days, the Company maintains a reserve of vehicles to allocate to competitive situations throughout its territory. Similarly, as a part of the Stagecoach Group, vehicles can be switched around the country at very short notice to deal with changes in local markets. This, of course, is the purpose behind that livery. As this book goes to press the nominal strength of vehicles allocated to Ribble use as given below.

The allocation given below also shows the nominal strengths at each garage. The actual vehicles to be found at each location are also subject to quite radical change in response to the competitive market place. The developments in the Manchester area described in the final chapter of this book appeared set to demand the transfer of some of the newest dual-purpose coaches to operate the Clitheroe express service from that city as but one example of the flexible use of resources.

Fleet Breakdown

145 double-deckers:-
92 Leyland Olympian, 28 Leyland Atlantean AN68, 26 Bristol VRT
146 single-deck buses:-
125 Leyland National, 20 Volvo 86, 1 Leyland Tiger
118 Minibuses :-
116 Mercedes Benz, 2 Optare Metrorider
31 dual-purpose coaches:-
27 Dennis Javelin, 4 Leyland Tiger
9 single-deck coaches:-
9 Volvo 81M

Nominal Depot Allocations

Blackburn 25, Bolton 85,
Bredbury 15, Clitheroe and Burnley 47,
Chorley 49, Fleetwood 15,
Lancaster 36, Morecambe 55,
Preston 98

Delicensed/Not allocated 34.

Still betraying its National Bus origins is this Workington-built Leyland Olympian with ECW dual-purpose body No. 2179 (C179 ECK) which still has Ribble-style fleetname, numbers and service number blinds alongside its newly applied Stagecoach livery.

Ribble Buses

PART OF THE STAGECOACH GROUP

Stagecoach Holdings PLC

Stagecoach (North West) Limited

Ribble Buses | Cumberland Motor Services | Stagecoach Manchester

'Ribble Buses'

The break in page style at this point signifies the sea change which beset Ribble Motor Services after its take-over by Stagecoach Holdings in 1989. The outward signs were the fairly speedy application of 'the white and stripes livery' to buses in the fleet but behind the scenes changes were afoot as the family tree demonstrates.

Although 'Ribble Motor Services Limited, still exists (as does 'Cumberland Motor Services Limited') these are both non-trading companies. Thus the name lives as the holder of the Operator's Licence used by a Trading Division of Stagecoach (North West) Limited. Consequently the legal lettering carried by many vehicles is still, at the time of writing, Ribble Motor Services...

The Stagecoach Group also has a much more flexible approach to vehicles – transfers between subsidiaries are commonplace and it is not unusual for new vehicles to be reallocated between despatch from the coach builder and registration. Older vehicles too can be moved around to respond to changing traffic demands. This may lessen interest for the Enthusiasts in some way but it nonetheless shows one of the means by which Stagecoach has become both a profitable group and also one whose shares have grown rapidly in value on the Stock Exchange.

Coaches Again

However, the Ribble Empire has begun to strike back ! Perhaps in a more measured style within the Stagecoach order, but nonetheless some degree of expansion is happening. Firstly, a small coach fleet has been established, primarily based on a few Volvo B10M drawn from either Cumberland Motor Services or Rainworth Travel of Mansfield. The latter was a coaching operation of another Stagecoach subsidiary – East Midland Motor Services. Ironically this activity was being wound up after the business of that Company's coaching division Midland Travel – was sold to Skills of Nottingham. A curious anomaly has arisen with certain of the Cumberland vehicles – they joined Ribble in the non-Stagecoach livery into which Cumberland had painted them. This was a tan and yellow scheme loosely based on the livery of an earlier Cumberland acquisition – Yeowarts of Whitehaven: the trading style was 'Coachline'. A couple were in National Express livery for local diagrams. If those vehicles were to undertake fairly routine local coaching, some further acquisitions marked a more determined return to the past. During 1993, in came some Volvo B10M/Plaxton Expressliner I vehicles, two from Skyliner, Mossley and a further three from PMT subsidiary Paramount Leisure.

Having some similarity to standard Stagecoach double-deckers Ribble 2217 (B893 UAS) is perhaps best described as one of the spoils of an earlier war. This epithet is gained as it was acquired by the Group after the successful raid on Inverness area services caused the virtual collapse of SBG subsidiary Highland Omnibus. Inverness Traction – Stagecoach's local company – had no wish to keep any of the vehicles which came with that victory as it had been presented with a wide selection of Group standard stock to conduct the battle. Curiously the vehicle looks somewhat native as the SBG destination display is the same in outline as the one Ribble gave up in NBC days.

Again there is a certain irony in that PMT was withdrawing from all forms of coach work at the time and the vehicles came with assignment of their contracts. This mileage was on some complex National Express diagrams which, inter alia, see nominally Ribble-owned vehicles in operation from Colne and Barrow to London once again. It is expected that these vehicles will be replaced by some Mark 2 Expressliners based on the new Plaxton Premier body shell during 1994. Livery is, of course, standard National Express 'Rapide' branded white.

The Lancaster Coup

The policy of the Conservative Government from 1992 has been to encourage Local Authorities to sell their bus companies. No actual power to force the issue exists but 'persuasive' measures to encourage this encompassed 'carrots' – letting them keep the cash proceeds of such sales and/or 'sticks' – excluding the staff affected from the Local Government Superannuation Scheme, if the Sale was not completed by the end of 1993. The latter was certainly to the detriment of many employees.

Lancaster City Council therefore resolved to sell out. Realising that it would certainly be precluded from bidding by the Monopolies and Mergers Commission (MMC), Ribble (Stagecoach) took pre-emptive measures by registering competing services to all LCT's principal routes. The effect was quite dramatic and LCT plunged into deficit to the point where a 'Going Concern' sale was virtually impossible. The City Council therefore made 'peace' in the best interests of its Council Tax payers (its overwhelming Duty in any event) by selling the garage and twelve (out of 60) buses to Ribble. Ribble therefore had 'acquired' the business of a competitor without much fuss at the cost of Real Estate at value – the properties – and a few buses. In a competitive world this was a 'first', a coup reflecting the skill of the parent company.

The Takeover that never was !

Inevitably the Office of Fair Trading sought to find grounds to challenge this scheme, probably because it was seen to set a precedent that avoided Monopolies legislation. A report was produced demanding that Ribble Buses enter 'Certain Undertakings' on its behaviour in relation to future competition. Presently this interesting challenge to the evolution of the bus industry remains unresolved.

Whither the 'bus ?

Stagecoach sets its subsidiaries quite severe, yet attainable, financial targets, including a minimum standard 15% profit on gross turnover before interest and tax. This notional indicator of performance is published in what amounts to a league table and is a key symbol of Management achievement. Inevitably this means subsidiaries must strive for maximum efficiency whilst securing both their own market objectives as well as any of those of their parent company. In some areas this means that Stagecoach subsidiaries, Ribble included, have reduced their involvement in the tendered market

Top: Another piece of 'booty' was this Optare Metrorider. One of 12 vehicles 'taken over' with the garage of the Lancaster Undertaking 450 (K450 YCW) is a standard narrow Metrorider new shortly before the takeover. At that time it bore an LCT cherished registration mark. It is seen in its erstwhile home town in March 1994.

Centre: Number 1162 (WLT 890) is a Volvo/Plaxton Paramount 3500 Mark 2 which came from Cumberland in 1993, although it originally belonged to Wallace Arnold. It has the registration mark of one of the LT Routemasters transferred by Stagecoach to Carlisle. It is seen in the Coachline tan/yellow livery whilst working a Rail Replacement service from Lancaster on March 31st 1994.

Foot: Also acquired from Cumberland was another ex-Wallace Arnold Volvo, with a later version of the Paramount 3500 body. This vehicle has been fitted with destination indicators. Perhaps regrettably, the demands of modern schedules and road conditions show it keeling over as it enters Preston bus station whilst trying to maintain its schedule for Sheffield. It is difficult to imagine a 1951 Royal Tiger appearing thus.

place, leaving that for either smaller companies or those chasing the apparent cash flow benefits of low priced 'socially necessary' tendered service contracts. Stagecoach policy has been to invest in high-specification modern vehicles whereby maintenance costs are contained, as well as public appeal maximised. These new vehicles have enabled the core network of traditional Ribble services to be continually upgraded to meet present market demands – such initiatives as the 'Network 2000' routes are the result. Ribble has therefore benefitted from this forward-looking policy throughout its operation whilst it has also been in the forefront of a number of territorial skirmishes described in both this and the first volume. From Barrow via Lancaster, Preston and now Manchester, both minor and major battles have raged with many won. As this volume goes to press, 28 11m Volvo B10M Alexander PS buses are due – possibly for a scheme similar to that which sister Cumberland implemented in Carlisle – every local bus was replaced overnight !

These battles have opened new challenges to the structure of the industry – and indeed Stagecoach in Lancaster will certainly be emulated elsewhere. In Colchester and Southend, Badgerline tried and failed to secure the destabilisation of the local Municipal Companies and British Bus won. This, however, is not the end of this particular tactic as time will undoubtedly tell.

Whatever may be said by those with a traditional outlook on local bus provision, and who prefer the order of the 1930 Traffic Act and its successors, Ribble seems to have an assured future with both commercial acumen and modern vehicles at its disposal. Albeit, its new Commanders-in-Chief have their home base in Perth and have but 15 years service compared with five times that of their operating subsidiary.

Above: Seen in use on the Lancashire Coastliner is Plaxton 'Interurban' bodied Javelin 139 (L139 BFV). This body is based on the 'Premier' coach vehicle. Days after this view was taken some of the batch were transferred to Manchester to meet the gauntlet thrown down in that city by GM Buses South.

Left: A transfer from Cumberland along with many of that company's National 2s was 379 (NHH 379 W) also seen in Lancaster in March 1994. It would not be alone amongst Ribble's 'short' Mark 2 Nationals.

One of the Alexander-bodied Volvo B6's, number 244 (L244 CCK), leaving the Hazel Grove terminus to return to Manchester via Stockport on a bright sunny day in February 1994. Note the Stagecoach Manchester branding above the doors and the route map on the side of the vehicle. The legal lettering reads 'Ribble Buses Preston'.

ACQUISITIONS

Much of Ribble's expansion during the late 1920s and early 1930s was achieved by acquiring the businesses of other operators. The list below shows what the company had to pay to get control of these businesses. Some transactions involved valuable properties, accounting for the great variations in prices paid. These were often subject to adjustment for spares, debts and other items. Records of transactions before 1926 have been lost. Detail in this section has been compiled from Ribble Minute Books, recently made available to the Authors.

Name of Operator	Date Acquired	Price	Remarks
J. Hodson, Gregson Lane, Higher Walton	6.6.19	N/A	Amalgamation
British Automobile Traction Co.Ltd	1.4.20	N/A	Amalgamation
J. Mashiter, Preston t/a Tra-Bon	.23	N/A	
Chorley Auto Co.Ltd. (including Parsons' Motors)	30.4.25	N/A	
Bullers Transport Ltd., Preston	6.25	N/A	
Kenyons, Coleman & Robinson Ltd.Blackburn (t/a KCR Services)	12.25	N/A	Stage carriage only
J.S. Bretherton, Ormskirk	27.2.26	N/A	
Lancashire Industrial Motors Ltd Blackburn (t/a Pendle Motors)	8. 9.26	£50,000	£18,500 in shares £6,300 as mortgage
Hodgson & Barnes, Preston t/a H. & B. Motors – transferred to Lancashire & Westmorland Motor Services Ltd.	9.26	£3,500	£500 in shares
The Pilot Motors Ltd. Preston	23.10.26	£40,000	£11,400 in shares
T.E. Smith., Elswick t/a Pilgrim Motors	1.7.27	£10,800	£2,000 in shares
Collingwood Motors (Liverpool) Ltd.	1.7.27	£13,515	
Skipton Motor Co.Ltd.	19.8.27	£2,000	
W. Webster, Wigan	5.11.27	£18,879	Jointly with Lancs. United. Ribble share £9,139.
Lancashire & Westmorland Motor Services Ltd.	1.12.27	£75,000	BAT merger
J.E. Loynds & Co. t/a Belford Service, Darwen	25.12.27	£13,500	
Waterloo & Crosby Motor Services Ltd.	3.1.28	£19,100	
W. Solloway & others t/a Eccleston Motor Co.	30.8.28	£3,500	
T. Wiseman, Skipton, t/a Old Bill Motor Service	9.12.28	£1,800	
County Motors (Lancaster) Ltd	1.2.29	N/A	Controlling interest 1.7.28. Management agreement 1.2.29 Ceased trading 31.12.30
Armstrong & Siddle Motor Services Ltd, Penrith	1.4.29	N/A	Transferred from Cumberland MS Ltd control by BAT. Remained separate until September 1929
Ideal Omnibus Services (Liverpool) Ltd.	3.12.29	£19,250	
W. Black t/a Imperial Motor Services, Liverpool	17.12.29	£1,250	Goodwill only.
S.P.& T. Adair, Carlisle	17.12.29	£1,250	City service only
Merseyside Touring Co.Ltd., Bootle	1.2.30	£120,000	Including Nor-West Bus Services Ltd.
Rishton & Antley Motor Co.Ltd. (including Calder Motor Co.)	1.3.30	£53,000	R&A subsequently bought Claremont Omnibus Services Ltd.
Matthew Wade (Majestic) & Preston & Longridge Motor Co. Ltd. (Empress)	3.30	£21,500	Bought by LMS Rly Co. To Ribble 10. 4.30
Kendal Motor Bus Co.Ltd.	12.4.30	£21,000	Plus £2,000 after 12 months if no competitor licensed to ply for hire in Kendal
Furness Omnibus Co.Ltd., Ulverston	18.5.30	£45,000	
H.Croisdale, Burnley t/a Brunshaw Motors	31.10.30	£7,850	Plus liability for 3 new AEC buses on order which Leyland Motors took in exchange.
F. Green, Chorley t/a Freeman's Silver Star	5.11.30	£7,500	Joint with Bolton Corpn.who paid £1,960 for part of goodwill and one Leyland Tiger.
Lawrence Motor Services Ltd Fleetwood	10.1.31	£6,000	Plus £185 for spare land next to garage.

PURCHASES ON BEHALF OF CARLISLE JOINT TRANSACTION

Name of Operator	Date Acquired	Price	Remarks
Carlisle & District Motor Services Ltd	1.11.31	£37,500	
White Star Motors Ltd.	1.11.31	£4,600	
G. Bristow	1.11.31	£3,350	
F. Waugh	1.11.31	£1,800	
Henry Hayton	1.11.31	£650	
R. Vickers	1.11.31	£400	
Carlisle & District Transport Co.Ltd.	22.11.31	£25,750	Including Richard Percival Ltd.

Name of Operator	Date Acquired	Price	Remarks
I.A.,E.A. & E.J. Wright, Armathwaite	27.11.31	£750	
H. Lace, Kirkoswald	22.12.31	£3,000	
A.E. Brennand, t/a Premier Motors, Chipping	20.5.32	£296	Goodwill & garage
W.C. Standerwick Ltd. Blackpool	11.11.32	£25,500	Jointly with North Western. Part sold to BMMO.
Wood Bros. (Blackpool) Ltd	1.2.33	£25,750	Jointly with North Western & BMMO. Liquidated 1937
Joseph Bracewell Ltd. Blackpool & Colne	1.2.33	£17,000	Jointly with North Western & BMMO
W. Armitage & Sons Ltd. Blackpool t/a Progress Motors	15.4.33	£10,700	Bought on behalf of Yorkshire-Blackpool Pool. Liquidated 10.36
Walker Taylor & Sons Ltd. Blackpool t/a Pride of the Road	7.33	£13,500	Bought on behalf of Yorkshire-Blackpool Pool. Liquidated 10.36
Red & White Services Ltd. Chepstow	7.1.34	£2,500	L'pool-Keswick service & E&T from Liverpool
Wright Bros. (Burnley) Ltd.	10.1.34	£22,500	Retained as subsidiary; liquidated 1948.
Lowland Motorways Ltd. and W.& G. Coachways (Manchester) Ltd.	5.2.34	£2,250	Manchester-Glasgow
Kenyons, Coleman & Robinson Ltd. t/a KCR Services, Blackburn	1.7.34	£9,600	Express & E&T
M. & H. Motors Ltd., Blackpool	9.3.35	£2,000	Goodwill only. Part North Western & LUT
J. Pearson & Sons Ltd. t/a Happy Days Motorways Including E.J. Jones (Liverpool-London) Ltd. Mrs S.S. Wilson (Liverpool-Blackpool service only) J.T. Harrison, Prescot (Old Swan-Blackpool service only) E. Horn, Birkenhead (to Crosville)	25.5.35	£23,442*	Joint with Crosville
East Lancashire Motors Ltd. Blackburn	6.6.35	£5,750	Bought by Standerwick. E&T Goodwill only
G. & E. Roe t/a De Luxe, Preston	8.6.35	£5,500	Preston-Gregson Lane service & E&T
Wm Salisbury & Sons Ltd., Blackpool	6.35	£15,000	Bought by Standerwick ; liquidated 7.37
H. & R. Spencer t/a Brookhouse Motors	1.7.35	£5,600	Preston-Bamber Bridge service & E&T
Dallas Services Ltd., Preston	10.7.35	£40,500	Goodwill only
Cadmans Services Ltd. Orrell	11.8.35	£25,000	Jointly with Wigan & St. Helens Corporations
W. Parkinson, Leyland	18.8.35	£5,000	Equally with J. Fishwick & Sons. Extra £500 if all licences granted.
J. & R. Singleton Ltd., Leyland	18.8.35	£16,375	Equally with J.Fishwick & Sons.Excluding E&T & P/Hire
A. Parkinson, Knott End	9.2.36	£500	Goodwill only
S.P. & T. Adair, Carlisle	2.7.36	£675	E&T & 1 coach
Parker Bros. Malhamdale Bus Service	8.2.37	£2,100	Equally with Pennine Motors
Lewis Cronshaw Ltd., Blackburn	1.6.37	£9,300	Jointly with Lancs. United & Bolton Corpn.
J. T. Harrison, Prescot	2.9.37	£1,800	Market services from Ormskirk & E&T from Prescot
Sidney Snape, Thornton Cleveleys	2.10.37	£1,769	Goodwill only
Arthur Christy (Bolton) Ltd.	12.4.38	£22,000	Lancs.United to contribute £1,000
F. Snaylam, Bolton	2.5.38	£10,000	Lancs.United to contribute c. £2,000
H. Sharrock, Halsall	19.5.38	£400	Goodwill only
J.T. Harvey, t/a Pilot Motors, Maghull.	26.9.38	£2,000	Goodwill only
H. Tennant & Co., Coppull	12.11.38	£12,650*	Jointly with Wigan Corpn. who paid £5,500
J. Edmondson, Clitheroe	13.3.39	£750	Goodwill only
Yarrow Motor Co. Ltd., Eccleston	3.4.39	£15,300	Fishwick to pay a share
J.B. Jump & Sons, Bretherton	1.1.40	£1,000	Goodwill only
E. Jones, Newchurch-in-Pendle and Barratt, Barley Omnibus Co.	1.11.45	£6,900*	Jointly with Burnley, Colne & Nelson Joint Transport
C. Head, Windermere t/a Magnet Bus Service	1. 2.46	£5,000	Goodwill only
J. Fawcett & Sons t/a Dallam Motor Services, Milnthorpe	1.12.50	£10,000	Goodwill only
Grange Motor & Cycle Co.Ltd. Grange-over-Sands	1.7.51	£10,000	Stage carriage services only
Viking Motors (Preston) Ltd., Preston	16.11.52	£3,000	Goodwill only
Oliver Hart & Sons, Coppull	25.5.53	£1,000	Goodwill only
Howard Coaches Ltd., Southport	13.8.54	£1,350	Goodwill only
Bolton-by-Bowland Motor Services Ltd. Clitheroe	26.9.55	£1,000	Sale originally agreed 1941but Regional Transport Commissioner would not transfer licences
Auty's Tours Ltd., Bury	1.1.56	£18,000	Operated as a subsidiary until 1.1.60 then liquidated
T.H. Parker, Hyde (t/a Bluebird)	26.3.56	£1,640*	Jointly with Yelloway, North Western, Standerwick & LUT
Northern Roadways Ltd., Glasgow	11.56	£2,871*	Glasgow-Birmingham service; jointly with Scottish Omnibuses, North Western, LUT & BMMO
M.Corless & Son, Charnock Richard	1.1.57	£17,500	Goodwill only
Grange Motor & Cycle Co.Ltd.	1.1.58	£9,500	£3,000 for goodwill of E&T & private hire; £6,500 for property.
F. Binns Ltd., Morecambe	26.6.58	N/A	E&T & private hire
Florence Motors Ltd., Morecambe	26.6.58	N/A	E&T & private hire
Kia-Ora Ltd., Morecambe	26.6.58	N/A	E&T & private hire

Name of Operator	Date Acquired	Price	Remarks
Geo.Moore & Sons Ltd. St. Annes	28.6.58	N/A	Acquired by Standerwick; offered for sale in 1944 but rejected.
Scout Motor Services Ltd. Preston	5.12.61	#	Including Eldon Coachbuilders (liquidated 1962) operated as subsidiary until 25.10.68
J. McGregor Ltd., Ambleside	30.6.62	N|A	
Parker's Motors Ltd., Grange-over-Sands	6.5.64	£3,750	Goodwill only. E&T & private hire
Lake Hotel Coaches Ltd. and Weightmans Coaches Ltd., Keswick	18.4.65	£2,500*	E&T, jointly with Cumberland Motor Services
P. Phythian & Sons, St. Helens	3.66	£16,000	Travel Agency Ltd. Co.formed and operated asa subsidiary.
R. Prescott & Sons t/a Bamber Bridge Motor Service	1.4.67	£24,400	
United Automobile Services Ltd. Darlington	2.1.69	£38,416##	Carlisle operations. Assets at book value.
Wm. Makinson (M/cr) Ltd. and North Manchester Motor Coaches Ltd.	6.69	£397*	Goodwill of Express service. Jointly with Yelloway, North Western, Standerwick & LUT.

E&T =	Excursions and Tours.
*	Ribble share of purchase price.
N/A	Not available
#	The sale price is not recorded. Scout came up for sale previously in 1951 and 1955, being withdrawn by the vendors in both cases. In 1955 it was valued at £340,000 but the following year it was said that its value had decreased. The nominal capital was increased from £245,000 to £325,000 in 1963 'to bring share capital more in line with the real capital employed in the business' and that probably gives a good idea of what was paid.
##	Net Book Value. No consideration in cash on Group Transfer Basis.

In later years, Ribble did not take over the rolling stock of acquired businesses, even when of types similar to its own. Viking Motors (Preston) Ltd had twelve vehicles when operation ceased in November 1952, which included two Leyland Titan PD1 models with Leyland lowbridge bodywork,of which No.10 (BCK 100), is seen here when new in December 1946. It was sold off with the rest, but Scout Motor Services Ltd, then still independent, bought it in February 1953, running it until December 1959 when it was sold to Tom Jackson (Chorley) Ltd, in whose fleet it ran until 1961. The remaining vehicles of the final Viking fleet, which included four Daimler double-deckers, found new owners distributed very widely across the country.

Some of the purchases were of concerns which had already taken over others, and hence some of the vehicles had quite rapid successive changes of ownership. This Leyland Lion PLSC1 with rear-entrance Leyland body was new to the Calder Motor Co Ltd of Great Harwood. Although not registered, the negative number suggests that it was almost certainly CW 6922, which had been registered for the operator by Tillotson, the Burnley dealer. Calder was taken over by Rishton & Antley Motor Co Ltd in October 1929, but in March 1930 that concern was acquired by Ribble, the £53,000 paid taking the inclusion of the Calder business into account. R&A was run as a separate business until September 1930, when the fleet was absorbed, CW 6922 becoming Ribble C983.

When the Furness Omnibus Co Ltd was taken over in May 1930, the £45,000 purchase price reflected the Furness policy of regular purchases of new standard Leyland buses, very similar to those chosen by Ribble itself, as well as a network of routes in the area indicated by the name, in those days forming part of Lancashire. The final batch comprised two Lion LT1 and three Tiger TS2, of which latter No.21 (TE 8686) is seen here when ready for delivery – it entered service in July 1929, later becoming Ribble C968. The setting is thought to be one of the royal parks near Leyland's Kingston-on-Thames works, indicating that this was one of quite a number of vehicles of that period that had Kingston-built Leyland bodywork.

When the Yarrow Motor Co Ltd was bought out in April 1939, the price of £15,300 did not include payment for any vehicles, Ribble having adopted a policy of not taking the buses of acquired businesses by then. In regard to this vehicle at least, the firm application of this might have seemed a little surprising, as ATC 269, a Leyland Tiger TS7, dated from August 1935 and was thus under four years old. However the Leyland metal-framed body fitted was of a type that had not proved very successful, and this may have contributed to the decision. The livery seen in this pre-delivery view at Leyland's South Works took the contemporary fad for 'streamline' markings to a remarkable extreme. The vehicle was sold to Macrae and Dick Ltd of Inverness, passing to Highland Omnibuses Ltd in 1951.

DEMONSTRATORS

Ribble was involved at a very early stage with the original Leyland Tiger – this photograph, dated 3rd September 1927, shows a pre-production example, chassis number 60005A, in Ribble livery even before the model was announced publicly. It had a longer rear overhang than the production vehicles delivered to Ribble the following spring and was effectively to the specification of the TS1 model as originally announced though very few examples of that variant were supplied before the TS2 became the normal model for operators in Britain. Minor chassis details differed from the production version, which would have meant that non-standard spares would have been needed, though in fact the vehicle had quite a long career, being registered TE 1635 and sold to Clydebank Motors in 1928 and later passing to OK Motor Services of Bishop Auckland in whose fleet it ran until after the 1939-45 war period. An interesting detail not repeated was a Tiger mascot on the radiator filler cap.

Like most major operators, Ribble tried out quite a number of demonstration vehicles at one time or another over the years. Its sheer size made it a tempting target, for clearly a fleet with over 1,000 vehicles, as was the case from 1938 to 1976, was likely to be placing big orders, as well as influential as a company widely respected for the quality of its fleet.

There was more to it than that, however, for being right on Leyland's doorstep made it particularly tempting a target. AEC, in particular, made repeated attempts to 'get in', as it were, and though some of them were probably not expected to succeed, the amount of trouble taken in some cases reflects more determination. Particularly in the years from 1928, there was no love lost between Leyland and AEC, following the 'defection' of G. J. Rackham as Chief Engineer from Leyland to Southall and the subsequent appearance of AEC models with many features which he had introduced at Leyland.

In later years, that 'needle' factor became less strong, though AEC was Leyland's main rival, and was competing strongly right up to the merger between the two in 1962 – indeed it was supposed to continue even after that, so far as home market sales were concerned, though in practice they co-operated increasingly from then.

Demonstration vehicles were by no means always operated in service, and some may simply have visited Frenchwood Avenue and been quite rapidly sent on their way. Others were in the nature of prototypes and, though painted in Ribble colours, and seemingly 'successful' in being followed by orders for similar vehicles, not taken into the fleet. Indeed, in general, for many years it was not Ribble policy to acquire demonstrators, save possibly where part of a taken-over business, and the only exception to this rule was the 1939 AEC Regal coach, KMG 593, taken into stock as 2380 under the exceptional conditions of the early wartime period.

Ribble was often closely involved in development work with Leyland, and in more recent times ran prototype examples of the Leyland National variants and the Olympian, in some cases on loan before they were added to the fleet, though this was in a somewhat different category from demonstrators as generally understood. These vehicles are detailed in the Fleet Summary.

Around the 'fifties and 'sixties at least, it became standard practice to put double-decker demonstrators into service in the Liverpool area, no doubt so as to assess them under the most difficult operating conditions with frequent stops and heavy traffic, the L3 or L30 routes from the centre of that city to Crosby being apt to be favoured. The 109 Preston-Chorley route was generally used for single-deckers, as it was convenient not only for access from Frenchwood Avenue but also to Leyland's works, as it passed through that town. A good coach test route was up the A6 to Carlisle in the days before the M6 was built, particularly because of the climb of Shap Fell, and the above-mentioned AEC Regal was on X21 Liverpool-Carlisle for much of its life with Ribble.

This selection of photographs gives some idea of the types of vehicle tried in service or used as prototypes at different times.

This well-worn picture from 'The Auto & Motor Journal' of 16th May 1929 shows an AEC Reliance (model 660) demonstrator, MT 3228, in Ribble colours, in use as a special timekeeper's box at the Brooklands motor race track on the occasion of the 'Double-Twelve' race. This was run in two spells of twelve hours, requiring extra facilities of this kind. The Reliance was AEC's first new model produced after G. J. Rackham left Leyland and there was doubtless a certain delight in sending one to operate under the noses of the latter concern. In fact, the model had little chance of causing Ribble to switch from the Tiger, for although having a very similar engine, the design of the rest of the chassis was more of the same generation as the Lion PLSC, using up stocks of parts from the earlier 416 and 426 types before the Regal went into general production. The vehicle in question was numerically the ninth Reliance, bodied by Hall Lewis and completed in March 1929 before being sent to Ribble in April. It was sold to the Great Northern Railway in Belfast in September 1929.

The new face. When Leyland introduced a complete redesign of the Leyland Tiger in 1933, setting the standard in terms of layout and appearance for the Tiger, Titan and related models for the period up to 1942. Ribble livery was chosen for the prototype, which carried Leyland-built bodywork. It is seen here when new in January 1933, parked outside Leyland's Social Club building which was often used for new model introductions or handing-over ceremonies. In fact this coach, the first completed to TS6 specification, was not supplied to Ribble, being sold in July 1933, to Leah Bros, of Huthwaite, Notts, registered AAL 486. The production batch built for Ribble from April 1933 was similar but had many minor differences – compare this view with that on page 81.

AEC came knocking on Ribble's door again in the winter of 1937-38, this time with an example of the Regal Mark II model, which was a slightly lightened version of the standard Regal with an engine of 6.6-litre nominal size, by no means as radical in terms of weight reduction as the Leyland Cheetah. The vehicle that was sent, EMF 94, was built in the summer of 1936 as an O862 type, with oil engine, that being the standard power unit for the model, but a petrol version of the same size was offered, and the presence of a starting handle (not usual for the type) suggests that such an engine might have been fitted to meet Ribble's preferences of the time. The vehicle had a Weymann bus body to the same design as a 1935 Show vehicle supplied to Rhondda Transport, but had been painted grey, as was sometimes done with demonstrators. It seems likely that Ribble was interested in it as the basis of a coach, and although no examples entered Ribble's fleet, the Standerwick order for batches of twelve and then ten similar petrol-engined chassis with Burlingham coach bodies supplied in 1939 suggest that a satisfactory impression was made. EMF 94 later went to Baker Bros of Warsop, Notts.

An unlikely-seeming 'Ribble' bus was KMD 306, the AEC Regent seen in this photograph taken at AEC's Southall works early in 1939; even though painted in the company's style, complete with elaborate lining out, and equipped with the correct front destination equipment, the legal lettering quotes AEC as the owner. The interest seems bound to have been centred on the engine, of AEC's then newly-announced A173 toroidal-cavity direct-injection version of the 7.7-litre type, though in fact the unit had been in limited production from 1936 and Ribble may well have been aware that Liverpool had been running ten from that date.
The vehicle had Park Royal metal-framed bodywork of a design clearly intended to resemble the curved-profile style Weymann had introduced as an option from 1938 – side route number and destination boxes, painted over in this view, imply that Ribble had not been in mind when it was completed in January 1939. It was allocated the fleet number 2019 but its period of demonstration did not last more than a few months, the vehicle being sold to the Gosport & Fareham Omnibus Co in December 1939, remaining in service until 1963. Unusually, the similarly powered Regal coach KMG 593 was taken into Ribble's fleet (see page 92), but no further AEC vehicles were bought – Leyland was developing its own toroidal-cavity engines, standard for post-war models.

There was very little need for demonstrators in the early postwar years, when almost all manufacturers could sell every bus they could build, but by 1952, the situation had altered considerably as replacement of over-age vehicles had largely been completed and demand fell. Leyland built a pair of the new Tiger Cub chassis, giving one each to Saunders-Roe and Weymann to body, the vehicles being registered OTC 738 and OTD 301 respectively. The body styles contrasted considerably, the former well rounded, (as shown left above, at Leyland's South Works) with front-end showing American influence, the latter quite similar to the Olympic in outline.

A Strachan-bodied Ford demonstrator, RNO 959D, made an unsuccessful visit and is seen here providing a splash of colour amongst the Cherry Reds in Chorley bus station on 29th June 1966.

The 1956 PDR1 prototype for the Leyland Atlantean, 281 ATC, was operated by Ribble on the Liverpool-Crosby services, as was to apply to other double-deck demonstrators in the following few years. There had been two earlier prototype rear-engined double-deckers built by Leyland, but this vehicle, displayed on Leyland's stand at the Commercial Motor Show in October that year, set the pattern for what is nowadays the generally accepted layout for double-deckers. It was also of advanced design in terms of technology, with integral construction, independent front suspension and low-floor layout, this last-mentioned allowing full-length centre gangways in both decks despite 'lowbridge' overall height. When the production PDR1/1 version was introduced in 1958, the design was simplified and all three of these features were abandoned; there is evidence to indicate that Ribble's management was disappointed in regard to the height aspect, leading to the adoption of the Albion Lowlander and then the PDR1/2 when they became available. The vehicle was dismantled by Leyland in the 'sixties.

Another new model first seen at the 1956 Show was the Bridgemaster, AEC's interpretation of a low-floor double-decker. The development work had been given to Crossley, by then part of the Associated Commercial Vehicles group of which AEC was the principal member, and thus 9 JML was officially a Crossley Bridgemaster, the second of the type produced, which had been in the demonstration park at the Show but is seen here in Liverpool operating on the L3 in December 1956. This model, with integral body structure designed by Park Royal and similarly delegated to Crossley's body department, achieved the combination of low height and centre-gangway layout conveyed by the name and also had independent front suspension, but otherwise was more traditional, with its half-cab layout. The vehicle was taken into stock by Birmingham City Transport in 1957.

Although Ribble did not place an order, the Ribble board resolution of 1st November 1962 on the vehicles to be ordered for 1964 delivery included a reference to 'Leyland Lowlanders or AEC Renowns', the latter model being of similar layout to the Bridgemaster, though more conventional. This may have reflected the influence of George Brook, who had just moved from his managership at North Western, where this model had been ordered.

The Guy Wulfrunian was another unorthodox double-deck model, introduced in 1959. This demonstrator, with Roe body to the design standard for the model, dated from June 1960 and toured the country visiting various operators, including Ribble, who put it to work on the L30 in Liverpool in the way that had become usual. The Wulfrunian represented a quite different approach to the design of a low-height double-decker, with engine at the front but with front wheels set back so as to allow the entrance to be opposite the driver. This was in much the same way as used on the Ailsa B55 of fourteen years later, though using the bulky Gardner 6LX rather than the latter's much more compact Volvo TD70 engine. The Wulfrunian incorporated many advanced features, notably disc brakes and air suspension, independent on the front wheels, perhaps too many new features to succeed. This vehicle was retained by Guy, withdrawn in 1964 and sold to the West Riding company, the model's only major operator, for spares in 1966.

ADDENDA
To Volume 1

Since Volume 1 was completed, access has been obtained to some of the company's minute books which have thrown additional light on some matters.

p. 9 (Picture) It is now apparent that EC 109 was also a Thornycroft, not a Clarkson.

p.12 J. Stacey & Co. should be J. Storey & Co.

p.21 Rishton & Antley Motor Co. Ltd. was run as a subsidiary to keep their operations outside the scope of the pooling arrangement with Accrington Corporation. R&A was wound up only when Accrington paid £2,250 towards the value of the goodwill.

p.21-2 County Motors (Lancaster) Ltd. was maintained as a subsidiary until the remaining shareholders voted to exercise an option to exchange 5 County shares for 4 Ribble shares. One of the shareholders was a coach operator, Morecambe Motors Ltd.

p.22/38 **Merseyside Touring Co. Ltd.** It is now clear that this company was taken over on 1st February 1930 not on 8th June as was thought but the sale was kept secret for several months, especially from Liverpool Corporation. After the Bootle bus services were handed over to the Corporation, £25,000 goodwill was written off. Ribble thought it worth the money to get the Liverpool agreement.

p.24 (Upper picture). Rutter was not connected with the Kendal Motor Bus Co. Ltd. but with Kendal Bus Services which was one of the constituents of Westmorland Motor Services on formation.

p.29 A. Parkinson's stage service was sold to Ribble at the insistence of the Traffic Commissioners as he had never applied for a road service licence. His coaching operations continued until 1946 when he sold out to Birch Motor Services Ltd.

p.32-33 **Producer Gas Buses.** The company was directed to convert 10% of its fleet to gas operation and 95 producer gas trailers were ordered and delivered in 1943-44. Ribble seems to have been more successful than some in dragging its feet and finding difficulties as only 11 vehicles were converted, 10 single deckers (8 petrol and 2 diesel) and one diesel double-decker which was converted back without entering service. There are reports of a Lion LT2 being used experimentally on service L1 Liverpool-Crosby. It was unusual for a four-cylinder bus to be adapted and it seems to have been unsuccessful. The steep hill of the Skelhorne Street city terminus would have been a severe trial. Park Road, Preston (AA) garage was reopened for the purpose, having been previously closed as a wartime economy measure and eight vehicles entered service there in June-July 1943. These were TS6 coaches. The identity of the diesel buses in unknown. The government halved the company's allocation to 47 trailers in January 1944 but abandoned the scheme on 12th September 1944; the gas buses were withdrawn immediately and the equipment, most of it unused was sold for what it would fetch. There must have been some problems in reversing buses with trailers off the bus station.

Company records show that in May 1941 as many as 252 vehicles were delicensed.

In addition to Liverpool Corporation taking over Ribble duties in 1942, Rawtenstall Corporation took over work on Bury-Rawtenstall services about the same time.

p.34 At the time Ribble was planning its new express network, Major Hickmott was approached by J.R. Tognarelli of Bolton who had started Bolton-Manchester, Manchester-London and Manchester-Glasgow services. He wanted Ribble to join him in the formation of a new company and offered the use of some Manchester premises as a terminus. The Ribble directors thought the Tognarelli premises too small and nothing came of the idea.

In August 1937 an agreement was signed by Ribble, Crosville and two parcel delivery firms with the object of setting up a passengers' luggage in advance scheme as was provided by the railways at that time. It failed to get off the ground.

p.37 The Claremont Liverpool-London service was taken over on 19th August 1929.

p.39 **Wood Bros.** For legal reasons, this company remained in existence until 1937. Ribble's shareholding was formally sold to Standerwick in 1936 and the goodwill of its Blackpool-Leeds service was sold to the Yorkshire-Blackpool pool operators in 1937.

p.41-2 **Wright Bros.** In the interests of accuracy, it would appear that the Coliseum was not owned by the Wright company but leased by them. Ribble were able to buy the property soon afterwards.

p.42 The Darlington-Keswick service ceased in September 1934 not 1935.

It is now known that the acquisition of Pearson's, jointly with Crosville, was a little more complex than previously thought. It was known that Pearson's had bought the businesses of E.J. Jones (Liverpool & London) Ltd. (t/a Imperial Motor Services) and E.Horn of Birkenhead but it is now clear that they had also bought the Liverpool-Blackpool services of Mrs S.S. Wilson and J.T. Harrison as well. The Jones fleet, comprising 15 vehicles and one chassis, was sold by Ribble for £625.

p.46 By courtesy of Mr W. Dodds, a full list of the Wigan Corporation buses hired by Ribble in July-August 1947 can now be given together with the Scout buses which followed them.

38	EK7906	Leyland TD1	71493	Leyland	L24/24R
39	EK7907	Leyland TD1	71494	Leyland	L24/24R
40	EK7908	Leyland TD1	71495	Leyland	L24/24R
41	EK7909	Leyland TD1	71745	Leyland	L24/24R
43	EK7911	Leyland TD1	71763	Leyland	L24/24R
45	EK7913	Leyland TD1	71793	Leyland	L24/24R
47	EK8039	Leyland TD1	71795	Leyland	L24/24R
48	EK8040	Leyland TD1	71796	Leyland	L24/24R
49	EK8041	Leyland TD1	71797	Leyland	L24/24R
50	EK8042	Leyland TD1	71798	Leyland	L24/24R
54	EK8087	Leyland TD1	71991	NCME	L24/24R
55	EK8088	Leyland TD1	71488	Massey	L24/24R
56	EK8089	Leyland TD1	71489	Massey	L24/24R
76	EK8330	Leyland TD1	72233	Leyland	L24/24R
29	EK8873	Leyland TD2	1736	NCME	L24/24R
25	EK9317	Leyland TD2	2730	NCME	L24/24R

After the Wigan buses went back, four Scout buses were hired; it is not known for how long.

23	CK4568	Leyland TD1	71964	Leyland L27/24R
30	CK4654	Leyland TD2	1544	Leyland L27/24R
25+	TF9462	Leyland TD2	1661	Leyland L27/24R
27*	RN8038	Leyland TD4	12625	Leyland L27/26RD

\+ ex-demonstrator 6/34

* originally petrol; converted to diesel 9/45. Doors fitted from new.

p.151 The system of destination equipment comprising a standard blind with the names of the principal towns, augmented by externally lit boards, was approved by the directors on 16th September 1926 and expenditure of £1,000 was authorised for external lamps, etc.

p.152 Blackpool Talbot Road garage opened in 1933 not 1928. The earlier garage is believed to have been in rented premises. Darwen out-station closed on 13th August 1988, not in 1989. Manchester (Trumpet Street) dates from much earlier than 1947 – possibly 1930 – but the exact date has not been ascertained.

INDEX

TAILPIECE

Portents: The arrow formed by the stripes points forward and the sub-title 'A Network 2000 Service' indicates the future. All in all, Ribble seems to have a sound future – as a member of yet another Grouping. Dennis Javelin number 145 heads for Clitheroe on Wednesday 30th March 1994, three days after the introduction of newly-revised services competing with Charterplan's incursion into East Lancashire Express Services, also running from Manchester's Chorlton Street coach station.

KENDAL MOTOR BUS CO. LTD.

Encirclement by Ribble – 1930

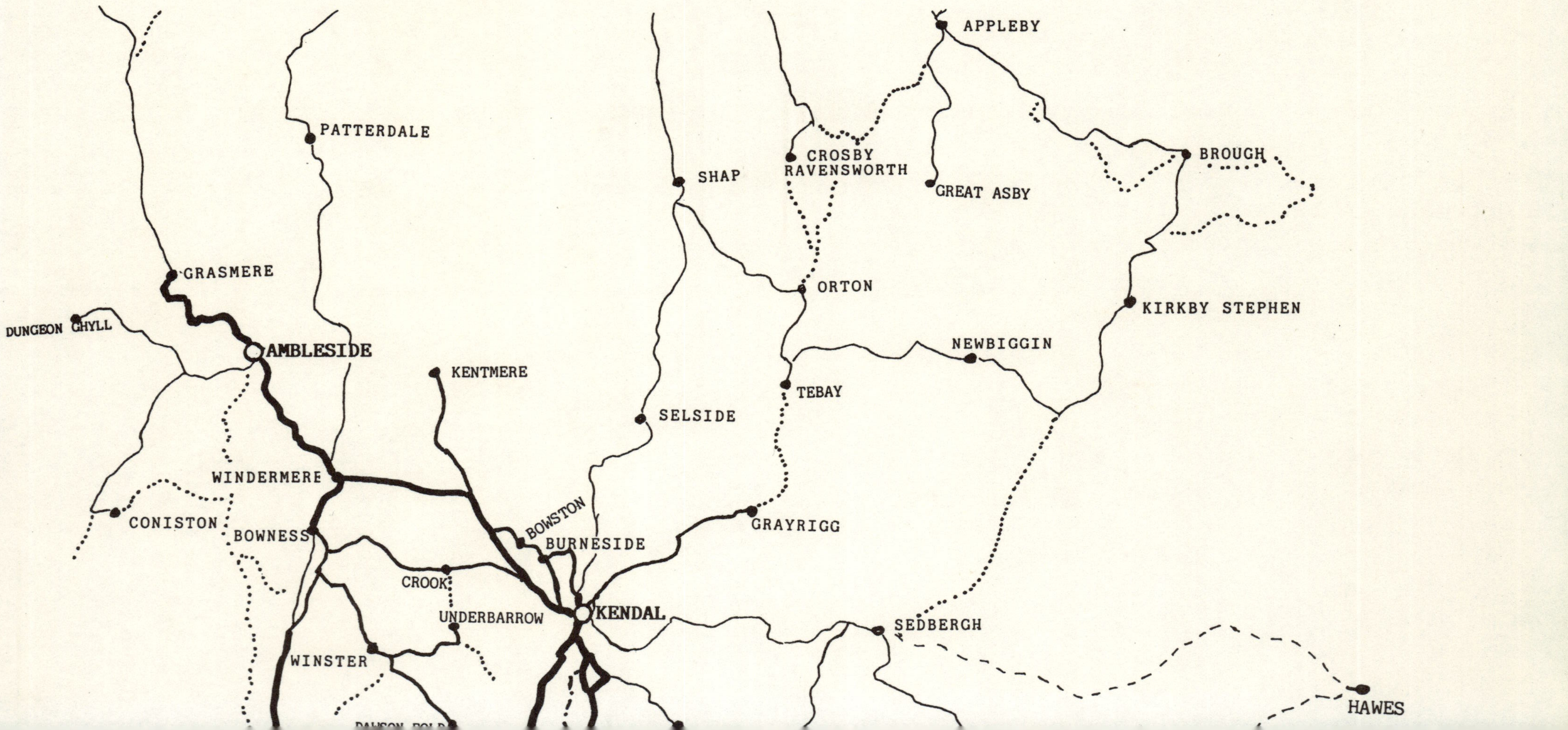